PRAISE FOR
It's All Relative

"Whether the author is being ruminative or rollicking, he is consistently thought-provoking in his 'adventure in helping to build the World Family Tree,' and his natural gift for humor lightens the mood of even the most serious discussion. A delightful, easy-to-read, informative book."

—*Kirkus*, Starred Review

"Whimsical but also full of solid journalism and eye-opening revelations about the history of humanity, the book is a real treat."

—*Booklist*, Starred Review

"In his latest adventure book, author and experimentalist A.J. Jacobs enthusiastically shares in the human quest for self-knowledge that drives so many of us around the world to search for—and find—our roots. The astonishing discoveries he makes not only reveal the compelling possibilities of genealogical and genetic research; they remind us of the common bonds that unite us as a single global family. As Jacobs's (however distant) cousin, I admit I may be biased in singing his praises, but as *It's All Relative* proves, who isn't?"

—Henry Louis Gates, Jr.

"A hilarious read from beginning to end."

—Adam Grant, *New York Times* bestselling author of *Give and Take*, *Originals*, and *Option B* with Sheryl Sandberg

"A.J. Jacobs is descended from pretzel vendors, dwarf pony breeders, and purveyors of bogus hemorrhoid salves, which may or may not explain why I love his books so much. Mostly it's because, like life itself, A.J. is deep and goofy at the same time. *It's All Relative* is the funniest, most thoughtful, most original and entertaining book about family that you will ever read and wish you'd written."

—Mary Roach

"I think it's A.J. Jacobs's best book yet!"

—Kevin Kelly, cofounder of *Wired* and author of *The Inevitable*

"Jacobs decides to hunt down his farthest-flung relations (Daniel Radcliffe, et al.) in order to host the world's largest family reunion. He fails to set the record, but succeeds in crafting a diverting chronicle of a country split apart and yet more self-consciously interrelated than ever."

—*New York Magazine*

"A.J. Jacobs has done it again! Having once lived the Ten Commandments for a year (even going so far as to 'stone' an adulterer with pebbles), his new book, *It's All Relative: Adventures Up and Down the World's Family Tree*, takes us on another unique adventure that pits idealism vs. practicality: Bringing about world peace and harmony by finding 'cousin' connections among people throughout the globe and then hosting a 'Global Family Reunion.' Jacobs again opens up to us his insightful (and hysterically bizarre) thought processes as he plots the end of hate and conflict through one massive first-of-its-kind event."

—Scott Fisher, host of *Extreme Genes*

"'The Sower,' the Simon & Schuster logo, is the perfect opening icon for this story about human seed sown by our common ancestors out of Africa and how you and I are related to the Jacobs clan. Like A.J.'s previous hilarious books, this one involves way-over-the-top performance art—this time the mother of all family reunions, at which I sang 'We Are Family' (and the rest of you 7.5 billion were expected to sing along). Genealogy is now, deservedly, tied for the top hobby, along with other ancient biotechnologies, gardening and sex. You could have no better guide than ace jovialist and awesome jester, A.J. Now, more than ever, we celebrate our connections, we read, we smile."

—George Church, author of *Regenesis*

"A terrific read, and A.J. is a terrific writer . . . funny and super-interesting."

—Michael Ian Black

"*Esquire* contributing editor Jacobs *(The Year of Living Biblically)* muses on the nature of family and the interconnectedness of humanity in this entertaining introduction to the world of genealogy. . . . With short, lively chapters and an easygoing voice, Jacobs keeps the story flowing."

—*Publishers Weekly*

"A.J. Jacobs's latest book embraces an entertaining and heartwarming search to discover 'Family.' His adventure is the natural curiosity in all of us to know where we are from. This book takes you along for the ride as A.J. discovers his family, and works to connect with all of us. His efforts culminate at the world's largest global family reunion. The reader if not already a family historian, will become one after reading this fascinating and amazing tale."

—David Allen Lambert, Chief Genealogist, New England Historic Genealogical Society

"Wonderfully smart."

—*The Washington Independent Review of Books*

ALSO BY A.J. JACOBS
Drop Dead Healthy
My Life as an Experiment
The Year of Living Biblically
The Know-It-All

It's All Relative

Adventures Up and Down
the World's Family Tree

A.J. Jacobs

Simon & Schuster Paperbacks
New York London Toronto Sydney New Delhi

To Julie, Jasper, Zane, and Lucas

 Simon & Schuster Paperbacks
An Imprint of Simon & Schuster, Inc.
1230 Avenue of the Americas
New York, NY 10020

Family Tree by John Forster & Tom Chapin © Limousine Music Co. & The Last Music Co. (ASCAP)

First Simon & Schuster trade paperback edition October 2018

SIMON & SCHUSTER PAPERBACKS and colophon are registered trademarks of Simon & Schuster, Inc. For information about special discounts for bulk purchases, please contact Simon & Schuster Special Sales at 1-866-506-1949 or business@simonandschuster.com.

The Simon & Schuster Speakers Bureau can bring authors to your live event. For more information or to book an event, contact the Simon & Schuster Speakers Bureau at 1-866-248-3049 or visit our website at www.simonspeakers.com.

Interior design by Silverglass
Index by Sydney Wolfe Cohen

All photos not otherwise credited are courtesy of the Jacobs family.

Manufactured in the United States of America

10 9 8 7 6 5 4 3 2 1

Library of Congress Cataloging-in-Publication Data is available.

ISBN 978-1-4767-3449-1
ISBN 978-1-4767-3450-7 (pbk)
ISBN 978-1-4767-3451-4 (ebook)

Contents

Introduction

Thanks for picking up this book.

You didn't have to, but it's a nice thing to do, seeing as you and I are cousins. Our shared ancestor would no doubt be proud.

Admittedly, I'm not sure exactly *which* ancestor we share.

If you're flipping through these pages at a bookstore on New York's Upper West Side, our shared ancestor might be our fifth-great grandmother, a seamstress in a Polish shtetl.

Or perhaps it's further back—our twenty-first-great grandfather, a goat farmer in the Euphrates Valley.

Or maybe we'd have to rewind all the way to our eight-thousandth-great grandparents, a couple of scruffy humans who hunted, gathered, and vigorously reproduced on the plains of Africa about two hundred thousand years ago.

These two über-grandparents were the real Adam and Eve. Their scientific nicknames are the slightly less catchy "Y-Chromosomal Adam" and "Mitochondrial Eve." And everyone on earth is descended from them—me, you, Miley Cyrus, the guy who took your parking space at Chipotle, the second-best dental hygienist in Singapore. Everyone.

Recently I've been thinking a lot about my eight-thousandth-great grandparents. Partly it's because I have young kids, and it's got me reflecting on the long family chain, both past and future.

I like to daydream about y-Adam and m-Eve coming to the twenty-first century. Maybe some budding Elon Musk could build a time machine, bring them here, and get them booked on the *Good Morning America* show.

Maybe George Stephanopoulos would ask them how they feel about having seven billion offspring. To which m-Eve would reply, "That's a lot of birthday presents," and everyone would laugh. (She's had some media coaching.)

Perhaps George would ask if they have a favorite eight-thousandth-great grandchild. To which they'd say, "Oh, they're all our favorites," but secretly they'd be thinking Nobel Prize winner Malala Yousafzai, because who in their right mind wouldn't?

Then George would ask y-Adam and m-Eve what they think of the state of their family today. They'd sigh and shake their heads. "We just wish all our family would get along better."

And they'd have a point. Because the world family is not getting along. At all. It's in crisis. It's more dysfunctional than I've seen it in my lifetime.

I'm well aware my time-travel idea is absurd on several levels.

First of all, y-Adam and m-Eve were probably not enlightened beings with wise advice. They were most likely xenophobic and paranoid and would attack George Stephanopoulos to steal his bagel. Second, they'd probably go with *60 Minutes* for the ratings.

So I know it's not realistic. But when I'm feeling despair—which is not infrequent these days—this is the kind of fantasy that takes over my brain.

Up until recently I figured humans were marching slowly but surely along a rational path. I figured we'd eventually shed primitive tribalism and join forces to try to solve the world's big problems. Instead, we seem to be more tribal than ever. We're obsessed with us-versus-them thinking. Blue state versus red state. Americans versus foreigners. Believers versus atheists. Black versus white. Patriots fans versus everyone else.

I see this trait in myself and it disturbs me. I try to be all noble and teach my kids to be good *Homo sapiens*. Over dinner, I'll tell them not to dehumanize anyone. Don't fall for hate. Be respectful and rational. And then ten minutes into the meal I'll find myself ranting about the issue of the day—gun control, isolationism—and slamming the other side as drooling, brain-dead idiots.

It confuses my kids. It confuses me, too.

But I'm trying to be more civil, more understanding. And in between bouts of despair, I think there might be hope, even without a time machine.

A few years ago I stumbled across a group of scientists and researchers working on a remarkable quest: to connect all of humankind in one big family tree. A World Family Tree uniting all seven billion cousins on earth. A tree built with the help of millions of DNA tests and thousands of historians and genealogists.

It's a crazy ambitious project, like mapping the human genome or building a colony on Mars. And as with many crazy ambitious projects, it's got huge implications.

The still-in-progress World Family Tree is already helping scientists track diseases and develop cures. It's changing the way we understand history and culture, race and ethnicity.

And maybe, just maybe, the World Family Tree will nudge us to treat our distant cousins a little more kindly. Or at least less awfully. Because for the first time in history, y-Adam and m-Eve's descendants can see the human family isn't an abstraction. It's real.

Granted, this may all be a fool's errand. I know it's got the whiff of naïveté and dorm room bong water. Maybe I should just go sit on a mound of patchouli and strum Peter, Paul & Mary songs on a sitar.

But I think the quest is worth a try. Because I'm feeling desperate. We need to do something. I want my kids to have kids (if that's their choice, of course) and for those kids to have kids and for y-Adam and m-Eve's family to continue for another eight thousand generations.

This book chronicles my adventure in helping to build the World Family Tree. It's been the most fascinating, exhilarating, and occasionally frustrating experience of my life.

It's allowed me to meet cousins from all seven continents (Antarctica included) and to drink a beer with a United States president. I've befriended a Hatfield *and* a McCoy. I've learned about the secrets and heartbreaks of my great-great-great-grandparents. I've sung in the Mormon Tabernacle Choir. I've had every nucleotide of my DNA decoded. I've found genetic links to Hollywood actresses and Chicago scoundrels.

And along the way, I've had my worldview transformed.

So if by chance you are reading this in the distant future, and you're one of my eight-thousandth-great grandchildren, sorry for all the things we messed up. Sorry for global warming, factory farming, and every reality TV show except *The Great British Baking Show*, which I've heard is quite good.

Also, I hope the family is doing better.

CHAPTER 1

The Eighth Cousin

My story begins three years ago with one of the strangest emails I've ever received.

"You don't know me," it says, "but you are an eighth cousin of my wife, who, in my opinion, is a fine lady."

Naturally I figure the next line will involve instructions on how to wire ten thousand dollars to a bank account in Togo, or inform me of the miraculous potency benefits of goji berries.

But instead, the emailer says his name is Jules Feldman. He explains that he's a dairy farmer on a kibbutz in Israel and has read some articles I've written. He wants to tell me about his life's project. For the previous fifteen years, Jules has devoted his time to building a family tree. A really big tree. More of a forest.

"We have in our database about eighty thousand relatives of yours," he says.

Eighty thousand. I try to wrap my head around that number. If he's right, my relatives could fill four Madison Square Gardens.

The email gives me profoundly mixed feelings.

On the one hand, as my wife, Julie, points out, I often feel like I have too many relatives already. I'd be happy to *trim* a few branches. I'm thinking of my cousin David, who, for his wedding, hired a little person dressed as a leprechaun to pop out from under his bride's dress and twerk with the guests. And then there's my brilliant but smug brother-in-law Eric, whose favorite phrase is the infuriating "I think what you're trying to say is . . ."

The point is, do I really want to be part of this mega-tree? Plus, the email has some creepy NSA-like privacy-invasion vibes. How did this dairy farmer know all this about me? And why should I trust him?

On the other hand, the less cynical hand, I'm oddly moved. Here I am, sitting in my home office in New York City, subjected to endless Internet headlines about our world's seeming descent into disaster—wars, racism—and up pops this startling news about how I'm connected to thousands of other humans across the globe. These newfound cousins would likely come in all shapes, sizes, and ethnic backgrounds: tall cousins and short cousins, white cousins and black cousins, carnivorous cousins and vegan cousins, gay cousins and straight cousins, cilantro-loving cousins and cousins who believe cilantro tastes like Satan's unwashed tube socks.

All of us different, all of us linked.

What I'm trying to say (as my brother-in-law explained to me later) is that I experienced a profound sense of belonging. I felt a part of something larger than myself. I glimpsed the Ultimate Social Network.

The timing of the email couldn't have been better. During the last several years, I've become increasingly obsessed with family, which might be an inherited trait. When I was a kid, my dad spent years building a family tree. Not quite eighty thousand, but it reached back multiple generations. He'd show me the names of my Polish and Ukrainian great-grandparents. He'd tell me about their lives. How they were farmers and general store owners; one even found a niche selling peacocks to nobles. How some fled the Russian pogroms by hiding in a haystack on the back of a cart. How my great-grandfather was supposed to pick up his wife and kids at Ellis Island but missed their arrival because he was eating a second bowl of soup. How the wife and kids had to stay overnight in the detention facility, confused, ignorant, and anxious they'd be sent back to Poland.

As a young man, I scoffed at these tales. I was an obnoxious little rebel who rejected all institutions, including family. I preferred to spend zero time thinking about my ancestors. Why should I care about these people, just because we happen to share some DNA by accident of birth? It's not rational. It's arbitrary. It's a relic of the past.

But as so often happens to people, I got older, I had kids, and I magically turned into my dad. Now I spend most of my time thinking about family: How can I give my three young sons a sense of belonging? What kind of wisdom and ethics from my ancestors can I pass along to my kids?

And then comes Jules Feldman's email. It stays in my mind the next day. And the next. And the week that followed.

CHAPTER 2

The World Family Tree

When I tell my brother-in-law Eric about the strange email from Jules Feldman, he, of course, thinks it sounds suspicious. He asks me how many of the eighty thousand relatives have hit me up for rides to the airport.

But he does have a suggestion. I should get in touch with a guy from California he'd recently met: Randy Schoenberg.

Randy—who I later learned is my fourteenth cousin twice removed—is a fascinating character. He's famous in the genealogy community. Also controversial (detractors use words like *stubborn* and *impossible*, which we'll get to later).

Randy's own family history is notable: he's the grandson of the great modern composer Arnold Schoenberg. Randy himself is more comfortable composing legal briefs. He's a lawyer best known for representing an Austrian Jewish woman whose family's Gustav Klimt painting *Woman in Gold* was stolen by the Nazis. Against all odds, Randy got the painting back from the Austrian government.

They even made a movie about his Nazi art case, with Ryan Reynolds playing Randy. Which makes sense, since both Ryan and Randy have abs that could grate Parmesan cheese (margin of error: plus or minus one person).

"So you're interested in genealogy?" Randy says, when I call him for advice a few days later. "I warn you. It's addictive."

I tell him I can handle it.

Randy explains to me that this is the most thrilling time in the history of genealogy. Which may sound a little like saying we're in the sexiest era of professional bowling.

I felt that way too once. But developments in genealogy actually have enormous consequences for everyone's life.

Randy tells me genealogy—on which Americans spend a mind-boggling $3 billion a year—is undergoing two revolutions, each with their own grand potential and heated controversies. First, the DNA revolution. You can spit into a tube, send it off to a service, and they'll send you back a list of cousins. We'll get to DNA in a minute.

The second revolution is online: massive Internet family trees.

"Like Ancestry.com?" I say.

"Well, yes. But there are other services. Ones with a different model that I like better."

Ancestry.com focuses on building your own private tree. The new model—found on sites like Geni and WikiTree and FamilySearch—is a more collaborative, Wikipedia-like approach. "Instead of everybody having their own little bonsai tree, you have this enormous forest of connected trees that everybody works on."

The secret is in combining the separate trees. You input your family tree. And if you have, say, a Jeff Bezos on your tree, and there's a Jeff Bezos on a different tree, and you realize it's the same Jeff Bezos, you have the option to merge trees. And you merge and merge and grow and grow.

"It's like everybody working on the same jigsaw puzzle," says Randy. "It's called the World Family Tree."

That does sound cool, if somewhat Orwellian.

"How many people are on it?" I ask.

"Let me check. They have a counter on the site." I hear Randy clicking keys in the background. "Okay, here it is . . . 70,420,308."

What? Seventy million? All of a sudden, Jules Feldman's eighty-thousand-person tree seems like a bush.

"Actually, it just got bigger," says Randy. "Three more relatives. Now it's 70,420,311."

There are cousins in more than 160 countries and counting. In a decade or two, Randy says, it's quite possible that we'll have a tree linking all seven billion humans on earth. That feeling of connectedness? It just went into overdrive. The Human family isn't just stoner talk. It's becoming a reality.

"Here's a fun game," says Randy, who isn't on Geni's payroll—he's just one of its biggest fans and its unofficial mayor. "You can figure out how you're related to famous people and historical figures. Give me a name."

"Dr. Ruth," I say. I'm not sure why the octogenarian sex expert was the first to pop into my head, but now it's out there.

I hear Randy typing into Geni. There's a long pause.

"Dr. Ruth is your wife's first cousin once removed's husband's fourth cousin's wife," he pronounces.

"Wait, so she's my cousin?"

"Well, by marriage. Some of them will be blood relatives, but others will be by marriage."

"So is she really family?" I ask.

"You consider your brother-in-law family?"

Reluctantly, I admit I do.

"Same idea, just a little further. It's like Six Degrees of Kevin Bacon, but everyone is Kevin Bacon."

I spend the next day inputting my own family tree into Geni and searching for famous people. I put Abraham Lincoln into the search bar and click the "find the connection" button. It takes twenty excruciating seconds, but up comes the chain. Cousin Abe is just seventeen steps away through marriage. Jackson Pollock is fourteen steps away, hence my kids' splatter paint skills. Actress Rachel Weisz is my twelfth cousin by blood. What about Mick Jagger? No path found. That's okay. I never liked that *Emotional Rescue* album.

I can't wait to start name-dropping my new relatives. That weekend, our friends Paul and Lisa come over, and Paul mentions that President Obama was in New York on Friday.

"Oh, Barack Obama? He's my cousin, you know," I say.

"Um. Yeah, you guys are dead ringers," says Paul.

"No, really."

Lisa laughs nervously, unsure how to respond. Julie explains that I've been planning this all day. I retrieve my laptop from my room and call up the page with Obama and me.

"He's my fifth-great aunt's husband's father's wife's seventh-great nephew."

"Wow, you guys are practically brothers," Paul says. "Not sure why you weren't appointed ambassador to the Bahamas."

Lisa is a bit more impressed.

I explain I'm also related to Einstein (just thirteen steps away) and Halle Berry (just twenty-four steps).

It's not all good news, I add.

"I'm also a distant relative of serial killer Jeffrey Dahmer."

"Oh my," says Lisa.

"But that's through Julie's side."

"Good one," Julie says.

"It's true," I say. "Through the Zuckermans. Just twenty-one steps away. So, if you ever hear that I've been chopped up and stuck in a freezer . . ."

"Very clever," Julie says. "You're also obviously related to Oscar Wilde."

Lisa wants to know how this works. "Is it legit?"

It's a good question: Is it legit? Depends on whom you ask. Collaborative genealogy is still controversial. It raises big questions about privacy—as in how safe is our data?—and concerns about accuracy: How are these huge trees monitored? What's to stop a prankster from making Paul Revere the son of Iggy Pop and Doris Kearns Goodwin?

It's reminiscent of the battle between Wikipedia and the *Encyclopaedia Britannica*. Some disparagingly call collaborative genealogy "fast genealogy," which has the same promiscuous connotation as fast women in the 1940s. In fact, a few traditional genealogists abhor Geni so much, they have gone in and vandalized the tree, disconnecting branches.

Randy remains a big defender. "Remember when everyone said, 'Oh, Wikipedia will never work?' And now we all use it every day." He says the World Family Tree has inaccuracies for sure, but there's also a committed team of "forest rangers"—volunteers who try to check the links. The big tree is getting more solid, he says, thanks to documentation and DNA. Scientists from Harvard and Columbia are conducting studies on the data. Plus, he argues, the upside is just too great. It's already an unprecedented record of the human race.

CHAPTER 3

DNA Sharing Is Caring

As I mentioned, the World Family Tree is just one of the revolutions in family history. The second is the use of DNA. You've probably heard of this, if not done it yourself: you spit into a tube or swab your cheek and send it off to a service such as 23andMe or Family Tree DNA.

A few weeks later, they send you back a report that includes the breakdown of your ethnic heritage (for example, 60 percent Northern European, 22 percent South Asian, 2 percent Native American, etc.) as well as a list of dozens, perhaps hundreds, sometimes thousands of cousins. These are people who share enough DNA with you to be considered your blood cousins—folks with whom you have a common ancestor within the last three hundred or so years.

I recently took the test, and after a few weeks, 23andMe sent me a list of presumed cousins. At my desk at home, I clicked on the list: 1,009 of them, mostly third or fourth or further. I scanned the list to see if I recognized any surnames—Glatt, Rose, Freeman, a lot of Anonymous. None rang a bell.

However, I did recognize one name.

"Julie Jacobs."

That would be my wife—the one related to Jeffrey Dahmer. I had asked her to take a test as well, and there she was. My cousin Julie. Huh. I'm a cousin humper.

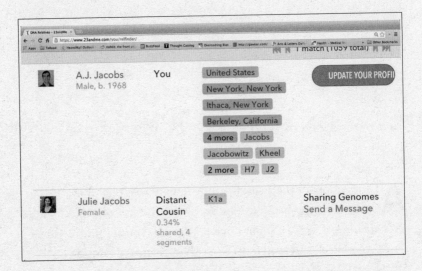

We aren't first or second cousins, so 23andMe labeled us "distant." Probably around seventh cousins, which means our sixth-great grandparents are the same people. I actually laugh out loud when I see my wife's name pop up on my computer next to all these strangers.

It seems so delightfully taboo. Maybe it'll spice up our marriage, I think. The forbidden fruit. Maybe my family and friends will whisper nervously—as if I'd married a burlesque dancer with a face tattoo or someone who frequently quotes Ayn Rand. Maybe Julie and I will grow closer as we hunker down against their disapproval.

I bring my laptop into the living room, where she is watching *Game of Thrones*.

"Julie, I have something to show you."

I point to the screen. "We're cousins!"

She leans in and examines the screen. She doesn't laugh. Instead, she makes a face like she's just found a dog hair in her ravioli.

"That's just weird," she says.

Over the next few days, I tell some friends. One starts humming the "Dueling Banjos" song from *Deliverance*. I get a couple royal-family-hemophilia comments. An acquaintance asks about our kids—do they have two heads or something?

No, we have three sons—a ten-year-old and two eight-year-old twins—and all are fine and monoheaded.

Julie's mom later tries to reassure her by telling her that Julie's great-grandparents were also cousins. First cousins.

"That's not helping," says Julie.

I do some research, and it turns out our result isn't too out of the ordinary. First, we're both descended from Eastern European Jews (Ashkenazi). Our ancestors were a highly endogamous population, which is a polite way of saying they loved to inbreed. Julie and I just carried on their tradition. Julie and I are distant enough that there's little risk of birth defects.

Plus, if you go back far enough, everyone is a blood cousin. Humans are a startlingly close-knit species. By some estimates we all share 99.9 percent of our DNA with one another. The farthest cousin you have on earth isn't so far off. According to some scientists, you are at most seventieth cousins with all other humans. (More on that in chapter 13.)

Eventually, Julie gets used to being married to her cousin and even starts bringing it up herself at parties. But I don't want to focus on her too much. She was just one of my thousand-plus cousins from 23andMe and one of seventy million from Geni.

I've been thinking: Is there anything I could do with this astounding bounty of new cousins? Reach out to them all? Ignore them all? Ask investment advice from my cousin Warren Buffett (eighteen steps away, through the Kingsbachers)?

CHAPTER 4

A Great (or Possibly Terrible) Idea

A few weeks after I got that email from my eighth cousin Jules Feldman, I set up a video call with him in Israel. He appears on my laptop screen—a kindly face with big tufts of white hair and big black glasses.

"Can you understand me?" he asks. "You don't have a problem with my South African accent?"

"I can indeed," I say.

Jules moved from South Africa to a kibbutz as an idealistic young man in 1971. He's married, has a degree in anthropology, five grown kids, and four hundred cows.

I ask him what he does with his list of eighty thousand relatives. Does it serve any purpose in his life? Jules says he loves connecting people—both on the tree and in real life.

One highlight came when he introduced a brother and sister. The sister was estranged from the father and didn't know she had a sibling. Jules got them in touch with each other. They met at a restaurant in Jerusalem. "The sister was so emotional she couldn't drink a glass of water."

But it worked out. "Now the brother loves being able to say, 'My sister this, my sister that.' That's what makes it feel worthwhile, like you've touched people's lives."

"How many of the people on your tree have you met?"

"Well, we had a family reunion a few years ago. Had more than three thousand here at a big hall in Jerusalem."

Wait. That stopped me. Three *thousand*.

The biggest family reunion I'd ever attended had about a hundred people. It was ten years ago at a restaurant in New York's Chinatown. My sister, Beryl, and my dad organized it. (Incidentally, the restaurant got confused, and when we all arrived, there was a huge sign congratulating my sister and my dad on their marriage. It was disturbing.)

But this was different. A mega-reunion.

Interesting.

After we finish, I start to think. If Jules could organize one, maybe I could too. An even bigger one. A *worldwide* reunion. Like Woodstock, but with more pants and antiperspirant. Sister Sledge could come and sing "We Are Family." It could be huge. It could be historic. It could be a nightmare.

Later that night, after we put the kids to bed, I ask Julie, "What if I threw a reunion for my seventy million relatives?"

"Why?"

I tell her maybe it'd send a good message. An absurd message, but a good one.

"I mean, not all of the relatives would come," I say. "Some will have doctor's appointments or squash tournaments. So it wouldn't be quite seventy million." I'm actually hoping for five thousand.

"Still sounds a bit overwhelming," she says.

I nod.

"Maybe make a list of pros and cons," she suggests.

Good idea. I get out a notebook and start with the pros.

THE PROS

1. I COULD BREAK A WORLD RECORD.

My dad is a world record holder. He's a lawyer and he loves to write long legal articles. More than that, he loves to footnote them. A few years back, he wrote an article with 4,824 footnotes, more than double anyone else in history, establishing himself as the Wayne Gretzky of footnotes. He sent his accomplishment in to the *Guinness Book of World Records*, but legal footnotes don't get the same respect as eight-foot-long fingernails. So he had to settle for a mention in Harper's Index.

Point is, breaking a record would be firmly in the family tradition. It'd be a tribute to my dad's love of outlandish but (ostensibly) impressive pursuits.

I click on the Guinness website, and, unlike with footnotes, there is a category for Largest Family Reunion. The record holders are the Lilly family from West Virginia. In 2009 their reunion drew 2,585 people. (Jules Feldman never submitted his.) Big, but certainly breakable.

2. IT'D BE GOOD FOR MY KIDS.

I recently read a parenting magazine article that said the best way to bond with your family is to do projects together, like build a treehouse or a gazebo. I don't own a power drill and I don't know the meaning of words like *joist*. So this could be my version of a gazebo. Our big family project.

And the topic would be good for my sons, too. I read a study from Emory University that found that kids who learn their family history are happier and healthier and never grow up to be meth addicts or *Bachelor* contestants. It gives them a sense of belonging. It enmeshes them in the world.

3. IT'S A FOOLPROOF PLAN TO END ALL WAR AND RACISM.

Okay, perhaps that's overreaching. I'm not Bono.

But maybe the we-are-all-family message would resonate with a few people. Maybe it'd increase the total kindness quotient in the world by four or five metric kindness units. Maybe it could put a tiny chink in the us-versus-them mentality. Maybe it could move my karma toward positive territory, counteracting all the times I used the handicapped bathroom.

4. I COULD STRETCH THE IDEA OF FAMILY TO ITS BREAKING POINT.

It occurs to me that I've got two paradoxical goals. First, to celebrate family. And second, to deconstruct family.

The notion of family was never simple, but it's now blurrier than ever. We live in the era of gay marriage, surrogates, sperm donors, open adoption, and eggs fertilized with three people's DNA. We create ad hoc families of friends and coworkers, what novelist Armistead Maupin called the "logical family" as opposed to the "biological family."

I'm all for this. I say, kick the door open on that definition. As my grandfather's niece's husband's sixth cousin Hillary Clinton says, it takes a village. The more potential parental and sibling figures, the better. I know some of my conservative cousins disagree. But maybe at the event, they'd meet some unorthodox families and see that they are worthy cousins.

5. I COULD DO A DEEP STUDY OF MY NEARBY BRANCHES.

Genealogists love to quote Alex Haley, author of *Roots*: "In all of us there is a hunger, marrow-deep, to know our heritage—to know who we are and where we have come from. Without this enriching knowledge, there is a hollow yearning. No matter what our attainments in life, there is still a vacuum, an emptiness, and the most disquieting loneliness."

I honestly didn't have much of that hunger until recently. But as my kids have gotten older, my appetite has grown. I want to figure out what to tell my sons about their heritage. I'm blessed with some colorful characters on my immediate family tree, but I've been embarrassingly ignorant of their stories. I want to know more about my grandfather, a labor lawyer and civil rights pioneer named Theodore Kheel. And my great-great-grandfather, who ran for office on the Bull Moose Party ticket. There are suffragists, animal rights activists, anarchists, and embezzlers. Lots to tell my kids.

6. IT WILL BE THE ULTIMATE LINKEDIN.

I can play the cousin card and reach out to anyone I want—presidents, rock stars, titans, eighties TV actresses on whom I had crushes. (This tactic turned out to be shockingly effective or surprisingly alienating, depending on the cousin.)

———

So, SIX PROS. Not bad. On another sheet of notebook paper I make a list of the negatives.

THE CONS

1. THE MONEY.

Never having hosted anything bigger than a twenty-person birthday party for Julie, I've got no idea how to budget this. My friend Paul—who puts on conventions for a living—said the hidden fees are endless: "Insurance. Poster design. Duct tape. You can't believe how much duct tape these things require."

That was concerning. I'm not out to make money on my reunion, but I don't want to use up my kids' college fund on adhesives.

And yet this hurdle can be overcome, right? I mean, it's a party for the whole world. I can sell tickets. And get sponsors! Yes, maybe Coca-Cola will sponsor it, and all the cousins will join hands and sing "I'd Like to Teach the World to Sing (In Perfect Harmony)"! Sure, I don't allow my kids to drink Coke because it's corrosive dirt-colored sugar water, but maybe for the greater cause?

2. IT'S A RIDICULOUS AMOUNT OF WORK.

When I later tell Jules Feldman about my idea, he pauses for a long time. "I'm a bit concerned your plan might just be a tad ambitious," he says at last. To say he is using understatement would be itself an understatement.

He explains that his reunion took six years of planning and the help of thirty near-full-time volunteers. It required committees and meetings and gargantuan spreadsheets and reams of Post-its.

3. IT COULD BACKFIRE SPECTACULARLY.

First, if I am doing this partly to bond with my kids, what if it fails? Will I embarrass them? Will they be scared off from ever attempting big projects?

The risk of public humiliation is high. Imagine if fourteen people show up. Or if a bunch of my cousins get food poisoning from bad fish tacos. Or if, instead of peace and harmony, there's an all-out brawl, perhaps started when Taylor Swift shin-kicks Katy Perry.

My brother-in-law Eric, for one, doesn't buy my whole premise. He thinks families fight as much as strangers.

"Maybe you're right," I say. But I have an instinct he's wrong. As much as families bicker, I think humans have a built-in bias to treat cousins— even distant ones—better than total strangers.

I've dubbed my theory the Judge Judy Effect. I came up with it after figuring out that Judge Judy is my eighth cousin twice removed. For years, I'd hated Judge Judy, the TV personality who rolls her eyes and berates the guests on her show. I found her borderline evil.

But when I discovered our connection, I could feel my perspective shift. Rational or not, I said to myself, Oh, Judge Judy. She's not so bad. She's just doing her shtick. Underneath all that bluster, my cousin Judy is probably a sweetheart.

This is a trivial example, I know. It's a long way from that to world peace. But I want to prove Eric wrong, and this would be a start.

I TAKE A look at my lists of pros and cons. The cons are big and scary and make me sweat. But the pros? Some huge ones there too. And look at the number of them. So . . .

Yes!

I pump my fist, or at least mentally pump it. *It is on!*

After which I immediately second-guess myself.

CHAPTER 5

A Pandemonium of Genealogists

There's an annual genealogy convention in New York called, fittingly enough, the Genealogy Event. I figure I should go. I can meet some family history power players, get ideas for my own event, and, perhaps most important, learn how to research my blood ancestors. My adviser Randy says that growing your own bonsai tree—your great-aunts, your grandparents et cetera—is crucial to merging with the Amazonian forest of distant relatives.

When I walk into the convention hall, I see booths for all types of ancestry—Irish, German, Jewish, African-American, Italian, and Colonial New York. I see signs for lectures on decoding DNA and searching vintage newspapers. I see rows of computer terminals displaying documents—census forms, birth certificates. I see a higher-than-average number of men in Hawaiian shirts.

As for the crowd in general? Well, you wouldn't mistake this for Coachella.

Despite the tech revolution, genealogy still skews a bit toward the mature side. Lots of snow-white hair, as well as the occasional oxygen tank. After chatting with one genealogy enthusiast, I ask to exchange emails. "I don't use email much, but I have a fax number. You want my fax?" (I know. Replace *email* with *Snapchat* and that's me in ten years.)

The aging crowds make sense. You get older. Mortality looms. You ponder your legacy. You hope your descendants remember you. You realize you should do the same for your ancestors so you can set a good example. It's a matter of respect. As one genealogist told me, "If there is a heaven, I want to have something to say to the people up there."

But an older crowd doesn't mean the event lacks for thrills. I'm pleasantly surprised by the amount of sex and violence I encounter at the Genealogy Event.

I attend a lecture about searching newspaper archives, and the lecturer brings up article after lurid article. "Our ancestors lived in violent times," she says, as she shows us a story about a man who brought a gun to a wedding and shot a fellow guest. "There was always an ancestor of mine being killed or arrested." Another exhibitor is dressed in a black-and-white-striped prison jumpsuit topped with a striped cap. He specializes in researching ancestral black sheep.

The convention hall is packed. As anyone will tell you, this is a boom time for family history. There are TV and radio shows, cruises and ancestry superstars like Henry Louis Gates Jr. According to a 2012 *Bloomberg* article, "genealogy" is the second-most-searched topic on the Internet, topped only by porn. Frankly, I'm skeptical of that statistic. Not the porn part. That's quite believable.

But regardless if it's number two or number twelve most-searched, it's an enormous field and it's growing fast. People want to feel connected and anchored. They want to visit what has been called the "Museum of Me."

After a couple of hours, I make an appointment with a trained genealogist for the afternoon. Her name is Barbara Sontz. She's a retired IT professional with sandy-brown hair and glasses.

We meet at a table in the conference center.

Barbara eyes the pen and paper they've given us. "Let me get a pencil," she says, retrieving one from a nearby table. "I'm a pencil person."

"Pencil seems like a good idea in genealogy," I say.

"It's good for everything," Barbara says. "I don't like to commit."

I know the feeling. Committing to this reunion has been traumatic.

The Vilna Gaon. (Courtesy of the Yivo Institute)

"What do you know about your family history?" asks Barbara, peering over her glasses.

"Well, I'm told that I'm a descendant of the Vilna Gaon," I say.

The Vilna Gaon is a famous eighteenth-century Lithuanian rabbi, and according to the tree my dad compiled, he's my sixth-great grandfather.

"Are you sure?" she says. "Or is that family legend? Because everyone's descended from a famous rabbi or the tsar's doctor in their family lore."

"I'm moderately sure. I wouldn't want to put it in pen."

We go online on my laptop and find a list of Vilna Gaon descendants on a Jewish website that seems reputable. There are thousands of names, and right there, if you scroll to the *J*s, is my name. The Vilna Gaon is my mother's mother's father's father's father's father's father's father.

"What *yichus!*" Barbara says.

Yichus is the Yiddish word for breeding, pedigree, blood.

I have conflicted feelings about this *yichus* of mine. On the one hand, I'm flattered. In some Jewish circles, being a descendant of the Vilna

Gaon is the Semitic equivalent of having an ancestor from the *Mayflower*. Look at me! I'm fancy.

On the other hand, I've always found societies like the Daughters of the American Revolution off-putting. They seem highly undemocratic. The dormant high school rebel in me is offended. The whole point of my reunion is to show we're all related, to flatten the family tree, not to celebrate supposed genetic elitism.

Plus, is my *yichus* really that impressive? Consider this. The Vilna Gaon is my sixth-great grandfather. I have two parents, four grandparents, eight great-grandparents. By the time we get to the Gaon, he's just one of 256 sixth-great grandparents. (It's slightly less than that, because of cousin marriage, but we'll get to that later.)

So yes, I might have a smidge of his DNA. But I also could have DNA from the 255 other men and women in his era. The farmers, the peddlers, the horse thieves, the layabouts, the button merchants. Why the focus on the one guy? It seems a slap in the face to my other ancestors. Maybe instead of the Gaon's Talmudic genius, I inherited the tailor's hand-eye coordination and ragweed allergies.

The point is, most family histories play favorites. We celebrate the fancy and elite. We fixate on the fact that we have a drop of blood from Pocahontas or Grover Cleveland or Genghis Khan, and ignore the thousands of Regular Josiahs.

I flip-flop between the two points of view. One moment I'll take pride in my scintilla of ancestral celebrity. The next, I'll shake my head with disappointment at my ridiculous sense of self-importance. I don't tell Barbara any of this. But I do tell her about my plan for the reunion. She seems intrigued.

"How are you going to find thousands of cousins?" she asks.

I tell her partly through DNA testing, partly through collaborative sites like Geni.

She looks concerned. "Geni is controversial among traditionalist genealogists," she says.

She asks when the event is. I tell her I'm considering next summer, June 6, a Saturday.

"Saturday? You're not going to get observant Jews to come on a Saturday."

Damn. She's right. I'd forgotten about the Jewish sabbath. Then again, if I have it on a Sunday, it will be a problem for any out-of-town cousins with long flights.

Family is complicated.

REUNION COUNTDOWN: 51 WEEKS

After talking to Julie, I'm sticking with Saturday, June 6—about a year off— and hoping my Orthodox friends will forgive me.

I need a name for my event. I read Julie some options I've written in a notebook. "How about CousinFest?" Julie says it somehow sounds kinky. "Kinnection?" Too punny. "The Mother of All Reunions?" Too Saddam Husseiny.

"What about just calling it what it is: Global Family Reunion?"

"Maybe," Julie says. "It does have clarity."

I ask my event planner friend Paul what he thinks of the name Global Family Reunion. Sounds pretentious, he says. I disagree. It may be pretentious, but it also suggests importance. We're just like the Clinton Global Initiative, because we both have the word *global* in the name. It sounds like we know what we're doing. It's definitely not just a guy with no experience throwing a massive event without a real plan or budget.

CHAPTER 6

Historical Voyeurism

Inspired by the Genealogy Event, I've been researching my ancestors' lives. I'm fascinated but also feeling a bit like a creepy voyeur.

There's a genealogy podcast I listen to that has the motto "Your ancestors want their stories to be told." Which sounded good when I first heard it. But upon reflection, I'm wondering if it's true. Maybe some of them just want to be left the hell alone. And if they do want their stories told, perhaps they want a highly sanitized version.

Consider my grandmother, my mom's mom: Ann Kheel, who died twelve years ago. I adored my grandmother. She was an unforgettable character. She had six kids, whom she organized by color coding (one got green towels, another red, and so on). She wore wool caps and mittens when biking in August. She spent her free time fighting for civil rights. I still treasure the copy of Martin Luther King Jr.'s book that he signed for her, thanking her for her hard work on the cause.

But she wasn't a fan of the unvarnished truth. She liked the truth fully varnished, with a tinted glaze and a doily on top. In her Ford Fiesta, she covered up the digital clock on the dashboard with masking tape. "I don't want to be reminded of how fast time goes by," she used to say. She avoided movies with any hint of tragedy.

She was an amazing archivist—I have a hard drive full of newspaper clippings and letters and photos that she kept—but there's no doubt it's a whitewashed archive. Just look at the *Family News*, a pagelong update she mailed to the extended family every other month for forty years. I have them all collected in a three-ring binder, and it's the size of a Jonathan Franzen novel. Just a huge amount of information. There are births, job promotions, vacations. What you won't find is much scandalous information. It's sort of like *Pravda* under Khrushchev, but with fewer stories about turnip farms. You won't read about cousins losing their jobs or kids experimenting with hallucinogenic mushrooms.

Some family members don't even exist in the *Family News* universe. In the 1980s, my aunt married an ex-cult leader; he was a Jewish guy from California who converted to Hinduism, then Christianity, then to Hasidic Judaism. He did the religious rounds. In the 1970s, he had seventy followers who lived in yurts outside Ithaca. His name was Gil. My grandmother despised him so much, she couldn't even bring herself to type his name into the *Family News*. She referred to him only as "he," as in "He and Kate will be visiting in March," which I always found an ironic echo of the Orthodox refusal to write the name God (usually written *G-d*).

Same with the family tree my dad worked on. When she helped him compile the tree, certain relatives simply disappeared, such as the first husband of her sister Frances. "She was married to him for only a year," my grandmother said. Which didn't explain why my grandmother was absolutely fine with including the sister of violinist Yehudi Menuhin, even though her marriage into the family lasted only six months.

I wonder if my grandma Kheel would be appalled that I'm poking around the family history, looking for both the good and bad. In one way, it's lucky she died before the Internet Age, in which it's much harder to control your family's narrative.

The Internet, of course, has birth and marriage and death records. But it also has online newspaper archives—billions of pages with the most ridiculous minutiae you can imagine.

After just a few hours of searching, the newspapers are already turning up fruit. On Newspapers.com, I find a reference to my third-great uncle Solomon Kingsbaker. It's just a single mention, but it's an interesting one. It's a 1904 advertisement in the *Roanoke News*, and in it, Uncle Solomon expresses his passionate endorsement of . . . a hemorrhoid cream:

> S. Kingsbaker of 80 East Ohio Street, Chicago, writes: "I had a bad case of Piles for several years. BANNER SALVE cured me quickly and permanently after several doctors had failed to relieve me."

Part of me is delighted, since I have hemorrhoids myself. Look at that! A profound echo across generations! We are connected by our rectal discomfort! This is what genealogy is all about.

But part of me feels terrible for Uncle Sol. That's his entire public legacy: swollen butt vessels. Is that how he wanted to go down in history? Is that the story he wants told? Did Banner Salve even get my uncle Sol's permission? Doubtful. (Note: Banner Salve was later busted as a quack potion by the US government.)

BANNER SALVE

is the most healing salve in the world. It cures Sores, Cuts, Burns and all Skin Diseases. It positively

Cures Piles

S. Kingsbaker, 80 East Ohio Street, Chicago, writes: "I had a bad case of Piles for several years. BANNER SALVE cured me quickly and permanently after several doctors and remedies had failed to relieve me."

GUARANTEED. Price 25 Cents

Fannie and Gerson Friedenheit, circa 1858.

I find another surprise when searching my great-great-great-grandfather Gerson Friedenheit. His name appears on an obscure antique auction site. There's a photo of six mottled silver spoons from 1868; the caption says the owners were "Fannie and Gerson Friedenheit. Gerson fought in the Civil War."

Hold on. My third-great grandfather was a veteran of the Civil War? I find that hard to believe. Wouldn't I have known about this? I wasn't even aware Jewish soldiers served in the Civil War, though I suppose it makes sense. (Turns out about ten thousand Jewish Americans fought in the Civil War: seven thousand for the Union, three thousand for the Confederacy.)

I've heard of Gerson. My grandmother knew her great-grandfather personally: when she was four years old, she attended Gerson's sixtieth wedding anniversary.

Certainly she would have mentioned he fought in the Civil War if it were true? Half an hour of frantic Google searches later, I'm not any closer to confirmation.

At the Genealogy Event, one lecturer told me about a special subscription database for wartime records. I grit my teeth, pay the eighty-dollar annual fee, and join Fold3. Gerson has several citations. The first is a handwritten letter to the Union Army with the signature Gerson Friedenheit.

In the letter, Gerson explains that he owns a general store in Missouri, and one of his customers began praising the Confederacy in his presence. The customer talked about the death of a Union soldier and "expressed much gratification, that this was good news."

So Gerson reported the customer by name. Ratted him out. Lesson: You do *not* talk sedition in front of my ancestors.

I click on the next document. It's a military record: Private Gerson Friedenheit from the Twenty-Fifth Regiment enrolled in the Missouri Militia in 1864.

"Whoa!" I'm alone at my computer, but I actually blurt it out loud like Keanu.

I call up my mom. "Did you know you are the direct descendant of a Civil War soldier?"

"Really?"

"Gerson Friedenheit! Missouri Militia!"

"Good for Gerson!" my mom says. Her tone is eerily similar to the one she used when her grandkids finished a twelve-piece *Finding Nemo* jigsaw puzzle.

That night, while doing dishes, I mention my discovery to Julie.

"You know how America almost split in half in the eighteen hundreds but then was saved?"

"Yes, I've heard about that."

"Well, my family had a lot to do with that. So . . . you're welcome."

I know it's absurd to take credit for the accomplishments of a man born two centuries ago. I didn't help him. I didn't grind his coffee or shine his boots—just as I had nothing to do with the Vilna Gaon's genius. Who knows what sliver of his DNA came down to me.

And yet, here I am, gloating. I can't help it.

I always pictured my ancestors as victims of the Cossacks, which I'm sure many were. But here's one ancestor who was a freedom fighter, the one doing the ass kicking. It felt empowering.

I should mention that the rest of the military record wasn't quite as inspiring. Gerson enrolled in late August of 1864 and was discharged for "medical reasons" in early October of 1864.

Six weeks. Okay, not an epic amount of time.

But that's six weeks longer than I ever served in the Union Army. And maybe in those six weeks he saw a lot of action. Maybe the medical reason was a bullet wound he got from jumping in front of his fellow soldier. Hopefully it wasn't hemorrhoids.

I SPEND THE next day scouring for mentions of Gerson in my grandmother's archive, which my aunt Jane scanned and loaded into an orange hard drive a few years ago.

There's lots of Gerson info. The archive reveals Gerson emigrated from Germany in about 1845. He arrived in New York and worked as a peddler. He started dating Fannie's sister, but soon switched siblings (no mention of the discarded sister's reaction).

There's a photo of young Gerson and Fannie all dressed up. He's got an Amish-style beard, no mustache. She's got a middle part and a trace of a smile. Gerson and Fannie apparently had a happy marriage—or at least a prolific one. Fourteen kids, eight girls and six boys. He supported his large brood first with his general store, and later switched to the insurance business.

Still no mention of the Civil War.

Finally, after half an hour, I notice another document. It's the text of a speech from Gerson and Fannie's sixtieth wedding anniversary—the one my grandmother attended.

The speech, written by the grandkids, is organized as a timeline of

Gerson and Fannie's lives. Some of the events are real, some exaggerated. In the section on 1864, I find this:

March 5   Grandpa enlists in Army of Union

March 7   Jewish holiday, Grandpa refuses to fight

March 8   Day of rest for Grandpa

March 9   Grandpa discovers a way to prevent his gun from going off

March 10   The Colonel tells Grandpa, "You're a hell of a soldier; go home."

Okay. So it's become clear to me that Gerson was not a major Civil War hero. You won't find granite statues of Gerson Friedenheit astride his steed, his bayonet poised.

And yet, oddly, this little morsel of family satire gives me a new reason to be proud of him. He obviously was secure enough to let his grandchildren bust his chops. He had a sense of humility. Gerson Friedenheit, Civil War veteran and father of fourteen, could take a joke.

REUNION COUNTDOWN: 49 WEEKS

I've sent off my first batch of save-the-date notices. Using the message function on 23andMe, I pinged 100 third, fourth, and fifth cousins I've never met.

"I know this sounds odd," I write in the message, before telling them about my event, and that they are welcome to come.

The reaction is decidedly varied.

"Is this a scam?" responds one.

"This sounds horrifying," says another. "I have enough relatives. I would rather spend my weekend in Gehenna." (I reply, "So how many should I put you down for?")

Other family members are more open-minded. "Par-teeee!!! I am so there," writes a fourth cousin from Florida. Another quotes John Donne's "No Man Is an Island" and says he thinks that the event will show we're all "part of the main." A Cleveland woman says, "I want to meet all these marvelous people with whom I share one or two drops of blood. Do you also have blue eyes? Do you have curly hair? Were you a blond child? Do you love to laugh? Out loud, from the belly?" (No, no, no, yes, and sometimes.)

Several people promise to bring casseroles or potato salad for three thousand.

CHAPTER 7

Genetic Jambalaya

I'm reading a sci-fi book to my kids called *Space Case*, about a bunch of families living on the moon. It takes place twenty-five years in the future, and nearly all the kids are massively mixed-race: The twelve-year-old narrator has a black mom and a white dad. His friends include "The Brahmaputra-Marquez family (Indian mom, Latino dad) . . . Kira (Asian mom, black dad) . . . Riley Bock (Korean-Italian mom, Irish-Sri Lankan-Peruvian-Choctaw dad)." The lily-white kids are the outliers.

The idea is that all these DNA mash-ups have reduced racism in the future. It brings to mind the slightly less kid-friendly quote from the movie *Bulworth*. Warren Beatty plays a senator who comes up with this proposal to solve the racial divide. "All we need is a voluntary, free-spirited, open-ended program of procreative racial deconstruction," he says. "Everybody just gotta keep fuckin' everybody till they're all the same color."

A quarter-century of free-spirited procreation probably won't be enough, but the data says we are at least on the road toward a blended world. In the last thirty years in America, the rate of intermarriage between spouses of different races or ethnicities has doubled. Most of my nieces and nephews have pie charts with multiple slices: Peruvian, Colombian, Korean, Indian, Native American, as well as Jewish.

Even many of us adults are far more varied than we'd expect. As Harvard professor Henry Louis Gates Jr. says, "There's no such thing as racial purity. . . . There has almost never been an African-American person tested by one of the three major DNA companies who is 100 percent Sub-Saharan. The average African-American has 24 percent European ancestry."

I wanted to see my own blend. So I spat and cheek-scraped for pretty much every consumer DNA service that would send me test tubes. Before I reveal my mix, a very quick primer on these DNA tests:

The first DNA tests for consumers started in 2000 and came in two flavors: Y-DNA tests that focused on your paternal line, and mitochondrial DNA tests that focused on the maternal line. These two tests have the astounding ability to reach thousands of years into the past.

The Y-DNA test—which only men can take—reveals the makeup of your male sex chromosome, found on the twenty-third pair. It's an unusual chunk of DNA because it very rarely changes. It's passed down from father to son to son to son virtually intact. It's like a genetic version of a bronze cup from thousands of years ago.

The mitochondrial DNA is similar, but for the mother's line. It's the DNA stored in little pockets in the cells, passed from mother to offspring nearly unaltered for thousands of years.

These tests allow you to see where your distant ancestors roamed—North Africa? Central Europe? Australia?—because the DNA from different areas had telltale markers.

So, in one sense, an amazing insight. In another sense, a very skewed insight.

Here's why: Say you have 256 sixth-great grandparents. The Y-DNA would only give you information on one of those (your dad's dad's dad's dad's dad's dad's dad). So if that ancestor was from Iceland but your 255 other sixth-great grandparents were from Mongolia, you'd still show up as Icelandic. Mitochondrial DNA has the same weakness.

In 2007, 23andMe began offering a third type of test: autosomal DNA. This was a big revolution. This test analyzes the mix of DNA from both your mother's and father's lines. As author Christine Kenneally says, think of your DNA as a handful of sand. Each great-great-great-grandparent contributes a different color sand, and autosomal DNA tests let you see multiple grains. Which is why the services can send you pie charts with, say, 54 percent Western European, 26 percent Asian, 5 percent Native American, and so on.

Okay, now to my results. I took a wide range of the DNA tests, and it turns out . . . I'm Jewish. I know! Your mouth is agape. I'll give you a minute to process.

But here's the thing: the tests said I'm not 100 percent Jewish. Yes, my mom's mom's mom's mom's (etc.) side came from the Middle East and my dad's dad's dad's dad's dad's (etc.) side came from North Africa—both of which are consistent with Jewish patterns of migration. But the third test—the one that measures the mixture from all ancestors—had a little twist. That test said I was also 13 percent Scandinavian. I was elated. I love being Jewish, but I figure there's nothing wrong with a little variety.

"Break out the snowshoes and gravlax!" I told Julie. "I'm Scandinavian!" It empowered me, gave me courage to face the winter—my hardy Swedish genes would see me through the bitter New York chills.

A few months later I logged in to show a friend my results and got an unpleasant surprise. My Scandinavian DNA had plunged to 3 percent.

I called some geneticist friends about the mystery of my disappearing Swedish ancestors. Turns out the estimates of your ethnicity are based, in part, on comparing your DNA with the DNA of other customers in the company's database and what those people report about their origins from oral history and traditional trees. So if your pool of customers skews too Scandinavian, it can mess with the results.

"It's better than astrology," says genealogist Judy Russell, who brings some much-needed skepticism to the field of DNA ethnicity tests. "But it's far from perfect science."

The good news is, the greater the number of people in the DNA databases, the more accurate the estimates will become.

Last I checked, all of the databases show me as highly Eastern European, though with tiny dashes of other ethnicities, including Asian and Native American. One database rated me 96 percent Jewish but with 2.5 percent Arab and Egyptian ancestry, which made me happy. If it's true, I've got both sides of the world's most intractable ethnic conflict inside me, even if one side is just a sliver.

So I'm a mutt—just a tiny bit of a mutt, but a mutt nonetheless. I'm a big fan of muttiness. I'm hopeful that embracing our genetic jambalaya will erode tribalism for all of us. I know this is Mr. Rogers-ish, but at least I'm not alone. Bennett Greenspan, who founded Family Tree DNA, puts it this way: "I really do think that if someone finds out they have a little Jewish DNA, they'll be less inclined to stay quiet when someone tells an anti-Semitic joke."

There are instances of this happening. One story could have been scripted by J.J. Abrams: A radical nationalist politician and outspoken anti-Semite in Hungary found out he was part Jewish. He abandoned the far right and became an activist against discrimination.

I spoke with CeCe Moore, a genetic genealogist who spends her days connecting lost relatives. "When direct-to-consumer DNA testing was introduced, many academics were concerned people might use it to divide themselves. We've seen the exact opposite. People are learning of their diversity." Both ethnic diversity and political, she says. She worked with a Texas meteorologist who found his biological mother through DNA testing. He's gay and she's evangelical Christian. It could have gone terribly. But in a book he's writing, he explains that his mom overcame her bias and fully accepts him and his husband.

"I think it's tremendously important," Henry Louis Gates Jr. told me in an interview about how DNA tests reveal our ethnic jumbles. Gates, who is African-American, discovered through DNA testing that 50.1 percent of his DNA traces to Europe. His great-great-grandfather, for one, was white, probably of Irish descent. Gates's grandfather had light skin as a result. When Gates was nine years old his grandfather died, and Gates remembers seeing the body in the open casket. "When he was alive he was so white, we called him Casper behind his back. So you can imagine how white he was when he was dead. It looked like he'd been covered with alabaster and sprinkled with baby powder. I wanted to know how I, with this phenotype, could be related to a man who looked like a ghost."

It was one of the main reasons Gates became obsessed with family history at an early age. Gates says his mixed heritage helps him to see himself as having multiple identities. It expands his compassion.

That's not to say the fears of ancestral DNA testing are totally unfounded. The most disturbing instance I ran across was described in a *Vice* article. The reporter uncovered white supremacists having online contests to see who had the highest European DNA percentages. If they didn't get the so-called purity they wanted, some of them spun conspiracy theories. One white supremacist said that the DNA services are "rigged" to spread "multiculturalism and make whites think that they are racially mixed."

And DNA results can be traumatic. One article in *Fusion* quotes an African-American woman who discovered she was 15 percent white, which drove home the likely trauma of her slave ancestors, who, even if they weren't forcibly raped, were subjected to a monstrous power dynamic. "I cried a lot," Florida mom Nikiah Washington said. "I'm thinking about not just the biological things that are passed down, but the spiritual things, the experiences." In the end, she was glad she took the test. "You feel a little depressed, but it shows you how important you are, how out of something so terrible, you made it."

So it's complicated. It's no panacea. DNA testing is a tool, and like all tools, it can be used for good or ill. But as intermarriage increases, I'm hopeful the positives of DNA testing will outweigh the bad. And I'm also hopeful that the cousins at the Global Family Reunion will be of every hue possible. I want the event to look as diverse as a photo in a liberal arts college catalog.

REUNION COUNTDOWN: 47 WEEKS

Where should I hold this already overwhelming event? I've visited several venues. I checked out a retired aircraft carrier, the *Intrepid,* in the Hudson River (my ancestors did come over on boats) and the New York Mets ballpark, Citi Field (a fun idea, but the rental fee was decidedly nonfun).

I gave a talk recently at a museum called the New York Hall of Science in Queens. It's on the grounds of the 1964 World's Fair, which has nice symbolism. In my dreams, the Global Family Reunion is the runty brother of the World's Fair. This museum could be the one.

Turns out the woman who runs the Hall of Science is a friend's aunt, so there's sort of a family connection. Several phone calls later, she gives me a deal on the rental fee, which I'm praying I can cover with ticket sales and sponsors (my next step). And that's it. It's booked. It's getting real: The Global Family Reunion, June 6, 2015, on the grounds of the Hall of Science, Queens, New York.

Dear Lord.

CHAPTER 8

Groundhog Sam and My 2,585 Southern Cousins

I decide to do some event espionage—check out the competition. I'm going to join thousands of revelers as they descend on West Virginia for the Eighty-Fifth annual Lilly Family Reunion. As you might remember, the Lillys are the current Guinness World Record holders with 2,585.

The website says all are welcome, Lilly or not, so I take them at their word. I fly into Richmond airport and drive three hours—past clover-filled fields and gorgeous mountains blanketed with haze—to the town of Flat Top, West Virginia. I pass an exit that features two signs, one for Southern X-Posure Gentlemen's Club and one for Appalachian Bible College. Highly efficient: You can sin and repent at the same exit.

I turn left onto a mud-puddled road and see a banner hanging on a chain-link fence that reads "World's Largest Lilly Family Reunion: Guinness Record 2009."

As I pull up to the entrance, the first thing I see is an American flag flapping in the breeze. Beyond the flagpole is a small village of tents, several dozen picnic tables, yards of red-white-and-blue bunting and thousands of Lillys, young and old, tall and short, bearded and fresh-faced.

I head to the mess tent, where tins of mashed potatoes and egg salad sit atop red-and-white-checkered tables. I fill my plate and scan the room, trying not to look awkward. Which isn't easy, because I feel quite awkward, like a pole dancer at a revival meeting.

I spot a group of Lillys who look to be in their seventies.

"Mind if I sit down?" I ask.

Not at all, they say, scooching over on the bench to make room.

They ask me where I'm from. I explain I'm a native New Yorker writing a book about family, and I came down here not knowing a soul.

"Well, I've never met a stranger," says a smiling woman with wire-rimmed glasses.

Look at that. The Southern hospitality stereotype is getting support in the first five minutes. And of all Southern stereotypes, it's the one I most want to be true.

We chat for a bit, and I ask, "How'd you get a family this big?"

A man named Cecil answers. "There wasn't much to do up here except breed, and we were pretty good at that."

They all laugh.

So there you go. I wasn't going to bring up breeding, or interbreeding for that matter, but they seem to embrace the stereotype—or at least Cecil does—so I'm not going to argue.

World's Largest Family Reunion!
Groundhog Sam, Fighting Bob,
Jim Cute, Beaver Jim,
Bear-wallow Bob, Big George,
Lying Lewis, Hickory Bill,
Curly Joe, Preacher Will,
Grinning Jim, Kansas Bob,
Sock-head Andy,
Jerusalem Jim,
Miller Bob, Shady Jim,
Cousin Abe, Gentleman John,
One-armed Bill, Crazy Ike,
Randell Bob, Blind Joe,
Devil Sam,
Tom Ticklebritches,
Shooting Bob or
Snake-Bite John

After lunch, I wander around the colony of tents and barbecue pits and iPhones playing Taylor Swift. I pass a woman who is introducing two men to each other. "James Lilly, I'd like you to meet James Lilly." They chuckle.

Many of the Lilly men sport big beards, suspenders, flannel shirts, and trucker hats. Give them a glass of absinthe and a Zadie Smith novel and they could pass for hipsters in Brooklyn.

I arrive at the tent selling Lilly Family Reunion merchandise. There are huge family tree posters, books, and baseball caps. My favorite is a T-shirt with a list of some of the legendary Lillys of history. Among them: Groundhog Sam, Beaver Jim, Bear-wallow Bob, One-armed Bill, Tom Ticklebritches, Sock-head Andy, and Fighting Bob (not to be confused with Shooting Bob, also on the list).

Now *those*, I think to myself, are nicknames. I'm ashamed for my family, whose most inventive nickname is my father-in-law's "Larry Boy." His name is Larry. And then they added "boy" on the end.

The T-shirt also lists a man named Snake-Bite John.

"So I'm guessing John was bitten by a snake?" I ask the woman selling the shirt.

"Yep. He got bit when he was in the outhouse."

"On the . . . part that you use in the outhouse?"

"Yep."

I'm a little suspicious that they created these yarns and nicknames to please Northerners like me, the way the German waiters at Epcot wear lederhosen. But I buy the T-shirt anyway.

I meet an elderly Lilly relative named Bobby. He's a retired bus driver with hair the color of circus peanuts and eyes creased with deep crow's-feet.

Bobby appoints himself my tour guide. He tells me about the very first Lilly Family Reunion he attended in 1934. It was even bigger back then, like a state fair with twenty thousand people.

"There was a Ferris wheel and rides. The governor would come. Preachers would come. I remember a preacher who would land his pro-peller plane, make a sermon, then get on the plane and take off again."

He tells me tales of moonshiners and bathtubs filled with beer. Bobby raised three kids. "I never cussed in front of them, never drank in front of them," he says, as we sit on a bench.

"Never?"

He shakes his head. "I didn't want them to say to me, 'But you did it!'"

So it's confirmed: I'm a terrible father. I drink and cuss in front of my kids. They're only eight and ten, but they already sound like characters in a Tarantino film.

"I did smoke a pipe," says Bobby. "And I regret it."

He tells me that one of his daughters started smoking as a teenager, and she died of cancer when she was fifty.

"I still wonder if I had anything to do with that."

Bobby stays silent for a minute, then tells me about bringing up his boy.

"I remember one day my boy came home with a bruise on his head. So I ask him, 'Where'd you get that?' And he says that the preacher was beating the kids."

So Bobby goes down to the church. He grabs the preacher, puts him in a headlock, and the preacher's legs are flailing. And then Bobby starts punching him.

"And the preacher says, 'That hurts!'" remembers Bobby. "And I say, 'Oh, you notice that it hurts?' After that, the preacher stopped knocking the boys' heads."

I'm not a fan of violence, and if I were in Bobby's position, I'd have probably channeled my anger into filing stern reports and organizing urgent meetings. But I have to admit part of me admires Bobby's reaction. If anything can turn you into a vigilante, it's someone who hurts your kids.

We walk back to the mess hall and check out the Wall of Lilly Fame. There's a framed photo of Bob Lilly, the Dallas Cowboys defensive tackle. There's Tick Lilly, a pilot who they claim broke the sound barrier before Chuck Yeager did but who was denied proper credit by a government conspiracy. (Every family has one of these wronged heroes. In my family, it's my great-uncle David, who I was told invented a better color television that the TV industry squashed.)

After a couple more hours—during which time he introduced me to about forty-two Lillys—Bobby leaves to go home. As it turns to dusk, I wander among the tents myself. I pass a table with tins of yams and burgers.

"Did you eat?" asks a woman with a leg brace.

"I did."

"Well, I didn't see you eat, so you're going to have to eat again." She laughs. "You thirsty?"

"Actually, yes."

"How about a Coke?" She opens her cooler and hands me a soda.

"Can I—" I reach for my wallet.

"No," she says. "Absolutely not. We're all cousins here."

IT STARTS TO rain lightly, then hard. Puddles of water collect on top of the tarps, sagging down the tents. I join some of my fellow reuniongoers and push on the drooping parts, splashing the water onto the ground. I'm a cousin, after all. And then I say good-bye.

As I drive off back down that dirt road, I try to figure out what lessons I can take away. Certainly my event will need lots of music. The open-air stage where various Lillys sang and played violins and banjos was a center of energy. And nicknames: I need to start brainstorming nicknames.

But I'm having trouble concentrating, because I'm also feeling guilty. My goal is to crush the Lillys. Take their title.

And yet, here they were, welcoming me and calling me a cousin and friend. My goal doesn't feel so family-like anymore. It actually goes against the very thesis of my project. It feels Grinchy.

In the plane, I come up with a solution: Share the glory! What if we combine the Lilly Family Reunion and the Global Family Reunion, so they can still say they hold the record? I've already found a link to a couple of Lillys on the World Family Tree. Okay, it's settled. I'll be inviting hundreds of Lillys.

REUNION COUNTDOWN: 46 WEEKS

When I get home, Julie asks me how my reunion will be different from the Lillys'. She's an event planner—her company, Watson Adventures, puts on scavenger hunts—so she wants details.

"I'm thinking a TED conference meets Lollapalooza meets a family reunion," I tell her.

"I don't know what that means."

I don't either, really. My vague plan is to have a bunch of speakers talking about family from all angles—family food, family history, family genetics. We'll have music and games and contests and trivia and break records. And of course, scavenger hunts. And we won't have to pay for any of it, because they're all family.

"I'm stressed out just listening to your list," Julie says.

CHAPTER 9

Embracing Failure

We're in a rental car on our way to visit friends in Connecticut. We drive past Exit 22 on the Henry Hudson Parkway, which leads to a semisuburb called Riverdale. "Hey, that's where your great-grandparents used to live," I tell the boys. One Sunday a month, I say, my parents and sister and I would go there and eat turkey, play Nok Hockey, bounce on the pogo stick, and listen to Great-grandpa Kheel tell stories about colorful politicians.

"Great-grandpa Kheel was very important," my son Zane says.

"Well, yes. Everyone's important," I say.

"But he was *really* important," Zane says.

"Well, he did a lot of stuff he hoped would make the world better."

"Like he solved the train strike so the trains started working and people could go to their jobs."

"That's true," I say. "But remember, for every success he had, he also had a lot of failures. Probably five failures for every success." I just made up that statistic, so I'm hoping Zane doesn't check my math. But the general idea is true.

"Like what?"

"Well, he tried to open a hotel in the city of Budapest, but that went bust. He invested in a Broadway play that flopped. He invested in a farm that bred midget ponies—"

"What are midget ponies?"

"I think they're supersmall ponies. I never got to see one, because the farm went out of business so fast."

As I continue to list the schemes gone sour, Zane begins to look confused. Like he's thinking, Why does my father keep trash-talking my great-grandfather?

I can explain.

I blame it all on Marshall Duke, a professor of psychology at Emory University. Duke is the coauthor of the single most famous study in genealogy. The 2010 paper, which appeared in a psychology journal, concludes that kids who know their family's history are happier and more adjusted than those who don't.

Genealogists love to bring up this study. Talk for half an hour to a professional genealogist, and the study will inevitably make a cameo. The subtext: If your kid doesn't have a subscription to Ancestry.com, she'll wind up burglarizing vending machines for a living.

But if you read the study, the conclusion is a bit more nuanced. Kids don't get inspired simply by learning the names, dates, and birthplaces of their ancestors. The key is the family narrative.

Here's how author Bruce Feiler describes those findings in his book *The Secrets of Happy Families.*

Psychologists have found that every family has a unifying narrative . . . and those narratives take one of three shapes.

First, there's the ascending family narrative that goes like this: "Son, when we came to this country, we had nothing. Our family worked. We opened a store. Your grandfather went to high school. Your father went to college. And now you . . ."

Second is the descending narrative: "Sweetheart, we used to have it all. Then we lost everything."

"The most healthful narrative," Dr. Duke continued, "is the third one. It's called the oscillating family narrative: 'Dear, let me tell you, we've had ups and downs in our family. We built a family business. Your grandfather was a pillar of the community. Your mother was on the board of the hospital. But we also had setbacks. You had an uncle who was once arrested. We had a house burn down. Your father lost a job. But no matter what happened, we always stuck together as a family.' "

So that's what I want to do. I'm trying to give Zane the oscillating family narrative to teach him resiliency, though I'm probably spending too much time on the southward side of the oscillation. I'm making my grandfather sound like Kramer from *Seinfeld*.

Maybe I'm overcompensating. When I was growing up, I saw my dad as invincible—the smartest man I knew, the greatest lawyer in America, never a career stumble. So anything less than perfection on my sixth-grade math quiz gave me a stomachache. What's wrong with me? I'd ask myself. Why can't I be more like my dad? I had a lot of stomachaches.

So I love talking with my sons about failure, such as the big fat folder of rejected book ideas on my computer. Or about the time when I was trying to sell my first book and a publisher I'll refrain from naming expressed interest but asked if I could send in a photo.

"Why do they want a photo?" I asked my agent.

"Oh, just to make sure you don't have three noses or something. They want to know that you can go on some talk shows when the book comes out."

So I sent in the photo. Two days later, the publisher said, "Thanks, but we're passing." (It was Crown. That was the publisher.)

I imagine my sons' friends asking, "What does your dad do?"

"Oh, he's a failure. He has a bunch of bad ideas that don't work out, and a few decent ones that do."

I have to remind myself to mention my occasional successes too, lest they think I don't oscillate at all.

Now that I'm researching my family history, I hunt for any and all of my ancestor failures. The other day I found one that made me positively gleeful.

It was an advertisement in a 1912 edition of the *Brooklyn Eagle* showing a photo of my great-grandfather—Samuel Kheel—looking intent and serious, wearing a high-collared shirt and tie. The caption reads "A Clean Man on a Clean Ticket."

The ad was for my great-grandpa's run for New York State Assembly on the Bull Moose ticket. He was soundly defeated. Came in third.

But it was a noble failure. The Bull Moose Party—the Progressive Party, as it was officially called—was formed by Teddy Roosevelt three years after he finished his term as president. His Republican protégé William Howard Taft was in the White House, and Taft's administration had taken a turn to the right. Roosevelt was infuriated and started his own third party.

The Progressive Party was indeed progressive for its time. Its platform included women's suffrage, campaign finance reform, and the minimum wage law for women.

It was also controversial. There's a famous story of how Teddy Roosevelt, during a campaign stop in Milwaukee for his new party, got shot with a Colt revolver by an unemployed saloonkeeper. The bullet penetrated Roosevelt's chest but not too deeply, thanks in part to the thick manuscript of the speech in his vest pocket. (See? Print media saves lives, I tell my kids.) Despite the blood soaking through his shirt, Roosevelt insisted on giving a ninety-minute speech.

Great-grandpa Sam didn't get shot. But he did face threats of violence.

Sam helped organize a 1912 Bull Moose fund-raiser in Brooklyn that some angry Taft-supporting Republicans threatened to disrupt. "Many attended in fear of bloodshed," the *Brooklyn Eagle* wrote.

Fortunately, the fund-raiser was violence-free. According to the newspaper, the only hiccups came when a "fair damsel . . . slipped on the dancing floor at 1 a.m." and "Sam Kheel of the Dinner Committee did not get anything to eat because he was too busy attending to others."

A failure as a politician, perhaps, but a gracious host. I hope I inherited his skill as an event planner.

REUNION COUNTDOWN: 45 WEEKS

Thank God we got our first speaker: George Church. He's a brilliant Harvard genetics professor with a big white beard to rival Charles Darwin's and a gene for being a mensch. I met him at a conference, and he said he'd be happy to speak, even though I can't afford to pay anything. He also said he'd provide a "low, soothing background voice for twelve hours chanting 'all one' or 'resistance is futile,' *Koyaanisqatsi* style." I told him I'd consider it.

George is heading up his own mega–family tree project, the Personal Genome Project, collecting DNA from thousands of volunteers who will allow their data to be used for science. I promised him I'd give him my blood in exchange for his speech.

He also told me that if we really want to unite the world, we should take advantage of human tribalism and have us all come together to fight a common enemy. In other words, if I can threaten an alien invasion, that would help.

CHAPTER 10

Should Family Be Abolished?

Today I do a Google search and discover that a woman filed a lawsuit against my great-great-uncle David Herzenstein in 1908. She claimed he skipped out on a $1,000 loan.

I'm immediately suspicious of this woman. I'm sure the situation was much more nuanced. I mean, chances are David had a totally reasonable excuse and would have paid her eventually. And who is this woman anyway? Can we trust her?

I type her name—Bella Usefof—into a search engine. There's only one other reference to her on the Internet. It's a newspaper article about her son. In 1918 Bella's son was convicted of killing a subway ticket agent and sent to the electric chair.

See? I say to myself triumphantly. *That's* what happens when you mess with my family, Bella. Bad things happen to you. Stay away from us, you Usefofs.

I'm positively gleeful. For about twenty seconds. Then I'm horrified at myself.

What kind of primitive tribalism hijacked my brain? A woman's son died a century ago, and I find pleasure in it? I know almost nothing about Bella or Old Uncle David except that David shared a smidgeon more nucleotides with me.

This is not good. This is the worst part of family—the us-versus-them mentality. The idea of the in-group and out-group. It gets to a big question I've been wrestling with: Is it possible family is actually a bad thing? Does it do more harm to society than good?

Most of us have been taught that families are the backbone of civilization. But some philosophers argue that the idea of "family" is an unfortunate evolutionary holdover. It helped us survive when we were small bands of cave people. But now it means we're programmed to choose our family's well-being over the Greater Good.

Here's how philosopher Stephen Asma describes this dilemma: "If some science-fiction sorcerer came to me with a button, and said I could save my son's life by pressing it but then (cue the dissonant music) ten strangers would die somewhere . . . I'd have my finger down on it before he finished his cryptic challenge."

I'd probably press the button too. Then I'd live a life of torment knowing I'm a mass murderer and self-medicate with a quart of Smirnoff every day and be too wasted to attend any of my kids' soccer games. So there's no winning in that scenario.

The dilemmas don't have to involve dying strangers. I read a *New York* magazine article by Lisa Miller called "Is Ethical Parenting Possible?" It includes this example: A mom is faced with a choice. One night she discovers lice in her kid's hair. Technically the kid shouldn't go to school the next day. That's the school rule. But the mom knows her kid has a crucial standardized test the next day, and missing school could mess with his future. So she chooses her own kid's well-being and exposes the rest of the class to lice.

Family leads to deceit. It leads to nepotism. It leads to feuds. It leads to lack of compassion for those who aren't nearby on your tree. In his HBO show, John Oliver acidly mocked those who see the world only through the lens of family. He showed clips of football players and sportscasters outraged by recent incidents of domestic violence because they said they could imagine the victim being their daughter or wife. Oliver shook his head in disbelief. "Or here's a crazy idea. You could put away your magic face-switching machine and just be upset by the incident as it actually happened. Because you should not need to insert a relative into a horri-fying situation to make it horrific. For instance, I hate SeaWorld's treat-ment of whales on principle alone, not just because my father is an orca."

So what's the alternative to this primitive bias? Well, we could get rid of family altogether. One Internet commenter wrote the following in response to an article I did on the Global Family Reunion:

> By the end of the century we'll be producing babies in factories so none of this "family" stuff will matter. We are all born alone and die alone and all of this family stuff is just clutter in between anyhow. We all have our own destinies and nobody should have to be tied to, nor obligated to anyone else. No, I'm not my brother's keeper, nor seek to be kept.

Beryl? Is that you?

Whoever you are, you're not alone. Many radical thinkers have also floated the idea of dissolving family ties altogether. One wrote an influ-ential 1999 paper called "Is the Family to Be Abolished Then?", which discussed whether families were antithetical to justice. Many antifam-ily activists believe we need to return to a more "natural" state. In *Sex at Dawn*, authors Christopher Ryan and Cacilda Jetha contend that our hunter-gatherer forebears had a much different kind of family. They had communal kids and multiple sex partners. They tell of a seventeenth-century French missionary in Canada who tried to explain traditional monogamous marriage to a tribesman. The tribesman replied, "Thou hast no sense. You French people love only your own children, but we all love all the children of our tribe." Ignorance of their kids' paternity apparently makes for a more compassionate society.

Still, the idea of abolishing the nuclear family gives most of us the creeps. It's the stuff of dystopian novels, like *The Giver*, which my son read for school and which features a society where babies are assigned to family units by a "Committee of Elders."

It brings to mind the vilest aspects of totalitarian societies, where the State becomes your true family. In the Stalin-era Soviet Union, for instance, kids were urged to alert the authorities if Mom or Dad showed any signs of dissent. Consider the tale of the thirteen-year-old Soviet weasel who turned his dad in to the Stalinist police and became a hero. His name was Pavlik Morozov and he reported his dad for allegedly selling documents to "enemies of the Soviet State." The dad was executed. In revenge, Pavlik's uncle and grandfather killed the boy. After which Pavlik became a national celebrity, a "glorious martyr." The Kremlin built statues of the little bastard. Pavlik was the subject of six biographies, plays and poems, even an opera. His school was turned into a shrine that Soviet students visited on field trips. It's unclear how much of Pavlik's tale is true and how much was Stalinist propaganda. But the message was clear: Stalin comes first. Mom and Dad are way down the list, maybe top one hundred if they're lucky.

Perhaps I'm too bourgeois, but I believe the notion of family is too deeply ingrained in human nature to be eradicated. We're stuck with it for now. At least until we become cyborgs and rewrite our own brain software. To be clear: I'm not saying that we thrive only in families with biological parents of opposite sexes. Not at all. A happiness-producing family can come in all sorts of shapes: stepparents, in-laws, extended family, gay parents. But there has to be some small, close-knit group, not just a communal pool.

Here's how philosopher Sam Harris puts it in his book *The Moral Landscape*:

> Communal experiments that ignore parents' special attachment to their own children . . . do not seem to work very well. The Israeli kibbutzim learned this the hard way: after discovering that raising children communally made both parents and children less happy, they reinstated the nuclear family. Most people may be happier in a world in which a natural bias toward one's own children is conserved.

So until we reengineer human nature, how can I be a more ethical member of the greater human family?

One tactic is to think of the nuclear family as a sort of moral training ground. That's the Confucian way. According to the book *The Intellectual History of Asia*, Confucius saw the family as a way to build up your ethical biceps. You have a duty to show kindness to your parents and siblings. Then you must take this kindness and apply it to the rest of your life—your colleagues, your neighbors, your customers.

So those football commentators in the John Oliver monologue? They were actually Confucian scholars!

Charles Darwin had a similar idea. He urged us to expand our circles of moral concern. Start with compassion for your family, then your street, then your town, then your country, then your world.

Or else you can remind yourself that, if you go back far enough, we're all cousins. Even Bella Usefof. And, to paraphrase the Bible, maybe you should treat your forty-third cousin as you would yourself.

Since the Usefof Incident, I've been making a conscious effort to widen my circles of compassion. Results have been mixed.

Consider the recent soccer game of my oldest son, Jasper. I'm on the sidelines with Julie. Things are going great. The weather is warm, the air is fresh (or as fresh as it can be when the field abuts the West Side Highway), and Jasper is playing well on defense. His team, the Sharks, is crushing the Titans. This is in large part due to Jasper's teammate, Number 8, a little blond kid who kicks the ball with the power of a surface-to-air missile launcher. The score is 5–0.

At which point I realize: I should start rooting against my son's team. The Titans are humans too. They're my distant cousins. And look how their heads droop as they trudge back to midfield after every goal. It's devastating.

I want to give the Titans a little taste of joy. I want to have the score be 5–4. Well, that's too close. Maybe 5–3. Okay, 5–2 is fine.

The Titans make a break for it. They shoot, the angle looks good—and then the ball caroms off the goal's top bar and bounces out of bounds.

"Noooo!" I shout. "Dammit!"

Julie gives me a look. "You know Jasper is on the gray team, right?"

I explain that if I'm thinking of the Global Family, I want there to be the most amount of happiness for the greatest number of people. I want to give the Titans a little sense of accomplishment.

"Okay, but maybe keep it down."

Five minutes later, the Titans have a corner kick, which hits a kid's shoulder and rolls into our goal.

"Yessss!" I whisper-shout, pumping my fist.

Julie looks at me again. Yeah, she's right. Screw the Titans. They got their goal. Now crush them, Sharks.

REUNION COUNTDOWN: 43 WEEKS

It's official: we've got a rabbi, a minister, and an imam. No joke. I went on a radio show in Florida hosted by the trio who call themselves the Three Wise Guys. They've agreed to come to the reunion and give a joint blessing.

I was thrilled. But then I started to worry that my atheist cousins would feel left out, so I asked Nando Pelusi, a friend who belongs to the NYC Atheists club, to give a secular sermon. He agreed. But then what about the Eastern religions? A friend who knows a man named Lama Surya Das has arranged for him to give some Buddhist reflections.

Oh, but what about the Mormons? The Mormons are hugely into genealogy, and I don't want to insult them. I called Cherie, a contact I have at The Church of Jesus Christ of Latter-day Saints, to ask if they'll be offended if they aren't included in the faith block. She says they'll be fine.

CHAPTER 11

The Good Cousin

Julie has a point. For the past few weeks, she's been saying that if we're going to gather several thousand people, why not turn it into a benefit for a good cause? Raise awareness, raise money—and make it clear we're not trying to start a doomsday cult or a pyramid scheme to sell water filters.

I've settled on my cause: Alzheimer's. My paternal grandfather, Charles Jacobs, a lawyer like my father, suffered from Alzheimer's. I remember visiting him at Century Village in Florida, and he'd tell a story about a novel he was reading. Then ten minutes later, he'd tell the exact same story. My sister and I would look at each other awkwardly, not knowing if it was a joke. We weren't mature enough to process how heartbreaking it was.

Alzheimer's robs people of memories, and memories are at the heart of families. So it seemed the perfect fit for my event.

The next day, I announce on Facebook that any and all proceeds from the Global Family Reunion would go to Alzheimer's.

"I chose Alzheimer's because of Grandpa Jacobs," I say to my father on the phone that night, hoping he'd be proud.

"Okay. But he didn't have Alzheimer's."

"Wait. He didn't?"

"He had vascular dementia."

Well, this isn't good. Alzheimer's is a type of dementia, and my grandfather had another type.

Should I change the cause? I've already announced it. That wouldn't look so good. Sorry, Alzheimer's charities! Turns out my grandfather didn't have your particular terrible disease, so I no longer care.

After lying awake for several hours, I arrive at a rationalization. We'll stick with Alzheimer's, because the Global Family Reunion is about my whole human family. I can't play favorites. Alzheimer's affects more than forty million distant cousins, even if it didn't affect my own grandfather.

One thing is clear: I don't know enough about my father's father.

He died when I was in college, and I remember just a bit. He wore a gray homburg hat. He had deep-set eyes that seemed gentle but far from carefree. We'd play chess together silently.

At the next family gathering—the bar mitzvah of a second cousin—I sit next to my aunt Carol, and while the DJ plays Rihanna songs, I ask her about her dad, my grandfather.

"My father grew up very poor. His father—that's your great-grandfather—was a pushcart peddler. He didn't have a happy childhood."

Which was an understatement, judging by what Carol tells me next.

My grandfather's mom died when he was young, and his eventual stepmom sounds like a Disney villain. The stepmom locked the icebox and hoarded the limited food for her own biological kids, so my grandfather went hungry, which might account for his short stature.

The stepmom gave my grandfather a nickel every day and told him, "You can spend it on lunch or on the bus fare. Your choice."

If he bought lunch, he'd have to walk home and was often beaten up by the neighborhood thugs. If he took the bus, he'd spend the day hungry.

So to earn lunch money at age thirteen, my grandfather started selling pretzels on the street. He apparently had no permit and was arrested.

"Did he go to jail?" I ask my aunt Carol.

"Yes. He spent one night in jail. He said, 'It wasn't a very pleasant experience.' He said it with a whimsical smile."

*My paternal grandfather, Charles Jacobs, with
his wife, Harriet, and son (my dad), Arnie.*

"Wow," I say. It's the fourth or fifth "wow" I've said in this conversation, but I'm not sure what else to say. I'd never known how tough he had it, and I feel like an ingrate for never asking. Plus I'm imagining what he thought when my sister and I complained that, say, my grandmother bought Hydrox instead of Oreos.

"He went to law school," Carol continues. "He struggled for many years: he and my mother didn't have a kitchen sink and would do the dishes in the bathroom." He eventually built up a steady business.

With this background, it'd be understandable if he had kept his hard-earned money close. But my aunt says that wasn't the case.

"I remember we were in a car, and there was a guy at the traffic light who was being drunk and belligerent and demanding money. My father rolled down the window and gave him money. And he turned to me and Arnie and said, 'The poor guy has lost his self-respect.'"

My aunt remembers another story, which her mom told proudly.

"When he was sick with dementia, she overheard two women talking at the supermarket. One was saying, 'I need to draw up a will.' And the other said, 'I recommend Charlie Jacobs. He's so careful and caring, and he hardly charges anything.' And my mom said to the woman, 'I'm Charlie Jacobs's wife. He isn't in the position to do the will, but thank you for the kind words.'"

He was less glamorous than my maternal grandfather, Theodore Kheel. As a kid, I paid less attention to my dad's dad. Unlike Grandpa Kheel, Grandpa Jacobs didn't tell funny stories about staring contests with Lyndon Johnson or dress in crazy red-and-white-striped blazers or take me to meet Howard Cosell.

But doing this project, I've come to realize: he too was a great man, just in a quieter way. And I feel like a fool for not realizing this earlier. My father, in his eulogy, said he was "the kindest man he'd ever met." I like to imagine he'd be happy that I'm supporting the fight against Alzheimer's, even if he didn't suffer from the disease himself.

A few weeks after talking with my aunt, I look for my grandfather in the census records online. In the 1920 census, there he is, a twelve-year-old, alongside his sister, Rose. This is right before their mom died. I scan down to look at their mom, Celia. It says "Children: 3. Living: 2."

Oh man. My poor great-grandmother. A child who died. No explanation why or how. What a life.

The next time my dad comes over to visit me and the boys, I show him the census record on the computer.

"Did you know you had another aunt or uncle?"

"I didn't know that," says my dad.

That's it. Like my grandfather, he'd rather focus on the good. And right now his grandson is challenging him to dominoes.

REUNION COUNTDOWN: 42 WEEKS

So far I've sent out thousands of invitations to distant cousins I've tracked down on DNA services and sites like Geni. I've gotten three hundred yeses.

Which is something but a long way from a record-breaking twenty-five hundred, which might explain my constant stomachache.

One RSVP is from a man who wants to come to the reunion dressed as Deadpool, the Marvel comics antihero. He'd wear a red mask and have swords strapped to his back. He'd also spread the word to the entire Deadpool community so that dozens of other Deadpool impersonators all show up at the same time. I tell him that although Deadpool is most certainly a cousin, and that although I do need more attendees, an army of Deadpools at the reunion seems a little off message.

Whether or not he and his clones show up, the email makes me realize how little control I have over this event. It's terrifying.

CHAPTER 12

Adam and Eve

If there's one family reunion I wish I'd attended, it was my friend Tyler's. It happened a few years ago. Without telling anyone in advance, Tyler's dad hired two elderly actors to portray his own dead parents, Tyler's late grandparents.

The actors arrived in character at the reunion. They were the spitting image. They shuffled around the room, complained about the whitefish, pinched a few cheeks, and thoroughly freaked out everyone in the family.

Tyler said his relatives were slack-jawed at the display of ghastly bad taste. It was his family's *Springtime for Hitler*.

Hideous as it was, Tyler's dad's trick planted a seed of inspiration. What if I hired two actors to play Y-Chromosomal Adam and Mitochondrial Eve? As you might recall, I've had a fantasy of using a time machine to bring our ultimate ancestors to twenty-first-century New York. That's not going to happen. But two actors? I could pull that off. They could wear some fur, grunt at the attendees, stand in line patiently for some Belgian waffles.

I've been told by several people this is not a good idea. And it almost certainly isn't. But it's on my mind again today, because I've volunteered to be a chaperone for Lucas—one of my twins—and his classmates when they take a school trip to the Hall of Human Origins at the American Museum of Natural History.

The Hall is a dark space filled with dioramas and stone axes and fossils. There's a display called "Our Family Tree," featuring an arrangement of skulls of various hominid species, with *Homo sapiens* on the upper right side.

Lucas and his friends gravitate to a diorama of a long-haired, loin-cloth-wearing fellow. He's protecting a gazelle carcass from a hungry vulture.

"Looks like he's on the paleo diet," I say to Lucas. Lucas nods politely.

A few minutes later, I overhear a woman and her boyfriend as they walk by the same diorama. "Hey," she says. "That's the real paleo diet."

It's now clear that I was the 80,472nd person to make the paleo diet comment in the Hall of Human Origins. What's the evolutionary value of dumb jokes?

It's humbling. But the Hall is humbling for another reason. Whenever I'm in exhibits like this, I can't help but imagine what school kids ten thousand years from now will think when they look at their holographic dioramas of twenty-first-century humans. "Check out those adorable *Homo sapiens*!" they'll say. "With their cute little crania and primitive computer pads and their wars over liquefied organic matter."

The older I get, the more I'm aware that our current version of *Homo sapiens* is a link in a chain. Future links will think of us with a mixture of pity and condescension, the way we look at bonobos.

Lucas and his class stop in front of a model of a human from about two hundred thousand years ago. This is about the time of our ultimate human ancestors, our eight-thousandth-great grandparents, y-Adam and m-Eve. They made their home in Africa. Some scientists used to think it was East Africa, but a recent fossil discovery in Morocco indicates it might have been elsewhere on the continent.

This Adam and Eve are different from their biblical counterparts for several reasons. One, they were not the first *Homo sapiens* on earth. Members of our species likely appeared in Africa millennia before Adam and Eve were born. Adam and Eve lived among thousands of other humans— would-be Adams and Eves. The difference is, the other family lines petered out, but Adam and Eve's survive. Their descendants are your friends, lovers, parents, shopkeepers, and bookies, everyone you'll ever meet.

The second thing to note is that y-Adam and m-Eve weren't even a couple. They probably didn't know each other. They may not have lived in the same century. They had their own sexual partners. It's just that, separately, both Adam and Eve had DNA with tremendous staying power, DNA that remains with us today.

Their descendants took over the world. At first, some of their progeny moved a few dozen miles away in search of more food. And over generations, tribes spread farther and farther until one group ventured into the Middle East.

The idea of a real-life Adam and Eve has powerful implications. First of all, it negates the malignant notion that different races are different species. For centuries, many Europeans saw the other ethnic groups— Africans, for instance—as being part of a distinct species, closer to apes.

In the nineteenth century, this took on the sheen of science, with scholars arguing that humans had multiple origins. One influential American intellectual, Charles Caldwell, said that there are four species of humans: Caucasian, Mongolian, American Indian, and African. And you can imagine which was at the top of the pyramid, intelligence-wise. This different-species worldview made it easier to justify slavery and genocide and other horrible human behavior.

Adam and Eve's grand family tree has been charted, at least in broad strokes. Over the millennia, their descendants split into a few dozen clusters called haplogroups. Each member of a haplogroup shares genetic markers with every other member, and each haplogroup is associated with a different region.

The P haplogroup has strong links to Southeast Asia. Members of the A haplogroup are associated with sub-Saharan Africa. The DNA of everyone on earth can be categorized into one or more of these haplogroups. On my mom's side, I belong to the H haplogroup (Middle East and Europe). On my dad's side, I'm a member of the J haplogroup (Northern Africa, among others).

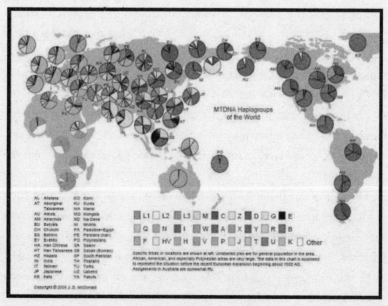

Haplogroups around the world.

Now back to Adam and Eve for a second. What were they like? Scientists agree they probably hunted and gathered and wore animal skins and ornamental jewelry.

But there's also a split in the academic community. On one side, you've got what I'll call the paleo apologists, who say our ultimate ancestors lived mostly peaceful and happy lives. On the other side are the paleo cynics (or realists, depending on your view), who say they were violent, brutish, short-lived louts.

You can read the paleo apologist argument in the previously mentioned book *Sex at Dawn*. The authors argue that the first humans lived in small bands, cooperated with each other, and had multiple sex partners. Basically what my neighbor did in Vermont in the sixties. They didn't even have to work that hard; they put in about forty hours of hunting and gathering a week. DMV hours. It was all very Rousseauian.

There's been an upsurge in paleo nostalgia in America recently. Witness the paleo diet and the paleo workout (which involves running through the woods barefoot). There's a feeling we need to return to a more "natural state."

On the other hand, the paleo cynics are not so wistful. Consider Harvard psychology professor Steven Pinker, who wrote the book *The Better Angels of Our Nature*. The thesis of his book is that life on earth has slowly but steadily improved in every way: Life expectancy, happiness, and intelligence have all risen, and violence has decreased. Hunter-gatherers like y-Adam and m-Eve had a violent death rate of about 15 percent, with some areas and eras reaching as high as 60 percent. Today, even with murders, terrorism, and war added together, the rate is less than 1 percent.

I tend to lean toward Pinker's side. For one thing, the bulk of scientists do as well. Plus it plays into my confirmation bias that life on earth is gradually getting better, current politics aside.

I believe the good old days weren't good. They were horrible. They were smelly, disease-ridden, deadly, and painful. I used to write a monthly column for *Mental Floss* magazine wherein I would recount the horrors of life in days of yore. I described surgery without anesthesia. I wrote about the "tobacco enema," during which doctors used a hose to literally blow smoke up your butt to treat a variety of ailments (and perhaps originating the phrase "blow smoke up your butt"). I wrote about childcare, including the medieval practice of leaving colicky babies in the woods, and about the nineteenth-century baby lozenges filled with opium. So I'm not the nostalgic sort.

And I don't glorify y-Adam and m-Eve. I imagine that if I met them, we wouldn't enjoy each other's company. I'd probably end up with a bashed-in face and require several opium lozenges to recover.

It's not just Adam and Eve, though. I'm skeptical of all my ancestors. Don't get me wrong: I'm incredibly grateful for them and the sacrifices they made. I know I'm a lucky bastard whose life is infinitely easier thanks to those who made the brave decision to immigrate and work soul-crushing jobs.

But my respect is complicated by the fact that, if I had a conversation with them, I'd be appalled. Take my fifth-great grandfather from Lithuania. In all likelihood, by today's standards he was sexist, racist, homophobic, ignorant, and laughably superstitious. He'd be equally dismayed by me. He'd yell at me for letting Julie dress like a harlot and show her knees.

In the same spirit, if my tenth-great grandson is reading this, let me apologize for all my ridiculous beliefs and unthinking cruel behavior. I wish my brain had a bigger cerebral cortex.

REUNION COUNTDOWN: 39 WEEKS

Another organizer of reunions has agreed to speak at the reunion. This is turning into a reunion about reunions. Very meta. His name is Dirk Weissleder, and he's seventeen steps away from me on the World Family Tree. He's from Hanover, Germany, and in 1990, six months after the Berlin Wall fell, he held a reunion of Weissleders from East Germany and

Weissleders from West Germany. Most hadn't seen each other for thirty years or more. Dirk and his East German cousin searched more than 138 phone books to track down their relatives. On a May weekend, they met in a small, mountainous East German town—about fifty Weissleders. "It was very emotional," Dirk tells me on videochat. "Lots of crying." He put both of his index fingers up to his eyes and mimed tears flowing down. "We weren't there to sell refrigerators. It was about the heart." Dirk can't bring all the Weissleders to my reunion, but I'm glad he'll be there.

CHAPTER 13

Kissing Cousins

This morning I got an email from a woman in Ohio.

> Hi AJ
>
> I've been reading all about you and your millions of cousins. I happen
> to date my second cousin and his family wants nothing to do with me.
> Is there a way I can show his mother and father that they are probably
> related as well, so they will accept me?
>
> Madeleine

I'm not sure how to respond to Madeleine. Yes, the point of my project is we are all cousins. And yes, it logically follows that everyone marries and/or dates their cousin, including me (as you might recall, Julie is, according to DNA estimates, about my seventh cousin).

But do I want to be an active proponent of close-cousin marriage? Is this the best cause with which to align myself if I want to reach a mass audience? It seems to have all the popular support of the right to eat cat meat.

On the other hand, I don't want to dismiss first- and second-cousin marriage just because it's unpopular and rates high on the ickiness scale. Morality should not be determined by what I find kinda gross.

Otherwise all sorts of things would be illegal—water parks, bowling shoes, and Bikram yoga to name a few. And Madeleine does seem to be in pain. I want to help her.

Before responding, I poke around the Internet to see what's out there. As expected, there are plenty of arguments against cousin marriage, most of them pointing to genetic defects. But there's also a surprisingly active pro-cousin-marriage movement. Advocates argue that the taboo is outdated. Love trumps ickiness. They say first-cousin marriage—like gay marriage—should be legal everywhere. They frame it as "Marriage Equality: The Sequel." Right now, the states are almost split down the middle. First-cousin marriage is legal in nineteen states (ranging from deep red like Georgia to deep blue like Vermont) but is illegal in the rest (such as Montana and Indiana).

I'm going to have to think about this.

Let's start with what both sides can agree on: close-cousin marriage has a long, long history. In fact, Rutgers anthropologist Robin Fox estimates that 80 percent of all marriages in human history were between first or second cousins. It's hard to confirm, but it makes sense, given that we spent most of our history in small tribes. As the scholar Stephen Stills says, you love the one you're with.

Everyone on earth is the product of cousin marriage. Try this thought experiment. You have two parents. Four grandparents. Eight great-grandparents. And so on. Keep doubling, and by the time you reach thirty generations, you should have more than 1 trillion ancestors—far more people than have ever lived on earth.

So obviously we don't really double our ancestors every generation. The reason? Cousins getting married. The twigs in your tree overlap. The child of two first cousins has six great grandparents at most, not eight. The official term for this phenomenon is *pedigree collapse*.

Europe's kings and queens had a habit of collapsing their pedigree, which both cemented alliances and resulted in the famed hemophilia of Queen Victoria's descendants. But nonroyals got in on it, too. H. G.

Wells, Sergei Rachmaninoff, and Edgar Allan Poe all married their first cousins (in the case of Poe, she was thirteen at the time, which is creepier than both the pit and the pendulum).

Cousin marriage varies by culture. Some cultures including the Amish and Orthodox Jews, have been highly endogamous (the proper word for inbred, as you might recall).

As humans became more mobile, close-cousin marriage went into decline. Taboos arose. Jokes were made. Laws were passed. Apps were invented. Or at least one app. In Iceland, a former endogamy hot zone because of its geographical isolation, potential daters can download an app that tells them if they are cousins (actual tagline: "Bump in the app before you bump in bed.")

Technically, of course, you can't avoid marrying a distant cousin, because we all are cousins. How far removed from you is your furthest cousin on earth? A 2007 analysis by an MIT computer scientist argued it could be surprisingly low: a mere seventieth cousin. Meaning any two humans—a New York hedge fund manager and a Papua New Guinea yam farmer, for instance—are seventieth cousins. They share a sixty-ninth-great grandfather. The MIT reseacher argued in *Nature* magazine that intermarriage between cultures has radically shrunk the cousin gap. Even if it's double that estimate—140th cousins—that's still a remarkable number. It means humanity's most recent common ancestors— y-Adam and m-Eve—lived a mere 3,500 years ago, in the time of the pyramids.

More cautious scientists think those estimates are far too small. They say your most distant cousin could be as much as a five-thousandth cousin (you and she share a five-thousandth-great grandfather, from about two hundred thousand years ago).

Whatever the maximum distance, it's clear that far-cousin marriage has risen while close-cousin marriage has ebbed. But close-cousin marriage hasn't disappeared. It's still practiced all around the world, including in the United States. As proof, you need only look at Cousin Couples.com. This is the official website for first and second cousins in romantic relationships. To get all the pros and cons, I figure I need to speak to the founder.

When I reach him by phone, he agrees to talk but asks that I not use his name. He's been in a couple of newspaper articles—and made an ill-fated *Jerry Springer* appearance—and it got him a lot of flak from neighbors and coworkers. He'd rather stay under the radar.

"So what should I call you?" I ask.

"How about K.C.? For 'Kissing Cousin.' "

K.C. is thirty-two years old and lives in North Carolina. Okay, let me stop right here. I'm not out to reinforce tired stereotypes or make you-might-be-a-redneck jokes, so I was kind of hoping K.C. was from Connecticut. But I have to play the cards I'm dealt.

K.C. is studying business and likes fishing and panning for gold. He met his first cousin/current wife when she was ten years old; until then, she'd grown up in a foster home. "The first thing I remember is her throwing water balloons at me. There was always some kind of chemistry. When we were teenagers, we just got to be inseparable."

"How old were you when you got married?" I ask.

"I was twenty-two, and she was seventeen."

Okay. Again, as a writer wary of stereotypes, I was hoping she was at least in her twenties. But to repeat, them's the cards.

As you might imagine, not everyone approved of their love. When K.C. and his fiancée announced their engagement, K.C.'s future mother-in-law actually chased him from the room screaming, "I want to kill you!" In the end, she didn't resort to violence. Just medication.

"She ate a lot of nerve pills that day," K.C. says, referring to their wedding day. K.C.'s mother-in-law agreed to attend the ceremony at city hall, since her daughter was under eighteen and a guardian was required. But she did it under duress. "The lady doing the ceremony kept asking her, 'Are you all right, ma'am?' "

With all the blowback, K.C. looked for support online and found little. So in 1998 he started his website CousinCouples.com to provide a community and helpful info. Since then, he's met dozens of couples from all over the country. "I've met lawyers, cops, schoolteachers. Gobs of schoolteachers. I don't know what's up with that."

If you look at the site, you'll see a guide to breaking the news to your parents. You'll learn some lingo, such as "cuzband." And if you're like me, you'll spend half an hour reading the stories on the message boards. Yes, partly because it's a cheap voyeuristic thrill. But it's more than that. The stories are heartbreaking—real-life forbidden love, like something out of a Puccini opera.

I read about a woman who saw her cousin for the first time in twenty years at a family reunion. "When I saw him there and gave him a hug, it was the oddest sensation of coming home. That hug felt like this was where I was supposed to be."

There's also the woman who confessed her crush to her cousin, and he broke off all relations. "I've cried every day for the last three months," she wrote. "This cousin is as much a part of me as an arm or leg. . . . We've been close since we were babies."

As K.C. and I wind down our conversation, I ask, "Do you see the attitudes changing?"

He says maybe a little. But overall, he says, the subject is still highly taboo. "I do get less hate mail," he says. "I used to get wild hate mail: 'God hates you' and 'You're going to hell.' I kind of miss that now. It was entertaining."

To me, the strongest argument against cousin marriage is the potential risk of genetic birth defects. Is it a real risk? The short answer is yes, but not as high as most people think.

The risk has been known for a long time. Charles Darwin married his first cousin, and three of his ten children died prematurely from health problems. Darwin worried endlessly that it was because of his decision to inbreed. It's a tragic scenario. His own theory of evolution gave him heartache.

According to *The Journal of Genetic Counseling*, the increased risk of birth defects from first-cousin marriages is about the same as that for women who give birth over the age of forty. The risk is even higher if there's a history of close-cousin marriage in previous generations.

But here's the argument that K.C. and other cousin marriage proponents make: Why should we target close-cousin marriage? What if two ostensibly unrelated people want to get married, but they both carry the gene that makes Alzheimer's more likely? Should they be forbidden to wed? Now that we can test our DNA for all sorts of health risks, it seems arbitrary to explicitly forbid first-cousin marriage.

It's a strong argument. So strong I've changed my mind. I find close-cousin marriage somehow unsettling in a knee-jerk way. But I can't say that I have a rational moral objection to it.

I announce my newfound enlightened stance to Julie. "I've decided I'm okay with first-cousin marriage," I say. "So if I die, you can marry David Zuckerman if you want."

"Good to know," she says, not looking up from her Kindle. This is not an issue she feels passionately about.

"But I don't think I'm going to make it a big theme of the Global Family Reunion."

"Probably wise."

Now, back to Madeleine. I send her an email suggesting she explain to her potential in-laws that cousin marriage isn't an aberration. It's quite normal from a historical point of view. I include a link to K.C.'s website and an article about fifteen historical figures who married their cousins.

A few weeks after that, I check in with Madeleine again. She thanks me for the info, but she has decided to end the relationship. She couldn't take the hostility. So in this case, at least, love did not win.

CHAPTER 14

The Greatest Generation (and the Upside of Cigarettes)

We're hosting my mother-in-law's birthday this year, and Julie's family is over, including her stepdad, David.

"You aren't the only veteran in the family," I tell him, as we sit on the couch before the meal. "I found out my third-great grandfather Gerson Friedenheit fought in the Civil War."

"Ah yes," says David. "I think I knew him. About yay high?"

David is an accountant who looks and acts like George Burns. He's ninety-four, a master of silly handshakes with my kids, and a genuine World War II hero.

"When's your big event again?" he asks.

"Next year," I say.

"Well, I won't be around for that." He laughs. "But have fun."

"You'll make it," I say. "You've got to. I need you to help break the record."

I tell him that I'd actually like him to speak at the event. He looks at me quizzically. "What in God's name would I talk about?"

"Just tell your story. About the war."

He shakes his head. "The new generation, they don't want to hear that."

I tell him he's wrong. I say that it's an amazing and inspiring tale, with themes of connection and kindness that'd be perfect for the reunion.

David Harrison in basic training, 1942.

"What's the story?" asks my son Jasper.

"See?" I say. "They want to know."

I ask David to tell it again, this time on tape.

"You want to record it in case I'm not around for the reunion?" he says, smiling, as I go to my room to get my voice recorder.

Julie sets up the story, explaining to the boys that David was a navigator on a B-17 bomber, which is delightfully ironic, as Julie's mom points out, since he's always getting lost when we drive to Hersheypark or the mall.

On his twenty-first mission, David's plane was hit with gunfire from a German fighter, and the engine caught fire.

"I went down on a mission to Hamburg," David starts. "We were shot up pretty badly. And I got the order to bail."

David jumped out the airplane door and opened his chute. "As I'm floating down, I see people running toward the spot where I am going to land. And sure enough, I landed, and there were four farmers running at me, all with shotguns.

"They searched me—roughly." He lets out a half laugh. "And then marched me to a barn. And there were other people gathered in the barn. There must have been twenty of them. And the men were getting very angry with me.

"And then I did something, and I'll never understand why." David pauses, gives a faint smile, and shakes his head. He takes a beat to gather himself and then continues.

"I found a cigarette. The people who packed the chutes, they'd put a cigarette in the harness. And I did a stupid thing. I put it in my mouth. And that started them off. The German farmers saw it as an act of defiance. And they started beating up on me. This guy, who must have been three hundred pounds—he hit me with a rifle. I didn't fight back. I just tried to defend myself.

"The men were all saying I was *schwein*. But there was this woman. It must have been the wife of a farmer. She said I was too young, I'm just a boy. I heard the word *jung*. And that saved my life.

"About a half hour later, a motorcycle pulls up with a man, and he puts me on the back, and off we go to a German army camp. From there, they put me on a train to a prisoner of war camp. I remember, it was three in the morning. And I'm sitting on the chair on the aisle in this train. And . . ."

David pauses for ten long seconds. He rubs his eyes with his palms, exhales, and continues.

"I was looking out the window. And I was completely depressed. I was a prisoner, and a Jewish one. I mean, this was the low point of my life. And there was somebody in the seat next to me. And it was a German soldier."

David's voice cracks. He's now practically whispering.

"And I look over, and he's offering me a cigarette."

David Harrison circa 2007.

David exhales. Gathers himself.

"That got me out of my depression. That was the most emotional moment of my life. That cigarette saved my life."

He turns to Jasper and his brothers.

"But don't take up smoking. That's not the point of this story."

Later I'll tell the point of the story to the kids. At least my interpretation: that even in the most inhumane of circumstances, you can still find little sparks of humanity. That maybe there's hope for our species after all.

At my prodding, David talks about the rest of the war. How he was stuck in a barracks with nine other Jewish prisoners of war. How they got a bag of potatoes to eat every couple of days and not much else, and would spend hours trying to divide the unevenly shaped potatoes into equal portions. How they'd spend their nights talking about food they'd eat when and if they were released. "That's where I first learned about Chinese food," David says. "I'd never heard of it."

And how, after several months, the Russian army came in to liberate them. One of the former prisoners broke into the camp's office and put a song on the PA system: Bing Crosby's "Don't Fence Me In."

Part of me feels guilty for asking him to recount his experiences. It was clearly hard for him. But I wanted my kids to hear. I wanted it on tape.

After everyone leaves the party, I search to see what records there are of David online. I log into Fold3 and, among the dozens of other David Harrisons, I find him in "Missing Air Crew Reports."

It is actually a questionnaire he'd answered after being rescued. There he is: David H. Harrison. 2nd Lt. Bailed out with pilot. He was uninjured, but the radioman received a bullet in the leg.

I never doubted David's story, but looking at it in courier font makes it more real. I notice the date of the mission: December 31, 1944.

December 31? I didn't know that.

The next day I call David in New Jersey. Julie's mom, Barbara, answers.

"I found some records of David's service," I say. "I didn't know he was captured on New Year's Eve!"

"Oh yes. He had a date with a British woman that night. He never made it because he was called up for the mission."

Well, that has to be the best excuse in history for standing up a date.

David gets on the phone.

"Did you get in touch with the British woman after the war?" I ask. "Did you tell her why you missed dinner?"

"I had a couple of other things on my mind." David laughs.

I say maybe I could track her down and have her come to the reunion and they could reunite.

David responds, "I'm not sure your mother-in-law would love that."

REUNION COUNTDOWN: 38 WEEKS

It's been a rough week, speakerwise. Three speakers who had previously agreed to talk have just dropped out. It has me down.

But then, at 3:35 p.m. on a Tuesday, I get an email. It's from a Harvard email address: Henry Louis Gates Jr. A few weeks ago I'd emailed him on a whim and had since given up hope. But today he writes back: "I'd be honored to speak."

Let me emphasize this: HENRY. LOUIS. GATES. JR. Yes, this news merits both capital letters and periods, possibly even a larger font, but I figure you get the idea. He's like the pope of genealogy. He's the host of *Finding Your Roots* on PBS and author of a shelf-full of books about history and race relations. In the geeky world of family history, this is like Bruce Springsteen agreeing to sing "Born to Run" at your birthday.

I'm thrilled but terrified. Now I can't screw things up. This is more nerve-racking than an army of Deadpool impersonators.

CHAPTER 15

Thank You for Having Sex

An unsettling thought keeps popping up in my brain. It concerns my very existence and the astounding amount of sexual intercourse that had to take place for it to happen.

My parents had to have sex—something I've known since the age of eight but have tried to keep buried in the Siberia of my subconscious.

But mom-and-dad sex, that's just the start. Their parents had to have sex, so add my grandparents' orgasms to the list (we're talking at the very least two orgasms by my grandfathers, but if I have to ponder it, I suppose I'd be rooting for double that, for my grandmothers' sake). The parents of my grandparents had to have sex, which adds four more sweaty copulations to the pile. Go back another generation and you get eight more grunting, passionate embraces.

And on it goes: 16, 32, 256 historical lovemaking sessions. So much sex. Go back five hundred years and you're talking an orgy the size of Sacramento. Go back ten thousand and you're talking more coitus than a Thursday night at Leo DiCaprio's vacation home. (I can make that joke because I'm his cousin.)

The point is, I used to see my foreparents in a certain role: staid ancestors, not giddy lovers. But lovers they were. Every time I look at the family tree, I'm reminded that each vertical line represents another sexual act.

I hope the intercourse was loving and mutual. Some of it was bad sex,

I'm sure, but other ancestors no doubt giggled and nibbled earlobes and had little inside jokes about the size of the wife's bustle.

It's not a comfortable notion, my fourth-great granddad in bed, naked but for his woolen socks and huge beard, shouting *"Tak, tak, tak!"* (Polish for "Yes! Yes! Yes!") while atop my fourth-great grandma.

And I'm sorry I put the image in your head. I know it's about as appealing as pondering the number of insect parts in your pizza sauce or a game of Escape the Room with Ted Cruz.

But it's also a concept I've come to embrace, because it fills me with gratitude. If my ancestors hadn't flirted and winked and eventually removed their undergarments, I wouldn't be here to be repelled by the thought of it.

So to all of them: Thanks for *shtupping* (as I believe they called it back in the Old Country).

Incidentally, if my kids are reading this: Don't worry. You were conceived by IVF, so your mom and I never had to have sex. I had to go into a room, lock the door, and . . . okay, that's not much better.

With all this in mind, I've been creating a list of the Seven Most Romantic Stories I've run across in my research.

1. HOTTEST COURTSHIP

I stumbled across one of the sweetest tales in my family's history right where you'd expect: my grandfather's FBI file. My grandfather Theodore Kheel, who died in 2010, had a nice juicy file, thanks to checking several boxes: liberal, pro-union, Jewish, lawyer. I got the report through the Freedom of Information Act (more on that later). And in it, an FBI informant provided this story about my grandfather's behavior at college in 1934:

> Confidential Informant T-1 advised that KHEEL had entered the room of one of the students, who was at the time in the infirmary at Cornell University, by means of a fire escape. The girl's mother was present at the time of KHEEL's entrance, and had requested that he leave immediately.

I'd heard the story before from my mom, but now I had J. Edgar Hoover's confirmation. The girl turned out to be my grandmother. She was sick with acute bronchitis. And my grandfather, who was dating her, was forbidden to visit her in the hospital on account of his gender. He refused to let prudish rules keep them apart until his future mother-in-law kicked him out. Luckily, the FBI declined to pursue this romantic gesture as un-American activity.

My maternal grandparents, Theodore and Ann Kheel.

Confidential Informant T-1 advised that KHEEL had entered the room of one of the students, who was at the time in the infirmary at Cornell University, by means of a fire escape. He stated that the girl's mother was present at the time of KHEEL's entrance, and had requested that he leave immediately.

Later in the afternoon, KHEEL had obtained permission to visit the girl at the infirmary, in her mother's presence, but in the evening of the same day, he again attempted entrance into her room by means of the fire escape, at which time the girl's mother persuaded him to leave.

Confidential Informant T-1 further advised that because of this occurrence KHEEL had been reprimanded.

2. STRANGEST MEET-CUTE

Here's how my great-great-aunt Sara met her husband in 1894, according
to a family oral history:

"Sara was engaged to a young man from a nearby town in Poland. The
day of the wedding came, the food was cooked, the rabbi waiting, and no
groom. After several hours of waiting, someone in the family saw a young
stranger walking about the town. They asked him if he was married. He
said no, so they asked if he would like to be. He said yes, and he and Sara
married then and there. Since she had never met her original intended, it
made no difference. The original groom showed up the next day, saying
his wagon had broken down, but by then it was too late. Sara and Shmiel
were married for over sixty years. They used to play pinochle in the din-
ing room every Saturday afternoon."

Of course, I wouldn't gamble my pinochle winnings on this being a perfectly accurate account. But even if it's a little bit true, it underscores just how
much randomness and dumb luck are involved in the shape of family trees.

3. MOST EFFECTIVE OBJECTIFICATION

Here's how my second-great grandparents Sophie and Morris Kingsbacher met, according to a family history:

In 1881 Sophie came to Pittsburgh to visit her sister, and is "espied"
by Morris when she walks by his jewelry store. "Seeing her approaching,
Morris calls forth his employees to gaze upon her beauty." So basically,
he ogled her, and then got all his buddies to ogle her as well. By twenty-
first-century standards, a little invasive, no?

I showed the story to Julie to get the feminist perspective. "I wouldn't
get too worked up about it," she said. "I think women of that era had
bigger battles."

"What about this?" I said. "When he saw her, he apparently shouted
out, '*Mein Gott*, what curls!' Which I'm thinking is the nineteenth-
century equivalent of 'What a rack!'"

*My great-great-grandparents Morris Kingsbacher and
his wife, Sophie (famous curls hidden under hat).*

"I don't know. If you're going to objectify a body part, hair is the
way to go."

I thank Julie for cutting my great-great-grandfather some slack.

4. CHEAPEST MEDIA HIT JOB

"Man Weds Sister-in-Law" reads the headline in the 1934 *Wilkes-Barre
Tribune* (Pa.). The article is about my second-great uncle Leo Sunstein.
And yes, he married the sister of his former wife, who had died years
before. Seems overly sensational. This stuff happened all the time. In
the Bible, it's even commanded that a widow marry her late husband's
brother (not that I approve of mandatory weddings). In short, this
could not have been a fun article for them to read on their honeymoon.

5. BEST WINGMAN

I found a letter to my great-grandfather Lazarus Sunstein from his friend, written when they were in their eighties. The friend was reminiscing about their pickup strategy, which was to boost the other guy's reputation. The two friends would call each other handsome and suave and eligible. He writes, "If pot and kettle call each other dazzling white, a few girls will be taken in. It was a great idea and it got us wonderful wives."

6. SWEETEST LAST WILL AND TESTAMENT

Amid the usual dry legalese in my great-grandfather Sam Kheel's will, I was delighted to discover the following two-sentence love letter:

> I make no specific provision for my infant children, not because of lack of love and affection; for the fact is that my dearest possession in life consists of my wife and two children. This is because of the absolute confidence and faith that I have in my beloved wife Kate Kheel, because she is blessed with a keen mind and is fair and just.

Sam left her all his money, with no instructions or restrictions. Very sweet, not counting the part where he calls his wife a "possession."

7. CLOSEST COUPLE

In that list of memorable family events from the sixtieth anniversary of the Friedenheits, I found an entry dated August 23, 1859: "Fannie and Gerson separated for 5 minutes."

I told Julie about this, and she said nonstop togetherness sounded dreadful. My wife needs her space. But I guess the system worked for my ancestors.

Would it be inappropriate to give a toast at the Global Family Reunion thanking my ancestors for their libidos?

CHAPTER 16

Biological and Logical Families

My mom, always on the lookout for important genealogy information, sends me a link to a 1940s song called "I'm My Own Grandpa."

It's a novelty tune based on a Mark Twain anecdote that is, in turn, based on a possible real-life incident in Norwich, England, in the early nineteenth century.

Here's how it works: The narrator marries a widow with an adult daughter. Then the narrator's dad marries the widow's daughter. So now the narrator is stepfather to his own stepmother. As Wikipedia puts it, by "tacitly dropping the 'step'-modifiers, the narrator becomes his own grandfather." Wikipedia points out that this arrangement is perfectly legal, in case you want to try it.

I spend the next half hour attempting to chart the I'm-my-own-grandpa tree on my laptop's genealogy software. In the end, my software refuses to cooperate. It essentially says, "I don't know about you, but I have better things to do with my time." Fine. Point taken, software. Asshole.

But the truth is, family tree software will need to become more flexible. Because our trees are becoming increasingly tangled and unorthodox. According to the Pew Research Center, the traditional nuclear family—two parents living with their biological kids—now makes up less than 50 percent of families. It's down from 73 percent in 1960.

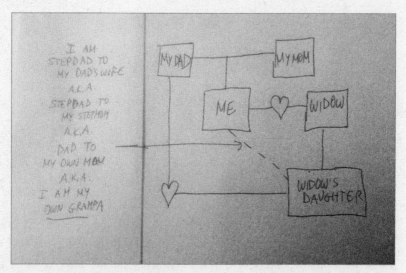

My hand-drawn attempt to diagram "I'm My Own Grandpa."

So what's on the rise? Blended families with various combinations of stepparents and stepsiblings. But that's just the start. We're in a boom era for creative and unorthodox family arrangements.

We're seeing more and more gay and trans parents. Open adoption. Surrogate moms. Group homes with multiple parents. Sperm donors. There's new vocabulary: *diblings* have a single sperm donor father but different mothers. They form Facebook groups and have half-sibling reunions.

There are other new arrangements: A few years ago, Bruce Feiler, the author of *The Secrets of Happy Families*, was diagnosed with cancer, which he thankfully survived. But when he thought he was going to die, he set up a "Council of Dads"—six friends who would mentor his daughters on a part-time basis. (Incidentally, Bruce has agreed to speak at the reunion.)

There's new mind-blowing technology: In 2016, for the first time, a baby was born to three biological parents. Scientists combined an egg from the mom, sperm from the dad, and some DNA from another woman to replace a section of the mom's genes that had a heritable disease. Mom, dad, and assistant mom. In *The Hitchhiker's Guide to the Galaxy*, two of the characters are related because they share three of the same mothers. This is coming to our galaxy soon. So get ready, annoyingly stubborn software.

Some of my conservative cousins find this new smorgasbord of family structures threatening, a sign of civilization's decay. Personally, I like the variety. My theory is this: The particular makeup of the family doesn't matter much. Could be two dads. Or a mom and a grandma. Or one adoptive dad and his ex-wife's uncle. The key is that the guardian or guardians provide a critical mass of love, attention, guidance, stability, and authority.

As always, it'd be great to have more studies to support my contention. The data available is wildly inconsistent, depending in part on who funded the study. What is certain is that the "traditional" nuclear family (mom, dad, a couple of biological kids) was not chosen by either God or evolution. It's actually a more modern arrangement.

In preindustrial society, the "traditional" nuclear family wasn't the norm. The norm was the extended family: the parents, the grandparents, perhaps a smattering of uncles, aunts, and cousins, all living under the same thatched roof. With the rise of industry, people began moving to cities for jobs and separated from the extended family. That ushered in the Nuclear Family Age, with mom, dad, and biological kids under a shingled roof considered ideal and "normal." But now that age is on the wane, thanks to several factors, including new reproductive technology, higher divorce rates, gay rights, and falling taboos against adoption.

One big result? The concept of "family" is slowly declaring its independence from DNA. You no longer need to share chromosomes to call yourself kin.

Taken to the extreme, this means you can choose your own family. As I mentioned, the writer Armistead Maupin calls these options our biological family and our logical family. Sometimes they overlap. Sometimes they don't.

Your logical family can be any group of humans with whom you share (nearly) unconditional love and support. It could be close friends. It could be your work "family." It could even be the parents of your ex-husband, as is the case with my friend Audrey. "I divorced my husband, not his parents. I still love them." Maupin's logical family was a close-knit group of gay men, since he came from a generation when the biological parents of gay men often rejected them.

The writer Andrew Solomon has different language. He talks about the "horizontal family" (who share your passion or worldview or condition) and "vertical family" (parents, kids, grandparents, etc.).

The World Family Tree gives a huge boost to logical and horizontal families. Everyone on earth is family, so go ahead and choose the humans you want to have in your inner family circle.

REUNION COUNTDOWN: 37 WEEKS

A disastrous week. I was checking the Guinness World Record website to have another look at the write-up for the Lilly Family Reunion, but it wasn't there. It has been replaced by a new record holder for Largest Family Reunion: the Porteau-Boileve family, from the west coast of France. Their reunion had 4,514 relatives. What? That's almost twice as many as the Lilly record of 2,585. This is terrible. Or *terrible*, as they say in French. My life has just become twice as hard. I have to get 4,515 relatives to Queens? That's about 4,000 more than have agreed to come. I've been telling potential sponsors we're going to break the record. Now I'm not so sure.

CHAPTER 17

Ellis Island

I'm on a mission to get my kids to appreciate their ancestors. It's Saturday, and Julie and I are taking the boys to Ellis Island. We want them to see the place where the SS *Lapland* arrived on October 9, 1910, carrying a Russian passenger named Chaya Flug—their great-great-grandmother.

"How long will it take to get there?" asks Lucas, as we walk to the subway.

"Probably forty minutes," Julie says.

"You know," I say, "your great-great-grandma's trip to Ellis Island was a little longer."

Lucas doesn't ask for details, so I tell him anyway. "Two months. It took her and her kids *two months* to get from Poland to here by horse and boat and on foot. And no screen time for the whole trip."

At the southern tip of Manhattan, we exit the subway and get in the line to board the ferry.

"You know your great-great-grandmother had to wait in line too?"

Jasper takes the bait. "What line?"

"They had a line at Ellis Island where they'd check you for diseases. And the doctors stuck a metal hook under her eyelids to check for eye disease. They didn't wash the hook much, so even if she didn't have an eye disease to start with, she probably got it there."

"Okay, A.J.," Julie says. "You're coming on a little strong."

She has a point. "I just want them to know how lucky they are."

"We get it, Dad," says Jasper. "We'll never complain about anything ever again."

The ferry sets off, and we chug past the Statue of Liberty. I've been reading a book on the history of immigration—*American Passage: The History of Ellis Island* by Vincent Cannato—and it turns out the U.S. government originally considered building America's immigration center on the same island as Lady Liberty.

But it never happened. The Statue of Liberty's sculptor, Frédéric Auguste Bartholdi, vehemently objected, writing a letter saying that it would be a "desecration." Instead, the government chose Ellis Island, half a mile away.

You have to marvel at the *pommes de terre* on this Bartholdi fellow. "Give me your tired, your poor, your huddled masses yearning to breathe free—just don't allow them to yearn near my beautiful statue. I don't want them touching my statue with their dirty yearning hands." There you have it: society's conflicted feelings about immigrants summed up in one anecdote.

As the ferry approaches Ellis Island, I decide to try again with my ancestors' tales. This time, I'll frame their journeys as thrillers. Because they do have several screenplay-worthy moments.

One of their ancestors didn't have the proper papers to leave Poland and had to hide her five kids under stacks of hay in the back of a wagon. Her eight-year-old boy sat in the front of a buggy, pretending to be the son of a German buggy driver. Boys were more strictly monitored, as they were the potential future soldiers for the Russian army.

And then there was their great-great-grandpa Harry Flug, who left Poland, which was then part of the Russian empire, and arrived in America in 1904. He was fleeing the violence of the pogroms, in which rampaging Russian soldiers killed thousands of Jews. Many of Harry's friends, neighbors, and even family members were murdered.

Harry worked as a tailor. After three years, he had enough money to buy tickets for his wife, Chaya, and their four children. Chaya and her kids got to Hamburg and boarded the steamship *Lapland* for a ten-day trip to New York. On a chilly October day, they finally arrived at Ellis Island and filed into its echoing main hall with 342 other passengers. The arrangement was that Harry would be there to pick them up.

He was nowhere to be found.

Imagine their state of mind: just arrived in a strange land, unable to speak the language, having been poked and prodded and interrogated. And they were alone.

Chaya was terrified. Did Harry abandon the family? Was he alive? One of Chaya's daughters started wailing, shouting that they'd all be sent back to Poland. The others joined in. They were given cots in the Ellis Island boarding quarters. I can't imagine they got much sleep.

So where was Harry?

Well, as I mentioned way back in chapter 1, he was eating soup. Harry was living with his sister in New Haven at the time, and she'd made him lunch. But while bringing the bowl to the table, she spilled the soup. "Let me make you another bowl of soup," she insisted. Harry got his second bowl of soup. But according to family lore, by the time he finished, he'd missed the train to New York.

I hope it was the best bowl of soup in the history of Eastern European cuisine. I hope it tasted like a Ferran Adrià special of the day. Because that soup caused a lot of anguish.

This story hit home with Lucas.

"She couldn't get in touch with him?" he asked.

"No cell phones."

"But she was okay in the end, right?"

"Yes, and she went on to have more kids, including your great-grandma Harriet."

He looked relieved.

"So what do you say?"

"Thank you, Great-great-grandma Chaya!" Lucas says.

He knows that's what I want to hear. And I know he's partly joking. But only partly.

We continue through the exhibit. In one glass case, we see the puzzles from the "mental deficiency" test that immigrants had to take. They had to match identical patterns and arrange a series of chicken-and-farmer images chronologically.

We see photos of the doctors examining immigrants for diseases. They had a list of more than 170 diseases that could get you sent back across the Atlantic. There was tuberculosis, flu, open sores, warts, and on and on. And according to *American Passage*, one unlucky soul in Ellis Island's history was sent back for masturbation. Which brings up so many questions. Where exactly did they catch this man pleasuring himself? While in line for his medical inspection? And what did he say to his friends when he got back to Europe?

"What happened, Vito?"

"Well, it's complicated."

On a computer, we fill out the same questionnaire that immigrants had to fill out by hand: *Are you a polygamist? Are you an anarchist?* I get tripped up on the question *Do you ever sing or talk to yourself?*

"You talk to yourself all the time, Dad!" says Zane.

It's true. I find it comforting. But apparently, in the early twentieth century, it was seen as a sign of mental infirmity. So I'd be on my way back to Poland.

While Julie and the kids finish touring the infirmary, I walk to the research center. "How does this work?" I ask the woman behind the desk.

"You pay seven dollars for access to the computer, and you can go online and look up your ancestors," she says.

"Okay. I'll take it."

"Just so you know, you can do it for free at home. It's on the Ellis Island database. Same information."

My great-grandparents Chaya and Harry Flug.

Huh. So we didn't need to schlep here, at least not for research purposes. But I wasn't about to tell my kids that. Besides, there's something much more authentic about doing research at Ellis Island. My ancestors didn't telecommute, right? They didn't check nypeddler.com to see what pushcart positions were free. They made the trip. And so did we.

REUNION COUNTDOWN: 34 WEEKS

A few years ago, two friends of mine, marketing geniuses named Dave and Carrie Kerpen, convinced a handful of companies to sponsor their wedding. A flower delivery service, a tuxedo rental store, and a bakery all donated stuff to the nuptials in exchange for mentions in the inevitable press coverage of a sponsored wedding.

Finding corporate sponsors is out of my comfort zone, but so is losing a lot of money. So I ask Dave to give me some advice. He says, "Land a big one, and the rest will follow."

I take his advice and go really big: Google. They seem to have a lot of money, so I figure maybe they'll give me some. I'm actually able to set up several meetings with Google executives in New York. I have a slide presentation. I use terms like "media impressions" and "step and repeat." In the end, they pass. What about Bing? No shame in Bing! They also pass.

After many phone calls and emails, I convince the massive genealogy company FamilySearch International to come on board as a sponsor. FamilySearch will help pay for the reunion and, in return, get its name on banners and posters. It'll also have a huge tent at the reunion. When I get the call with the news, I almost cry with relief.

Dave was right. Other ancestry companies soon follow. Findmypast, 23andMe, and Family Tree DNA all come on board. MyHeritage agrees to be a major sponsor—though on the condition that its big rival Ancestry has nothing to do with the reunion. We may all be family, but that's not the same as communism.

CHAPTER 18

Our Neanderthal Cousins

My son Zane—one of the twins—has a business idea. He recently read an article about hybrid animals and now wants to start a stuffed animal line of genetically jumbled creatures. He shows me photos of real-life *zonkeys*, the offspring of a donkey and a zebra. Zonkeys are odd-looking beasts, with a brown donkey torso but black-and-white-striped legs.

There are also examples of *tigons*, the offspring of a female lion and a male tiger. Which is not to be confused with *ligers* in which a male lion breeds with a female tiger (creatures made famous by Napoleon Dynamite).

I tell him I'm ready to invest.

"You know, we're kind of zonkeys ourselves," I add. "Because humans interbred with an extinct humanlike species called Neanderthals. We're kind of humanderthals."

Zane says that's interesting, but he doesn't think it fits into his marketing plan.

The first time I ever heard that *Homo sapiens* are part Neanderthal was at a medical conference. I'd just written a book about health and was asked to give a short talk about my experience.

I gave my speech and sat down to watch the next speaker, a geneticist who had sequenced the genome of heavy metal singer Ozzy Osbourne.

The scientist and Ozzy had both come to the convention and were sitting side by side onstage. I remember two things from their presentation:

(1) When the scientist asked Ozzy about his health, Ozzy said he strives to avoid processed foods. "I do agree with one of the guys over here who was saying the American diet is pretty bad."

It hit me: I'd discussed the American diet in my presentation right before Ozzy. I was "the guy" he was talking about. This was thrilling. Rock 'n' roll legend Ozzy Osbourne was quoting me. Sure, he couldn't remember my name. But the Godfather of Headbangers had acknowledged my existence, and he'd even gotten my gender correct. It's an experience this generic, unnamed guy will never forget.

(2) While discussing Ozzy's genome, the scientist revealed that Ozzy had a small percentage of Neanderthal DNA. In fact, most *Homo sapiens* have a small percentage—somewhere around 2.5 percent—because about a hundred thousand years ago, *Homo sapiens* interbred with Neanderthals. Neanderthals later went extinct, but we carry their genes with us.

Ozzy enjoyed having Neanderthal heritage, since it fit his self-conception as a rule-breaking, crazy-train-riding personality. Unfortunately for Ozzy's hypothesis, the idea that extra Neanderthal DNA would cause a wild, heavy metal personality—well, it's highly conjectural. For one thing, it's stereotyping Neanderthals. Maybe they preferred smooth jazz. Who knows?

A few years later, 23andMe sent me my own Neanderthal results. I learned I contain relatively little Neanderthal DNA, a smaller amount than about 63 percent of the world's population, a fact I tried not to see as emasculating, despite the taunts from my friends higher on the Neanderthal spectrum.

Who exactly are Neanderthals? I'd always thought they were a primitive hominid that, over thousands of years, got smarter and stood up straighter and turned into us. That's not the case. Neanderthals didn't eventually evolve into us. They died out. *Homo sapiens* and Neanderthals lived at the same time and were an entirely different species, in the same way foxes and wolves are different species, or moose and white-tailed deer. Neanderthals went extinct about forty thousand years ago, but not before some of them interbred with *Homo sapiens*.

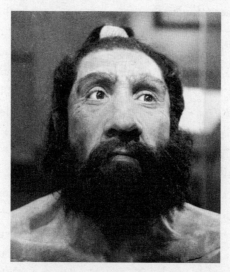

My Neanderthal ancestor at the Smithsonian. (Photo by Tim Evanson)

The Neanderthals, who were already living in Europe and Asia, mixed with the modern humans who migrated from North Africa. All humans today, with the exception of some sub-Saharan Africans, have Neanderthals in their family tree. At least one of my fifteen-thousandth-or-so-great grandparents was a Neanderthal. This, to me, is an astounding fact. For those concerned with purity and the mixing of races, it is, I hope, a wakeup call. In all likelihood, you aren't just one race. You aren't even one species. You are a jumble. You're a zonkey.

So how did we come to have Neanderthal ancestors? The romantic in me hopes it was a star-crossed lovers scenario. Romeo Neanderthal and Juliet Sapiens are smitten. Their parents disapprove and threaten to cut off their inheritance of clamshells and sharp rocks. But the two passionate primates go ahead and mate anyway.

Unfortunately, this was probably not the case. As one of my advisers, the

Harvard geneticist George Church, told me, "I don't think it was a sweet, consensual love affair." It's unclear which species was the assailant and which the victim. It's also unclear if it was just one couple or dozens of pairings.

Either way, according to the latest research, Neanderthals have gotten a bad rap. They weren't nearly as crude and primitive as their stereotype would have you believe. Some scientists believe that Neanderthals buried their dead, took care of their injured, and wore ornamental jewelry. Neanderthals possibly even had the gift of language. According to an article in the *New York Times Magazine*, "they probably had high-pitched, raspy voices, like Julia Child." (Free idea for Food Network: a paleo cooking show where a high-pitched raspy-voiced Neanderthal chef teaches us how to prepare mammoth stew.)

There's still a lot we don't know about this ancient branch of the family. For instance, what Neanderthal traits have we inherited? I've read articles claiming Neanderthal DNA contributes to everything from our depressive personalities to our nicotine addiction. But the evidence is murky at best. We also don't know how Neanderthals died out. Did *Homo sapiens* kill them? Did they succumb to disease?

But it's clear they did mate and we are the offspring. And here's the kicker: They aren't the only non–*Homo sapiens* in our family tree. There's at least one, and possibly three, extinct hominin species that bred with our paleo ancestors.

One is a population called Denisovans. They lived about 50,000 years ago and interbred with *Homo sapiens* in Siberia. Some humans in Southeast Asia and Australia have about 3 to 5 percent Denisovan DNA. And such DNA may contribute to the higher body fat percentage of people native to colder climates.

In his book *The Ancestor's Tale*, Richard Dawkins talks about the "tyranny of the discontinuous mind." What he's saying is that reality often lacks hard boundaries. Species blend into one another, as do the differences we interpret as races. The world does not consist of tidy cubbyholes. Almost everything is on a continuum. It's not only incorrect to reject the nuanced view of the world; it's dangerous. It can lead to racism and fundamentalism, to us-versus-them thinking.

So in that sense, Zane's stuffed animal line may actually be a good thing. It may help us see all the grays in between the blacks and whites. And it's certainly better than his father's Neanderthal cooking show idea.

REUNION COUNTDOWN: 33 WEEKS

Plenty of my jaded friends have mocked me for the Age of Aquarius vibe of the event. I've heard more renditions of "Kumbaya" than seem necessary. But I've also gotten feedback that it's a fascistic affair. Well, maybe not fascistic. But this week, while giving a talk at a New York high school, I showed images of, among other things, the Global Family Reunion logo. The logo is a tree in the shape of a globe, with the Western Hemisphere represented with leaves. After the talk, a student came up to me to ask why the logo showed only the Western Hemisphere. What about the Eastern Hemisphere? Why am I ignoring half the world? You know, she has a point. But I'm too exhausted to make two alternating logos.

Example #83 of the rule You'll never please everyone.

global family
REUNION

CHAPTER 19

Family Feuds

'm sitting on Jasper's bed emailing random cousins. He's at his desk reading *Romeo and Juliet* for English class. When he takes a break, I tell him I want to make two things clear about that play.

"First, please never act like Romeo. He's a terrible role model."

"Okaaaay," Jasper says, not sure where this is going.

"Romeo went way overboard. He acted like a crazy person. Falling in love can be a good thing. But if the relationship doesn't work out for whatever reason, just try to move on."

I believe this. If Romeo hadn't overreacted, he would've eventually met another nice Veronese lady with a puffy skirt and fallen in love with her. And Juliet would have rebounded too.

Romeo would probably bump into Juliet at a ball a few years later. They'd have a polite conversation, maybe chuckle about the time he woke the neighbors by shouting to her on a balcony like a tomcat near a tabby in heat. As he rode his carriage home with his new wife, Romeo would think to himself, Isn't it weird I was so obsessed with Juliet? I mean, she's sweet and all, but she could be so irritating. Remember when she kept making those pretentious falconry allusions?

"Okaaaay," Jasper says again.

I tell him I'm sort of kidding, but not really.

The thing is, I know I can't shield my sons from all heartbreak, but I can try like hell to cushion the inevitable blows.

When my first girlfriend—who I thought was The One—dumped me, it was an emotional Armageddon: weeks of doing little but weeping and watching cable coverage of a murder trial involving two tennis-playing brothers who shot their parents. A little perspective might have helped.

I blame, at least partly, the odious myth of the soul mate that permeates our culture.

"If I hadn't gotten married to your mom," I tell Jasper, "there are dozens of other women I'd be happy with. Maybe hundreds or thousands."

Jasper looks at me, his eyebrows raised.

"Does Mom know you think this?"

"Well, yes," I say, adding there's no need to bring it up with her.

I pause. Is this wise parental advice? Maybe in my quest to make his life less painful, I'm crushing his notion of romance before he even goes on a date. Maybe I should move on.

I'm much more certain of the second point in my *Romeo and Juliet* lecture: "The other thing you should know is, feuds are a deadly and terrible thing. Shakespeare was right. You have to learn to forgive quickly and easily. You shouldn't wait for some horrible event to reconcile."

Feuds and forgiveness have been on my mind since I began working on the Global Family project. And more so recently. Not long ago, I got an intriguing email from a fifty-one-year-old man in North Carolina. His name is Ron McCoy.

As in the Hatfields and the McCoys, the most famous family feud in American history. Turns out Ron has written a book on the topic, and he and his wife, Bobbi, want to release the book at the Global Family Reunion. (He's also about fourteen steps away from me on the tree, via Julie's mom.)

A couple of weeks later, I arrange a video call with Ron. He takes the call in his home, in front of a brick fireplace. He's got oval glasses and a red button-down shirt, and is as mild-mannered as an accountant, which is what he is.

"I didn't know I was one of *those* McCoys till much later in life," he tells me.

Ron's dad and grandfather both died when he was young and never told Ron about his heritage. They were stoic men, both in the military, and not eager to rehash the past. (Ron later learned his grandfather refused to even utter the name Hatfield.)

When he was thirty-five, Ron discovered a tattered book that had been in his grandmother's attic. It was a list of his ancestors' names. With some more research, Ron figured out that he is the great-great-great-grandson of a hog farmer named Randolph McCoy—the patriarch of the famous feud.

"So what was that like, to find out at age thirty-five?" I ask.

"I felt embarrassed I didn't know about my heritage. I hadn't realized how disconnected I felt from my past."

A few weeks later, Ron flew to Pikeville, Kentucky, drove to a remote area with knee-high grass, and climbed up to a cemetery on a hill. He wanted to visit Randolph's grave, a simple granite headstone.

"I remember kneeling in front of the grave, just weeping and saying, 'I'm sorry I didn't get here sooner.'"

Ron is getting choked up just telling the story. I don't want to press, but I tell him I'm curious why it moved him so deeply.

"I was surprised by how much it affected me," he says. "I think it's because it gave me a sense of purpose. I thought, My job is to pick up the mantle. It will be my duty and my pleasure to carry this story forward."

"Why's that so important to you?" I ask.

Ron takes a moment. "I think Randolph's sense of loss was just so deep. I can't fathom the grief and despair he lived with. I feel I owe it to him. He had a reputation for wandering the streets muttering to anybody who would listen about the feud and the loss of his family. It got to the point nobody wanted to hear."

The feud began in the 1860s and '70s. There were several inciting incidents. Among them: There was a dispute over who owned a hog. There was a soured romance between a Hatfield man and a McCoy woman. There was a drunken election-day fight where a Hatfield was stabbed twenty-six times. It escalated. Three McCoy brothers were tied to bushes and shot fifty times. The Hatfields attacked the McCoy cabin, killing two children and beating Randolph's wife with the butt of a rifle. The violence lasted till 1901 and claimed at least a dozen lives.

I ask Ron if he's seen the Kevin Costner miniseries about the Hatfield-McCoy feud.

"I have it on Blu-ray but haven't been able to watch it."

Why? Well, Ron has heard that the McCoys got a bit of a raw deal in the series. Costner, the star, plays the Hatfield patriarch, a charismatic lumberman named Devil Anse.

The McCoys have always had bad PR, says Ron. He writes in his book, *Reunion: Hatfields & McCoys*:

Over a century of feud accounts, "Ol' Randolph" too often has been portrayed in a negative light. He has been rendered as a slow-to-act religious fundamentalist, resentful of the economic success of his Hatfield neighbor; a man consumed by jealousy and so enflamed by hatred that he was willing to sacrifice the lives of his children to see his own vision of justice served.

By contrast, "Devil Anse" has been regarded as a man of noble character, an intrepid mountaineer, a skilled backwoodsman and pioneering entrepreneur.

The problem, he says, is the Hatfields were much more gregarious. When the reporters came around, the "McCoys didn't talk, whereas the Hatfields would take them in, treat them to dinner, and tell them stories all night."

I get the sense that Ron still smarts from the way the McCoys were treated, that some part of him still holds a grudge against the Hatfield ancestors. And yet here's the twist: Ron has spent the last twenty years working to get over that grudge.

Act two of the story began in 1998, when Ron teamed up with another McCoy cousin and they decided to hold a McCoy reunion. They told a reporter for a local AP bureau, hoping she'd write it up.

"Are the Hatfields invited?" the reporter asked. "Because that would be something."

A pause. Then Ron and his cousin said, "Of course!"

And thus was born the Hatfield-McCoy reunion.

"I'm a very flawed person but I see the need for reconciliation. It's the hyphenated nature of the two families. This is Hatfield *dash* McCoy. We have a joint history," he says.

Ron and his cousin approached some Hatfields, who signed on. The first time Ron met a Hatfield was at a media-friendly announcement of the reunion at a park in Pikeville, Kentucky. The Hatfield in question was an eighty-two-year-old named Paul.

"You don't hold any ill will against any McCoys?" a reporter asked Paul at the meeting.

"Not a bit," Paul said, though he added the McCoys should "shave them homes for disabled crabs."

It was a jab at the bushy beard Ron was sporting at the time. The Hatfields still knew how to charm the reporters.

A few months later, in June of 2000, the reunion took place on a big field in Pikeville. There were about five thousand people (though they never submitted it to Guinness). There was a barbecue and beer and a tug of war and a softball game, which the McCoys won 15–1. "I still have Hatfields accusing us of having ringers on the team."

Overall, Ron sees the reunion as a huge success.

"I'm proud to say I have lots of Hatfield friends. I've never had a Hatfield say a harsh word to me."

Three years after that initial reunion, Ron was approached by one of the Hatfields with the idea that they should officially and publicly end America's prototypical feud. So in 2003 at 8:30 a.m. at a gazebo in that same park in Pikeville, Kentucky, in front of nearly a hundred Hatfields and McCoys, they signed a treaty. "We're not saying you don't have to fight, because sometimes you do have to fight," Reo Hatfield said at the signing. "But you don't have to fight forever."

"The most meaningful moment was when my nine-year-old son signed it," Ron says. "I thought to myself: This is my legacy."

Ron tells me he's going to bring the signed treaty to the Global Family Reunion.

"I see people of different religions that are killing each other, and I just don't understand it," he tells me. "I'm seeing more and more division; it's alarming, really. It's a family feud run amok. I'm convinced that we are one human family. I hope people think, well, if the Hatfields and McCoys can do this, we can do this."

It's delusionally optimistic. But honestly, I'm all for some delusional optimism. Sometimes I think it's all we've got.

Before I hang up, I ask Ron whether his reunion continues.

Yes, he says. He's not as involved. But now there are actually two reunions every year. Two competing Hatfield-McCoy reunions: One is held each October in Kentucky, which is McCoy country. The other happens each June in West Virginia, which is Hatfield country.

I thank Ron and click off. I engage in my own delusional optimism and try not to focus on the fact that there are two separate Hatfield-McCoy reunions now. Oh man. Even the reunions can't stay united.

REUNION COUNTDOWN: 32 WEEKS

It's official. Sister Sledge has agreed to come sing "We Are Family" at the Global Family Reunion. I'm stunned and thrilled. One of the sisters, Joni Sledge, called me to tell me that she likes the idea of a global family. "It's not a good idea," she tells me. "It's a *God* idea." I've heard plenty of not-so-positive adjectives recently, so Joni is my new hero.

CHAPTER 20

Who's Your Father?

My sister Beryl calls on a Tuesday afternoon. I'm at my computer tapping out an email to a fourth cousin. Maybe a fifth.

"I got my DNA results," she says. I'd asked Beryl to take a DNA test a few weeks ago, figuring it would help me track down more cousins for the Global Family Reunion. She'd finally gotten an email back from 23andMe.

But I can hear something askew in her voice. She's on the road to full-on panic.

"Look at the page where it lists my relatives."

"Hold on." I sign on to her page and click the list of close relatives of Beryl Jacobs. There is my name, right at the top.

"See the second column?" says my sister. "It says we share fifty percent of DNA. What happened to the other half? Did mom . . ."

She trails off. She can't say it out loud.

"No," I say. "Can't be."

"It says fifty percent," says Beryl.

I study the page. My neck gets hot, my pulse ratchets up. She's right. Fifty percent. My sister and I are half siblings? I feel my worldview undergoing a sudden shift, like I'm watching the twist end of a *Black Mirror* episode. Mom had an affair? Dad might not be my father?

Beryl and I do look quite different. She has blue eyes. She has a much prettier, less angular face.

"Wait," I say. "Fifty percent. Hold on. I think . . ."

I do a quick Google search.

"Yes!" I say. "That's what we're supposed to be! Fifty percent. If it were one hundred percent, we'd be identical twins."

"Oh, thank God."

My neck returns to its normal temperature. Ten seconds ago I was feeling existential uncertainty. Now I just feel like a perfect idiot. Come on! I should have known that. I got caught up in the moment.

My DNA surprise was a false alarm. But it could have gone the other way. The more I immerse myself in the genealogy world, the more I hear stories of DNA tests unearthing bombshells.

The stories can go both ways. I've met sisters thrilled to have found new half brothers. I talked to an eighty-eight-year-old man delighted to discover a new sixty-six-year-old daughter. But I've also gotten emails like this one from a woman in Virginia: "We took a DNA test, and it turns out my brother is not related to my dad. It's tearing the family apart. My dad won't talk to my mom."

In genealogy, such surprises are called "nonpaternity events." That's the euphemism. Which I suppose is better than "Some-other-guy-slept-with-your-mom events."

How common are these nonpaternity events? One oft-cited estimate puts the number at 10 percent of births worldwide, meaning one in ten kids is the result of a stealth father, not the presumed father. This is probably inflated. A more recent estimate puts it at 2 percent of children.

That's still a huge number. Over a hundred million people worldwide. Just a couple of decades ago, we had to rely on rumors and whispers. The old catchphrase was "Mother's baby, father's maybe." But DNA has changed that. No more maybes.

As DNA testing gains in popularity (more than 2 million have had their genes analyzed as I write this), thousands of other trees will be redrawn. It will cause estate disputes and Maury Povich shows and Lifetime series. It may even mess with the royal family. The Queen of England recently announced that DNA evidence would be considered in a hereditary dispute.

A little after my call with my sister, I was listening to a genealogy radio show called *Extreme Genes*, hosted by a deep-voiced, Utah-based researcher named Scott Fisher, who has agreed to be an emcee at the Global Family Reunion.

Scott's guest that day had a story that was so startling, a story that so perfectly encapsulated DNA's potential for both happiness and heartbreak, that I had to hear more, and see if he'd be willing to speak at the reunion. I called the man up and asked if he'd tell me the whole tale. He agreed but asked me not to print his real name. The reason will become clear soon enough.

Michael, as I'll call him, is sixty-one years old, works in technology, wears a lot of plaid, and looks a bit like Bill Murray. He tells me that he grew up in a big family in Wisconsin—nine kids. His dad was a good man, though he was away a lot (he sold fire trucks for a living) and also prone to drinking. His mom had trouble with money—at one point she maxed out sixteen credit cards—but she was nurturing toward Michael.

Michael's first clue that his family might not be 100 percent traditional came when he was thirteen years old. His brother Kenneth was in a bad accident. "A tractor rolled over on him, crushing him and sending him to the hospital. A call went out for blood donations from all family members. But when my dad donated, he was told they could not use his blood because it did not match my brother's blood type."

From then on, the kids suspected that Kenneth had a different dad.

"So how did the family react?" I ask.

"We were really good at repressing," Michael says. "We didn't talk about it. We didn't want drama."

The next crack didn't come until thirty years later. One of the sisters got in a screaming fight with the dad. She went to her mom and said, "I wish he wasn't my dad."

To which the mother said, "I've got something to tell you. He's not."

Her real dad was a farmer who lived nearby. Not Kenneth's dad, but another man her mom had slept with. A second guy.

A couple of years later, yet another daughter confronted the mom about rumors over her paternity. The mom confessed. She'd had another lover. A third one.

Three of the nine kids were from different fathers. How much further could this go?

"In 2007 my father died and we were all gathered at the funeral home for his viewing," Michael says. "My brother Zachary pulled me aside and told me that after we bury Dad, we've lost any opportunity to get any DNA samples to test."

So Michael's brother asked the funeral director for a favor: could the director surreptitiously pluck out a bit of the dad's hair before the service ended. The director agreed. As the family left, Zachary was handed an envelope of hair strands. A little odd, but better than living with unanswered questions forever, Zachary figured.

Michael wasn't worried about his own paternity. He knew he was his dad's son. They had the exact same mannerisms, right down to the straight-legged robot walk. The DNA was to see if any other siblings had unexpected dads.

A few weeks later, Zachary called. He'd gotten some results. Michael's DNA and his dad's DNA did *not* match. Michael was, as you might expect, shocked. He flew to see his mother in Wisconsin. She denied it.

A day later, she called and asked him to come back over. "We need to talk." She confessed that Michael's biological father was a meatpacker named Bryan. Or maybe Bryan's brother. She wasn't sure. She'd been with both.

"I hate to say this, but the first thing that came to my mind was, 'Wow, my mother's a skank. She's a hoochie mama!'" says Michael. "I was so angry at my mom. I didn't know I could be so angry at a person. I felt so utterly and completely betrayed. I was probably not very kind or Christian or compassionate when I got the news."

Michael grew up without much religion. But in his twenties, he became a Mormon, which he remains today, and which might explain why the harshest phrase he used is "hoochie mama."

"The news kind of made me feel like, 'You're the product of an illicit affair.' I took it personally. The two people that I really cared for, and now it's like, 'Wow, that's not really my dad . . .' "

It wasn't over. Soon came more DNA evidence, and more of his mom's confessions and more surprise fathers.

By the time I talked to him, Michael had figured out the math: nine children, eight different fathers, and one mother. (Kenneth and another brother, Zachary, were the only ones who shared a biological father.) The father who raised all nine kids was the biological father of exactly zero of the children.

The dads were a mixed lot. One was a soldier who had a one-night stand with Michael's mom. One was the dad's best friend who would come over to "help mom move furniture." Another owned a candy store and always brought great birthday presents to one of the brothers but not the others.

Michael's biological dad fixed machinery at a meatpacking plant. He was athletic when younger. That's about all Michael knows.

Once the siblings learned the truth, bits of their past started to make sense. Michael remembered when their dad (the fire truck salesman) came up to his son Zachary at a holiday party, and said, "Zachary, there's someone I need you to meet. Zachary Peterson, this is Zachary Bennet. Zachary Bennet, this is Zachary Peterson." And Zachary Peterson said, "Oh, that should be easy to remember." Hahaha.

Zachary later told Michael, "It always seemed strange, until I understood that the Zachary, the guy he was introducing me to, was my father."

Other things fell into place. "I remembered that when I was a kid, some of my friends were not allowed to come to my house and play," Michael says. "I could never understand why that was."

"Do you wish you'd known as a kid?"

"No, I'm so grateful I didn't know. I would have been mortified."

So what was going on in that marriage? Was Dad sterile? Did the couple have an arrangement? How much did his dad know? Michael's mom wouldn't answer the questions. Michael will never know for sure.

All he knows is that he has one of the most complicated and gnarled family trees in America. "When I tell people, they say it's the weirdest story they've ever heard. Well, it's the weirdest story *I've* ever heard."

It is an astounding tale. But I found something equally astounding: Michael's ability to forgive. His compassion. One of the first things Michael said to me when I called was "I don't want to demonize my mom."

"For all her faults, she had some great qualities," Michael says. "She was a pretty good woman. She would never be anybody I would choose to be my friend, but she did some good things to help me as I was growing up. She could be amazingly nurturing."

"Like how?" I ask.

"When I was a kid I had a speech impediment and I was growing really, really fast, so I was incredibly awkward. I had to take second grade over again. Mom always made it a point to just let me know, 'Listen, Michael. You've got talents, you've got abilities, you can be whatever you want.' And in the end, I ended up with two master's degrees."

Michael called his mom every week until she died. He still tries to see the best in her. He says her own childhood was messy, and he suspects she may have been sexually abused. "She made mistakes, but God knows I've made mistakes too," he says.

Michael, being a member of the genealogy-loving Church of Jesus Christ of Latter-day Saints, knew a lot about his dad's family tree. So the news that these ancestors didn't share his DNA was especially jarring for him. "My great-grandpa came over from Norway and they were farmers and worked the land and were never wealthy, but they were all very kind, sweet, nurturing people. Salt of the earth. And I just had that feeling of, 'Wow, they're not my people anymore.'"

At least that was his initial response. "But then," Michael continues, "a friend told me, 'They are still your people. They will always be your people.'"

His dad will still be Dad. "He's the man who raised me and as far as I'm concerned, that's my father."

Not everyone took the news as well as Michael. One of the brothers broke off all contact with the mom.

"I look at my brother's lack of forgiveness for what Mom did," says Michael. "And what it's doing to his life, it eats you up."

Another sister wasn't told at all. "I just don't think she could handle it," Michael says.

That is why Michael asked me not to use his real name, and why, sadly, he can't come speak at the Global Family Reunion, even though he'd be fantastic (and has a ton of relatives he could bring).

As we wind down, Michael says, "When I look at my own [nuclear] family, I feel so boring." He and his wife have four kids. And they're definitely Michael's.

I ask Michael what he thinks the word *family* means.

"They tell me that the family unit is eternal, and I'm thinking, you're kidding me," he says. "So many of the families nowadays are so bizarre and so dysfunctional or so made up, so nontraditional. Maybe that's the best word. *Nontraditional.*"

REUNION COUNTDOWN: 31 WEEKS

One of my favorite corporate sponsors is a hummus company. Or was. When the marketing woman first called, she told me her angle: Food brings people together. "Maybe it's a stretch, but what is the one thing that people in the Middle East agree on? Hummus," she said. She had a point. Peace through chickpeas. Why not? The plan was for the company to give out samples to everyone at the reunion. Seemed fun.

Well, news just broke about a nationwide recall on this hummus. There's a widespread salmonella contamination. The marketing woman has since stopped returning my calls. It's looking like there will have to be another path to peace. And at least I won't poison my family.

CHAPTER 21

Son-in-Law of the
American Revolution

I've been invited to speak at the New York chapter of the Daughters of the American Revolution. You may have heard of the DAR. It's a club for women who are direct blood descendants of Revolutionary War soldiers (or drummers or fifers or tea throwers—anyone who helped upend King George III).

The official description of the DAR is that it's a "lineage society." It's probably the most famous lineage society, but it's far from the only one. There are hundreds of them. If you have the proper ancestral line, you can join . . .

The Flagon and Trencher Society: Descendants of Colonial Tavern Keepers

The National Society of Calvin Coolidge Descendants

The Royal Bastards: Descendants of the Illegitimate Sons and Daughters of the Kings of Britain

The Order of Descendants of Pirates and Privateers

The possibilities are endless. If I get enough interest, I'm planning on starting the Descendants of Brave Survivors of Piles, Fissures, and Other Hemorrhoid-Related Diseases. So please contact me if you want in.

In one sense, lineage societies are the exact opposite of my project. They are exclusive instead of inclusive—gated genetic communities. They proclaim their unique ties to history, whereas I say *everyone* is related to Revolutionary soldiers, if only by marriage or paleolithic forebears.

On the other hand, the DAR has 180,000 members. If I can get them involved in the Global Family Reunion, they could swell our ranks and provide several barrels of hard cider. So I happily accept their invitation.

The midday meeting is held in a room at the National Arts Club in downtown Manhattan. There are about thirty daughters (or actually seven- and eighth-great granddaughters) of the Revolution in attendance.

When I arrive, I see a lot of what I expected: decorative scarves and pearl necklaces and American flag pins. We say the Pledge of Allegiance. The women talk about their "obligation to their ancestors." They welcome a new member, who has emerged intact from the rigorous entry process (you need to provide documented proof—birth certificates, census forms, etc.—for each generation of your ancestry; DNA evidence is allowed, but only in addition to the papers).

There are, however, other aspects that I didn't anticipate. Such as the New York State's vice regent, Wilhelmena Rhodes Kelly. Wilhelmena is charming and warm, and practically insists on getting me a glass of wine.

She's also African-American.

This is surprising to me. I'd always thought of the DAR as one of the whitest institutions around, rivaling Elvis movies and Weezer concerts in its lack of diversity. In fact, the DAR was the subject of an infamous race-related controversy in 1939: The great African-American opera singer Marian Anderson tried to book a concert in Washington, DC's Constitution Hall, which was owned by the DAR. But the DAR, which was segregated at the time, had a "white performers only" policy. They rejected her.

First Lady Eleanor Roosevelt was appalled. Roosevelt withdrew her membership from the DAR and helped organize a concert for Marian Anderson on the steps of the Lincoln Memorial. The concert drew seventy-five thousand people.

The DAR later apologized, but the damage to its reputation had been done.

Given this history, I ask Wilhelmena how she got involved. She explains she was always interested in her family history, which includes Virginia and Brooklyn, black ancestors and white. She was at a genealogy conference fifteen years earlier, looking for information on a line of ancestors that went back to the 1700s. She spotted the DAR booth.

"I said to my sister, who was with me, 'I'm going to talk to the DAR folks.' And my sister was skeptical. She said, 'Do you *really* want to do that?' And I said, 'Yes, I need the information.'"

Not only did the DAR volunteers help her, but they tracked down an ancestor of Wilhelmena's who aided the Revolution—a farmer who donated two thousand pounds of beef to the patriots, along with some fodder and a rifle. Wilhelmena ended up joining, as did her sister.

Wilhelmena Rhodes Kelly, Daughter of the American Revolution. (Courtesy of Wilhelmena Kelly)

Their beef-donating ancestor is from the Anglo side of the family. Wilhelmena's African-American roots come via this man's grandson, a Virginia lawyer named Edward Hamlin. Edward was white, but his life-long partner, Dolly Scott, was an African-American woman, a former slave of Hamlin's family.

It's hard to know the power dynamics behind the relationship, but Wilhelmena says that it was a consensual love story and that Edward gave all his money to their children. Wilhelmena says Dolly once saved Ned's life. "It was the Civil War, and the Union soldiers came to their house and were going to hang Ned just for the heck of it. But Dolly came out of the house and begged for his life. The Union soldiers let him go. That's the family lore, anyway."

When I was a kid, my grandfather was the first Jewish member of a super-WASPy club. I remember some Jewish people couldn't believe he had joined. I ask Wilhelmena if she had any reservations.

She shakes her head. On the contrary. She says that in her small way, she's hoping to help heal the divide. "Part of my commitment to the DAR is trying to change the DAR's profile and keep this country from degenerating into a little revolution of its own. My goal is to stress that we all have a common heritage." She calls the Revolutionary War the true first world war. It involved not just the British and Americans but also French, Germans, Native Americans, Africans, and Latin Americans. She's been on a mission to recruit all of the above to the DAR.

The current DAR membership roll wouldn't be confused for the guest list at a BET Awards after-party. It's still pretty monochromatic. But I admire their efforts to broaden it. As another member told me, "When people give me crap for being in the DAR, I say to them I'm three-quarters Jewish and the head of our chapter is black. Done. End of argument."

I like Wilhelmena immensely. And my appreciation only grows when she says she'll give a talk at the Global Family Reunion. The DAR is on board!

At the luncheon, we eat our salads and cookies, and it's my turn at the lectern.

"I'm not a daughter of the American Revolution," I say. "And I may not be a son of the American Revolution. But I am certainly a son-in-law of the American Revolution. My uncle's wife's ancestor fought at the Battle of Trenton."

The Daughters nod their heads politely.

I talk about my Global Family project and also put in a plug for Haym Salomon, the great Jewish Revolutionary War hero who saved the United States by securing a $20,000 loan for George Washington and his troops. Salomon died in poverty because he was never reimbursed for the debt. He's my third cousin's wife's sixth-great uncle's grandfather.

At the end of my talk, the Daughters clap and seemed pleased. Though they probably would have clapped just as much if I'd spent the entire time playing air saxophone to the *Star Wars* cantina song. They're just too polite not to. So who knows.

Before I leave, Wilhelmena has one more question for me. She says, "Your project is all about uniting the world, and you use the phrase 'citizen of the world.' But being a citizen of the world—I worry that takes away from being a citizen of the United States."

It's an interesting concern. Can you be a patriot and also a global citizen?

"I hope I can be both," I say. "I'm all for multiple identities. I'm human but also American. I think having a sense of community is good, as long as it doesn't devolve into tribalism."

I'm not sure I satisfied her, but she nods, too polite to do otherwise.

REUNION COUNTDOWN: 29 WEEKS

I read a *New York Times* article about social networks this week. It said that, according to legend, if two medieval knights met on a road, they'd stop and recite their lineages. "If they found that they shared a great-uncle or one of them had been a vassal to the same king, they would dismount, hug each other, and swear loyalty. . . . But if they found they had no overlap, they would fight to the death."

Which made me think two things: (1) If medieval knights had had Wi-Fi and a Geni password, they could have avoided a lot of bloodshed. And (2) what about an app that would allow Global Family Reunion–goers to bump phones and see how they're related? I get in touch with a young genealogist and entrepreneur named Wesley Eames. He's been thinking along the same lines. We decide we'll work on an app together, by which I mean he'll do the coding and I'll send him occasional encouraging emails.

CHAPTER 22

The Mega-Tree Revolution

Julie and I take the kids on vacation to Los Angeles for the usual under-thirteen tour: gasping at the robotic *Jaws* at Universal Studios, trying to buy some T-shirts at the Santa Monica pier that don't extol the virtues of smoking weed.

And while we're here, Randy Schoenberg—my fourteenth cousin and one of the Geni pioneers—has invited us to his home for dinner.

It's a lovely house. In one room there's a framed poster of Klimt's *Woman in Gold* (the painting, stolen by the Nazis, that Randy famously returned to its owner). Randy's office wall is filled with photos of his grandfather, the composer Arnold Schoenberg. And most impressive to my kids, there's a Ping-Pong table with a cannon that spits out Ping-Pong balls so you can hone your backhand and forehand.

Over a roast chicken dinner, we chat about movies, table tennis, and Randy's last name. It happens to be the same as my wife's maiden name, though they haven't found a common blood relative yet, which means it might have been adopted independently by their respective branches.

After dessert, Randy's wife and kids drive off for an evening basketball practice. So Randy is left alone with my family.

"What happened to your arm?" Jasper asks, pointing to the sling around Randy's right wrist.

"I have tendonitis," Randy says. "Tennis elbow."

"Do you play a lot of tennis?" I ask.

No, Randy says. He explains he thinks he injured himself partly from too much typing. He spends hours and hours every week inputting names and birthdates into Geni.com.

"See?" I tell my kids. "Genealogy can be dangerous." Maybe this will make them see my new hobby as thrilling, sort of like motocross or ice climbing.

"Actually," Randy says. "I can't really do the dishes . . ."

"So . . . we're on duty?" says Julie.

"Is that okay?" he asks.

For the next half hour, Julie and I scrub the dishes and load the dishwasher. Which is a little unusual but also highly appropriate. The World Family Tree is all about collaboration and chipping in. It takes a village to connect humanity and clean up after dinner. Plus Randy might have hurt himself inputting my ancestors, so it's only fair.

As we clean, Randy talks about his Geni adventures. Geni is based in Los Angeles and, since it started in 2007, has acquired 11 million users. It's one of three monster collaborative trees online—along with WikiTree and FamilySearch—each with its own fervent fan base, each racing to connect the entire human species. Geni has, at press time, 114 million connected people on its World Tree. WikiTree has 13 million profiles connected. FamilySearch is technically the biggest, with more than 240 million people connected (though it can be harder to navigate connections). As I mentioned, Ancestry.com—the most profitable genealogy service—isn't in this race. Ancestry specializes in smaller private trees, the bonsai.

Randy explains that Geni has two magic powers. First, when you input, say, Max Planck, the Geni robot searches its millions of profiles to see if there's another Max Planck on the World Tree. If there is, and you agree it's the same Max Planck as yours (matching birth dates, etc.), you can merge your tree containing Max Planck with the other guy's tree. So suddenly your tree has grown new branches. You've gone from, say, one hundred relatives to two hundred. You continue merging and eventually link to the big tree and gain millions of cousins.

The second magic power is the six-degrees-of-Kevin-Bacon-like connections. If you're looking for a link between two people on the big tree, Geni will do billions of calculations to find the best path. Which is how you end up with Abe Lincoln related to Beyoncé.

Geni boosters say collaborative online genealogy is to traditional family history what a NASA rocket is to a penny-farthing bicycle. One Geni user, a New Jersey–based lawyer named Adam Brown, told me he searched the name of his wife's grandfather, who had been killed in the Holocaust. Adam's wife had thought she had no living cousins. She was almost certain all her blood relatives had been killed by Nazis.

Within hours, Geni had found a link to second cousins in Budapest she hadn't known about. She was blown away. The surviving cousins soon got together for a teary reunion. "It would have taken years to find them without Geni," Adam said. "If it could have been done at all."

A cadre of scientists are also fans of these worldwide trees. Yaniv Erlich, for instance, is a geneticist at Columbia University. He crunched the data from 13 million Geni relatives to figure out patterns of migration. Look him up on YouTube and you'll see Yaniv's stunning time-lapse animation showing how humans have spread out onto all continents.

Yaniv is also studying the Geni tree to find clues about heredity. He's working on a paper about what the World Family Tree tells us about the secrets of longevity. (I spoke to him, and he couldn't tell me the secrets yet because his *Nature* article hasn't come out yet. Hopefully it will be published before I die.) These trees, he says, will eventually help us understand and treat deadly diseases.

Meanwhile, scientists at the University of Utah traced a family's colon cancer gene back to a British couple who married in 1614. Their thousands of descendants have now been advised to get colonoscopies.

The Big Tree has come in handy for non-PhDs like me. The other day, my kids were learning about John Adams at school, and I was able to show them he's not just some boring dead white guy. He's linked to us. We're a part of history. He's Uncle John! I also got invited to give a talk to my sons' grade about how everything is connected. It went over pretty well. Until I demonstrated how Lucas and Zane are linked to Taylor Swift, which I was later told was the most embarrassing thing in the history of the universe.

Things are only going to accelerate. In twenty years, I imagine nearly all seven billion humans will be on a single tree. You'll go to a restaurant wearing your Wi-Fi–enabled contact lenses. You'll meet the friend of a friend. Your lenses will do a facial recognition search and link to the Big Tree. "Hey, nice to meet you, my fourth cousin three times removed."

It will be either fascinating or terrifying, probably both.

Even today, these mega-trees have plenty of detractors. A couple of years ago, I attended a panel at a genealogy conference called "Online Trees: The Root of All Evil?" Many feared these forests signaled the end of privacy. They're worried their data will be stolen. (I'll talk more about this in chapter 26.)

And then there's the accuracy problem. Accuracy has always been a bugaboo of genealogy. Family trees have been riddled with errors forever. Most are unintentional: human memories are notoriously faulty. Even official records can't always be trusted. Census takers spell names wrong. Copies are smudged. Alphabets are hard to transliterate.

Other errors are the result of outright fraud. In the nineteenth century, a group of colorful American hucksters made a killing by fabricating family trees for their wealthy, status-hungry clients. "See? This is how you're related to the Duke of Marlborough."

My favorite fraud was for a good cause. In the 1970s, the Soviet Union allowed Jews to emigrate to Israel, but only if they could prove that they had close blood relatives there. So the Israeli government set up a department whose job was to fabricate old birth certificates and census records to create nonexistent family links, allowing the Soviet Jews to escape.

Are these mega-trees any less accurate than a well-crafted private tree? Depends on whom you ask.

Randy thinks Geni's tree is actually *more* accurate than the average tree. "We've got millions of eyes on it looking for mistakes," he says. There's also a platoon of obsessives—nicknamed "the forest rangers"—who scour any new profiles to assess their veracity.

If you believe its boosters, the precision will only improve. The World Family Trees are adding documentary evidence—censuses, wills, etc.—to many of the profiles. And this is important: the tree is now meshed with people's DNA results, which will help ferret out false parentage.

But even Randy has to admit that the further you go back, the less reliable Geni becomes. In fact, at a certain point, some branches of Geni become purely mythological. Religious Geni users have added biblical characters without providing much evidence at all. My tree says that I'm the ninety-eighth-generation grandson of King David of Israel. That's a leap of faith I cannot take. I trust Geni only a few generations back. If I make a six-degrees connection to Melania Trump, it has to be recent and well documented.

Many traditional genealogists say King David's profile isn't the only problem. Despite the efforts of the forest rangers, they say, the mega-trees have errors everywhere, and the inaccuracies are so deep they're hard to fix.

They allege that most Geni users don't adhere to the Genealogical Proof Standard. This is a rigorous series of rules that hardcore gene-alogists say is necessary to verify an ancestor: census records, marriage certificates, DNA tests, oral tradition, and so on.

One detractor, respected genealogist Gary Mokotoff, wrote about sites like Geni in a genealogy journal: "Collaborative genealogy is not genealogy, and a new term should be used for it. Genealogy is not the activity of connecting all the people in the world and their ancestors on one common tree. . . . Connecting all the people in the world is not a scientific study."

To which Randy responded on Facebook: "Does anyone actually agree with this? I don't see how anyone can look at what we have done on Geni and not call it genealogy."

Randy says the problem boils down to control. "Some folks don't like the idea of other people changing what they think of as 'my tree,'" he says. "They confuse the word *my* and read it as possessive (indicating ownership) rather than attributive (indicating inclusion). But the same control issue is involved in any human endeavor. At some point, if you want to work on larger projects, you have to give up some control and start working with other people. That means being open to the possibility that your collaborators (whether partners or employees) will make mistakes that will affect you. But where would we be if that type of collaboration didn't exist? Living in caves gathering nuts and berries for food?"

The genealogist Adam Brown puts it more philosophically: "I would call our hobby 'quantum genealogy.' We can never truly know facts, we can only estimate their probability of being true."

Geni and sites like it suffer from one other big weakness. The World Family Tree is lopsided. Some cultures and ethnicities are well represented, including WASPs, Jews, and, for some reason, Norwegians. Other groups are underrepresented, including Asians and Africans. The genealogists are working hard to rectify that. But they've got a ways to go.

CHAPTER 23

Our Animal Cousins

I gave a talk about the global family at my synagogue. Afterward, a short woman with long red hair walks up to me briskly. She has a look on her face. It's not the look of someone who is going to ask me to autograph a book or tell me about her favorite great-uncle in Belarus.

"I disagree with your project," she says.

"How so?"

"You say we should care for members of our family. But what about those who aren't in my family? Should I treat them with less kindness?"

"But that's my point. Every person in the world is in your family."

She sighs and shakes her head. "No, you see," she says, "I'm an animal person. I love animals. What about them?"

I'd actually been waiting for this objection.

"But they're family too! Cats, dogs, monkeys, warthogs—we're all cousins if you go back far enough."

She still seems suspicious.

"We all share DNA," I continue. "So bring your animal cousins to the reunion! Actually, I should probably check with the venue on their pet policy. So let me get back to you." Judging from her demeanor, I don't need to get back to her soon. It's unlikely she or any of her cats or warthogs will be attending my event.

Percentage of DNA Humans Share with Various Animals

Bonobos..............98.8 percent
Mice.....................88 percent
Cows....................85 percent
Dogs.....................84 percent
Platypus...............69 percent
Fruit flies...............47 percent
Yeast....................18 percent

Sources: Javier Herrero, European Molecular Biology Laboratory, and Carl Zimmer, National Geographic
Magazine, American Museum of Natural History

But it's something I've been thinking for a while, that animals are our cousins. The family tree shouldn't be restricted to bipeds. Ideally, it should spread out to envelop every kingdom and phylum and species.

Charles Darwin talked about this way back in *On the Origin of Species*. All creatures, all forms of life, he wrote, are "cousins to the same millionth degree."

The numbers bear this out: Humans share 98.8 percent of our DNA with bonobos. We share 88 percent with mice, 84 percent with dogs, 47 percent with fruit flies, and 18 percent with yeast. Sending big hugs to you, Cousin Yeast!

I recently finished *The Ancestor's Tale*, by Richard Dawkins, and the book taught me a new word: *concestor*. This is the common ancestor linking two species. Dogs and modern wolves, for instance, share a concestor, a primitive wolf.

Dawkins's book is a reverse chronology. He starts with *Homo sapiens* and goes back and back, concestor by concestor, animal by animal, fish by fish, until he gets to the bacterium that started it all. "We can be very sure there really is a single concestor of all surviving life forms on this planet," he writes. "The evidence is that all that have ever been examined share . . . the same genetic code; and the genetic code is too detailed, in arbitrary aspects of its complexity, to have been invented twice."

Inspired by Dawkins and my animal-loving friend with the long red hair, I decide to put some ancestral portraits up in the living room. When the kids come home from school, I show them my new display.

"This is our wall of ancestors," I say.

I've printed out about twenty black-and-white images of our fore-bears and taped them to the wall. At one end is their grandmother, smiling, wearing a white cable-knit sweater. At the other is a close-up of a circular bacterium.

"Who's this?"

"That's our 1.1-billionth-great grandfather."

"He's round, just like you," Julie says, patting my tummy.

"Good one," I say.

"You got his genes," Julie adds.

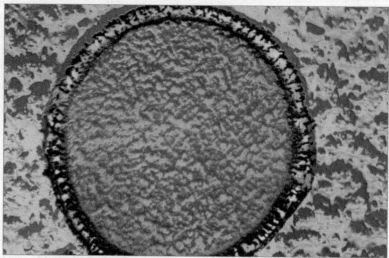

Luca, the one who started it all, probably looked similar to this.
(Wolfgang Baumeister / Science Photo Library)

"So his name is Luca," I say. "It stands for Last Universal Common Ancestor."

Lucas looks pleased at having a namesake in the family.

"Luca lived about four billion years ago. He liked to hang out in deep sea vents where hot magma was shooting out."

Zane says, "So you're saying that he's our great-great-great-great-great-great-great-great—"

"You know what'd be super, Zane?" says Julie. "If you did that in your head."

"—great-great-great-great-great-great-great-great—"

Over the sound of Zane's "greats," I take them on a tour of their distant ancestors.

I show them their 250-millionth-great grandfather, an unsegmented invertebrate that resembles a tapeworm.

I give them my best invertebrate impression, doing a classic Old Coot voice. "Back in my day, we didn't have your fancy respiratory organs. Your so-called lungs. We got our oxygen straight from the mud. And we liked it!"

No response, except for the continuing drone of "great-great-great."

"And here's your fifty-fifth-millionth-great grandfather."

I show them a picture of a shrewlike creature, the eutheria. "He lived about one hundred and five million years ago. All mammals descend from this guy. Some of his descendants got longer necks and became giraffes. Some got whiskers and became cats. And some got language and eyebrows and became human."

I take them through several other ancestors—their eighty-fifth-hundredth grandfather, a stooped and hairy fellow called *Australopithecus*. A less stooped, less hairy fellow called *Homo habilus*.

All the way past Gerson Friedenheit, their third-great grandpa, and Sam Kheel, their second-great grandpa, and Ellen Kheel Jacobs, their grandma. "So there they are! Your family. Aren't they a handsome group!"

55th million Great-Grandpa Eutheria.

I'm actually conflicted about this display. On the one hand, I want to make my kids aware that they are just a small part of the vast web of life. I'm hopeful it'll make them more compassionate, feel more connected.

On the other hand, I'm a little worried it will humble them *too* much. What if it makes them feel insignificant? As biologists often point out, humans are just a "slender twig" on the tree of life. Most of the branches are bacteria.

In the book *The Hitchhiker's Guide to the Galaxy*, there's a torture device called a perspective machine. You go into a booth, strap on a helmet, and it reveals to you just how inconsequential your life is when compared to the vastness of time and space and other living beings. People emerge devastated.

When I talked to creationists for my book about the Bible, this was their great fear about evolution. Evolution, one told me, says, "We evolved via pond scum. When we say that, we're not applying much value to humanity. If we say we're a product of accidents and random processes, how much purpose and hope does that give to our youth?"

I find creationist conclusions absurd, but I do understand the problem of retaining dignity when we're just "glorified lungfish," as Dawkins puts it.

A long time ago, when writing my book about the *Encyclopaedia Britan-*

nica, I read a quote by philosopher Robert Ardrey that brilliantly sums up why we should feel proud of our species, despite our mucky and primal origins. So I end my tour by reading it to my kids.

We were born of risen apes, not fallen angels, and the apes were armed killers besides. And so what shall we wonder at? Our murders and massacres and missiles? . . . Or our treaties whatever they may be worth; our symphonies however seldom they may be played; our peaceful acres, however frequently they may be converted into battlefields; our dreams however rarely they may be accomplished. The miracle of man is not how far he has sunk but how magnificently he has risen. We are known among the stars by our poems, not our corpses.

"Replace 'poems' with 'Super Mario Galaxy games,'" Julie says. That hits home.

REUNION COUNTDOWN: 26 WEEKS

This week I spend several hours trying to get a tourist visa. It's for a Norwegian man and his Filipina girlfriend, both living in Manila. They're engaged and they want to have their wedding at the Global Family Reunion, which would be awesome and delightfully on point. So I've been writing to various government agencies, hoping a little romance will melt their bureaucratic hearts. So far no luck. I'm thinking it won't happen.

I tell my kids about this likely failure, as I like to do with all my failures. Which have been many: Prince Charles will not be sending a video message. We will not be making the world's largest potato salad. For every idea that works, I tell them, there are ten that don't. So you succeed 10 percent of the time if you're lucky. (I'm not referring to the couple's marriage itself, which has more like a 50 percent chance of failing.)

CHAPTER 24

Big Love

The topic of alternative families keeps popping up. I read a *New York Times* article about a besieged family in Connecticut. Their neighbors want them out because of their unorthodox group-home setup: two couples, two single people, and five kids all living in a single-family house.

This led me to another article in a Massachusetts weekly called "Dishes, Dinner and Sex." It's about a polyamorous family—a group of four adults who share partners and coparent three kids. They go to parent-teacher meetings as a foursome: "Mama," "Daddy," "Mama Too," and "Bubba."

My project is about families of all shapes and sizes, and poly families seem especially au courant. A friend in the tech world summed it up with the catchy phrase "Poly is the new paleo." The sex columnist Dan Savage said that, in terms of acceptance, the poly community is where the gay movement was twenty years ago.

Not to mention that a few poly families at the reunion would do wonders for my attendance tally.

I see online that Open Love NY—the local polyamory support group—is holding a meeting with a perfectly appropriate theme: poly families. Two weeks later I'm in a large room in a midtown office building. About thirty people sit in a circle of fold-up chairs. Our leader tonight is Gette, who has glasses, purple Puma sneakers, and blue-streaked hair in a bun. She looks like she could play Lena Dunham's sister on *Girls*.

We go around the room introducing ourselves (name and whether you want to be referred to as *he*, *she*, *it*, or another pronoun). The crowd isn't much different from what you'd see at a LaGuardia Airport lounge— about half men, half women, ranging from twenties to seventies, a healthy sampling of tattoos.

I introduce myself as a "he" and say I'm not polyamorous but I'm writing a book on family. (I'll only quote them with their permission, I add.) The circle nods nonjudgmentally. That's one thing I notice. This could be the most nonjudgmental room I've ever been in. Later in the night, someone will utter the ultimate nonjudgmental phrase: "I'm not judging your judgment."

For those new to the group, Gette gives us a quick summary of poly-amory. The idea is, basically, "responsible and ethical nonmonogamy." In polyamory, you can have more than one partner—it can be two, three, seventeen—but you have to be honest with all involved. There are rules, guidelines, sometimes even written contracts.

Polyamory is often confused with swinging, but there's a big differ-ence. While swinging is all about sex, polyamory is about relationships— the feely was well as the touchy.

As the meeting progresses, I learn the poly life comes with at least four big challenges:

1. TIME MANAGEMENT

A woman who looks like the actress Amy Adams put it this way: "Love and praise are infinite. Time is not." People in poly relationships often share Google calendars that get as complex and multicolored as a Byz-antine mosaic.

2. THE RULES

When you draw up rules with partners, the key is to be specific. Chan-nel your inner lawyer. If the rule is "You need to let me know before you sleep with someone else," what does that mean exactly? Does a quick text right before hopping into a lover's bed count? Or do you need explicit permission the week before?

3. SOCIETAL ACCEPTANCE

Our country isn't always tolerant of polyamorous people. Europe is more open to it. "I heard that in France, there is health insurance for polyamorous relationships," says a woman at the meeting. We all nod. That sounds like France. The poly community is fighting the idea that they are unnatural. Actually, argues a bearded real estate salesman who was holding hands with his Asian partner, "Maybe monogamy is the kinky one."

4. JEALOUSY

This is a constant battle, as you might imagine. One man at the meeting—a bald guy named Kevin who became poly after three failed marriages—said the key is to embrace antijealousy. There's even a name for it: *compersion*. It means to get joy from your partner's joy, even if the joy comes from hooking up with someone else. I wish I were emotionally evolved enough to feel compersion. The thought of Julie kissing another guy fills me with lots of emotions—sadness, anger, insecurity—but nothing approaching joy.

"One of the big draws of polyamory," Kevin says, "is that you can get different partners to fill different needs." This past weekend, Kevin flew up to Buffalo to see one of his girlfriends. Who paid for Kevin's ticket? His girlfriend's other boyfriend. The shared girlfriend wanted to see a play, and Kevin is a theater fan. The other guy is decidedly not. So the other guy called in Kevin as a replacement. Polyamory provides you with a whole new type of family member. It's called a *metamour*: the partner of your paramour.

After some more chitchat, we turn to the main topic: poly families. Gette apologizes that we didn't get more poly families to come. A group and their teen kids were supposed to show up but had to cancel. We do, however, have a handful of poly parents. One of those is a former tattoo artist named Jessie Lou. She's wearing a pink sweater and has her blond hair in a ponytail, and she starts us off.

Jessie Lou says she and her husband have a nine-year-old daughter and another on the way. She also has boyfriends. She had a serious boyfriend for several years, but he moved to Texas recently, which was a tough split for both Jessie and her daughter.

Jessie Lou came out to her daughter when the daughter was very young. "I used four-year-old language. I said, 'Mama likes Dad. Is that okay?' She said yes. I said, 'Mama likes Robin [the boyfriend]. Is that okay?' She said yes. I said, 'Can Mommy kiss Daddy?' She said, 'Ewwww.' I said, 'Can Mommy kiss Robin?' She said, 'Ewwww.'"

Jessie Lou says, surprisingly, that being a poly mom is no big deal, at least in Brooklyn. "I get a lot of responses, and the responses are 'So the F what?' At our school, we're much less interesting than the gay couple who had twins with the Indian surrogate."

Another mom in the group chimes in. She's a bit older, has curly hair, and says her ride hasn't been as smooth. She says she's gotten negative feedback from nosy neighbors. Another dad agrees; he says that his kids were getting bullied at school.

Not everywhere is Brooklyn.

Jessie Lou says being poly doesn't affect her parenting. "Kids just want to know that you love them and support them in whatever crazy thing they're doing and will support them when they drop that crazy thing and move on to the next crazy thing and discipline them when they are wrong. Nothing else matters."

She makes a good case. While watching *Big Love* on HBO a few years ago, Julie became moderately obsessed with the idea of a sister wife. She thought it'd be great to have another woman around, especially one better than me at fixing dishwashers. Her ideal sister wife is Michelle Obama, she said. But that was all talk. Neither of us would do well in a poly relationship. For starters, the schedule sounds far too stressful.

And yet it clearly works for others, so I'm not going to judge them or their judgments.

I do have one concern, though. If polyamory becomes widespread, would it be bad for the nerds among us? One scenario in a poly world is that everyone shares partners equally. Another scenario is that the rich, attractive men and women get dozens of wives and husbands, and the rest of us get stuck with nothing. This happens in the wild all the time: the alpha elk gets a harem of female elk, and the other male elks spend their days butting heads. In this way, monogamy is unnatural but might be fairer.

I bring this up to Gette. She says she understands my concern. But I'm looking at it from a "scarcity mentality." Perhaps she's right.

REUNION COUNTDOWN: 25 WEEKS

I'm working with an event producer named Aaron. He's got spreadsheets and uses phrases like "run of show" and makes me realize just how little I know.

Both Aaron and Julie say we have to start going harder after the parents-with-kids demo. So I've signed up to do an exhibit at my sons' school's science fair. As part of it, I bought 1,000 jelly beans and put 999 jelly beans into one bowl and 1 jelly bean into the other. The idea is that, according to some estimates, humans share 99.9 percent of our DNA, so that single lonely jelly bean represents the tiny difference between you and every other person on earth. (I've always thought it unfortunate that the tiny difference affects traits that are highly visible—for instance, skin color. It might be better if that tiny percentage affected unseen traits, like spleen size. Then again, maybe that would just mean we'd be living in a world of big-spleen-only country clubs.)

I guess I should have predicted what would happen. The boys' classmates chowed down on the DNA, dividing humanity with each bite.

999 jelly beans verus 1 jelly bean to show what 99.9 percent looks like.
That is one estimate of the amount of DNA humans share (see note on
page 303 for more detail). Credit: Jasper, Lucas, and Zane Jacobs

CHAPTER 25

The Other Side of the Dash

Julie emerges from our bedroom. She's just been on the phone, and there are tears in her eyes.

I can tell instantly that these aren't your average my-client-is-being-an-inflexible-jerk tears.

"What happened?" I ask.

"It's David."

"Did he die?"

"Not yet. But close."

David Harrison—World War II hero, loving stepdad, terrible driver. Oh man. We just saw him a couple of weeks ago at a lunch at my brother-in-law Eric's house. He was reading his spy novel, making his granddad jokes. ("You're putting me on the cover of your book, right?" he asked me. "Which is my better side for the photo? Right or left?") Yes, he was ninety-four, but he seemed at least two decades younger. He was one of my favorite people of any age. Dammit.

It's a week later, David has died, and the funeral is in a synagogue in New Jersey. There are plentiful cheese cubes, lots of hugging and crying, and a half-dozen speeches from David's family and friends.

David's son-in-law (from his first marriage) gives a lovely eulogy that made me appreciate David even more. We learn about one of David's best-kept secrets. Turns out, every couple of weeks, David would get up early in the morning, sneak outside the house, and sprinkle a few nickels and quarters on the ground—in the driveway, in the garden, on the lawn.

This is because his wife, Barbara, loved nothing more than finding a quarter on the street. It just made her day. Put her in a good mood for hours.

So to brighten her life, David would seed the ground with several dollars' worth of change. He never told her. It was his furtive gift to his wife—and one of the most romantic gestures I've ever heard of.

Later a friend of David's from the army describes how David pulled off the most deadpan joke of all time. After he was captured in World War II, he was jailed in a prisoner-of-war camp in northern Germany. David was locked in a cell with eight other Jews.

On the first day, another prisoner, Jack Kirsch, came up to David and said, "Hey, you look familiar. Weren't you in the class of 1938 at Weehawken High School in New Jersey?"

"Nope," David said. End of conversation.

Several hours passed. The prisoners ate the scraps of potatoes. They sat in silence.

Finally, David looked up and said, "But I *was* in the class of 1939."

I love that he kept the gag going for several hours. I guess he figured they weren't pressed for time. Why rush it? David and Jack became best friends and had lunch at a Jersey diner every Wednesday until Jack died a few years ago. And now David is gone too. David had not-so-jokingly promised he'd die before the Global Family Reunion. I hate that he kept his word.

Even before David died, I'd been spending a good part of every day talking, thinking, and reading about death. It's a huge part of genealogy, since the vast majority of our relatives are dead.

Genealogists love a good graveyard. "I consider them outdoor art museums," says David Lambert, chief genealogist at the New England Historic Genealogical Society. "I've been going since I was a kid. I learned math by subtracting the birth years from the death years."

In the quest to verify names, birth dates, death dates, and offspring, cemeteries are as important as census forms and newspapers.

Tombstone spotting isn't quite as dangerous as BASE jumping, but it does have its hazards. I read a novel about a grizzled genealogist/ detective—it's called *A Tale of Blood*—in which we are supposed to know that our hero is the real deal because he has a scar from a dog bite he got while sneaking into a cemetery. It can happen in nonfiction too. Chip Rowe, a New York–based genealogist, tells me about the time he was on a family road trip in upstate New York and noticed a handful of graves in someone's backyard.

"I went up to the guy and asked if I could take photos of the graves on his property. The guy got super pissed. He said, 'You're trespassing!' I said, 'I'm only trespassing so I could ask you if it was okay for me to trespass!'" Chip got kicked out, but not before he snapped a grainy paparazzi-style photo of a couple of headstones.

(Sidenote: Chip has one of the odder career paths of any professional genealogist I've met. Before making the switch to full-time family historian, Chip answered sex questions from readers for *Playboy* magazine. When asked if there was any crossover, he says, "There were a lot of questions about contraception, so I guess I helped keep the world's family tree smaller. Now I try to make it bigger.")

Chip and others take photos of tombstones for a massive worldwide database called Find A Grave. It's a huge collaborative project, currently listing 159 million graves in more than a hundred countries. There's even a section on wacky tombstones, like the one with Scrabble lettering for a board-game enthusiast, and a *Star Trek* fan's epitaph saying the deceased will "boldly go where no man has gone before." (Which, come to think of it, doesn't make a huge amount of sense, since presumably billions of men and women have boldly gone to the same place before.)

True to its name, I find several of my ancestors' graves on Find A Grave. I figure, as part of my immersion in genealogy, I should go see at least one of them in person.

So on a Tuesday afternoon, Julie and I take a subway to Washington Cemetery in Brooklyn. And there, in Cemetery 5, Post 467, Row 1, Grave 3, among the sea of 56,860 other gray rectangular stones, is a simple gray block reading, "Samuel Kheel. Beloved Husband and Father. March 25, 1885—Feb. 20, 1945."

Julie and I stand on the browning grass and look at the stone in silence. In this place, seventy years ago, my ancestor was lowered into the earth.

On the subway home, Julie asks if I'm okay. I nod. I'm fine. Oddly, I wasn't particularly moved by seeing my great-great-grandfather's grave. I'm actually a little upset by how unmoved I am.

I know I'm an outlier here. I know cemeteries can be beautiful, poignant, and sacred places for many people. But it's become clear to me: What affects me emotionally isn't seeing the ground where my ancestors' bones lie. It's hearing their tales, seeing their images, reading their words. It's learning about the nickels they strewed on the ground for loved ones.

When I read about Aaron Kheel coming from Russia as a young man with thirty dollars in his pocket, opening a newspaper kiosk in the West Village, and making enough money to support an orphanage in the Bronx—that's what gets me. Even looking at photos of him gives me more connection than a graveyard visit. I see him and his well-groomed mustache and gray fedora and wonder what he had for breakfast and what he said to his wife when he left the house.

When my kids are a bit older, I plan to tell them that I don't particularly care what happens to my body after I die. If they want to save money, they can bury me in an IKEA dresser or keep my ashes in a Ziploc bag under the sink. Doesn't matter to me.

What I would love, though, is if, every once in a while, they could look at a photo of our family playing Marco Polo, or read a letter I wrote to them at camp, or watch a video of our family attempting and failing to play a didgeridoo.

REUNION COUNTDOWN: 24 WEEKS

One thing that's freaking me out: the Cousin Connect Project. I thought it'd be simple to link everyone to the World Family Tree, but that's not the case.

Thankfully, I've hired a genealogist named Eowyn Langholf, who lives in New Mexico. (*Eowyn*, by the way, is not a traditional New Mexican name. It's a traditional Middle Earth name: Éowyn is the name of a shieldmaiden in *The Lord of the Rings,* her parents' favorite book.)

Eowyn's job is Chief Cousin Coordinator, which means she wrangles dozens of volunteers to help research how potential reunion attendees are actually related. They use sites such as Geni and WikiTree. They use censuses and birth certificates and DNA. They create massive spreadsheets (Eowyn is a Michelangelo of Excel). And they use information sent in to our website. Thousands of people have filled out a questionnaire that asks for information such as their ancestors' names and the names of any famous or semifamous cousins, since notable people are often well documented and therefore easier to connect. (One woman is the actor Danny Bonaduce's wife. Another writes, "My grandfather started the second-biggest exterminator company in Iowa.")

Eowyn and her team can almost always connect folks, but each case can take hours, even days, for a connection to be made. Would it be cheating if we connect some cousins after the reunion?

CHAPTER 26

Privacy

"**D**o we have more privacy now than our ancestors had?"

The question is being asked by a genealogist named Thomas MacEntee, known for his Hawaiian shirts, cherry-red glasses, and online seminars. MacEntee has agreed to give a talk at the Global Family Reunion, so I'm watching one of his seminars on video to brush up on his ideas.

Back to his query: Do we have more privacy now than in the past? I suspect it's a trick question. Also, I know it's a trick question because last week I hacked into MacEntee's laptop and looked at all his Power-Point presentations. I kid! But yes, according to MacEntee, even with today's Facebook algorithms that predict the exact onset date of your wife's menopause, we still have more privacy in the twenty-first century than we did a hundred years ago.

MacEntee's argument is that our ancestors just didn't value privacy as highly. Life was lived much more in the open. Busybodies ruled the world. The local newspapers were packed with details about regular folks—details that would be considered startlingly invasive by today's standards. You could read about who was in which hospital and for what ailments (this was pre-HIPAA). The society pages listed the names of hotel guests and their home addresses.

I agree with MacEntee to an extent. While looking at old newspapers about my family, I came across some astounding privacy-encroaching nuggets. Consider the July 18, 1904, article in the *St. Louis Pioneer Republic* about my great-great-aunt's wedding. It was a pretty fancy affair. But I learned much more than that. The article had so much personal info, I half-expected the byline to be J. Edgar Hoover.

The *Pioneer* listed every guest by name. It described every female guest's dress and jewelry ("Mrs. Ben Blythe wore a handsome robe of serpent green Henrietta cloth, over a cream cloth petticoat, banded in gilt braid . . ."). It listed all the wedding gifts, including a bronze clock (useful) and a gold ice cream ladle (superuseful!).

And here's the oddest part: The article—which appeared in a public newspaper for all to read—listed how much money each of the guests gave the couple.

You've got the Nussbaums of Baltimore with a gift of fifty dollars. Nice!

The Rosenours of Maryland with twenty-five. Not bad.

But the Meyers of Baltimore? Oh, the Meyers. They came in dead last with twenty bucks. Thanks a lot, cheapskates! Hope you enjoyed your public humiliation.

So apparently, privacy didn't mean as much in the old days. But things are different now, and I've been thinking a lot about the issue of privacy in family history. It's a thorny one.

The first thorn: Do our deceased ancestors have a right to privacy? My mom sure thinks so. She was initially excited about my project but has become more and more nervous. She got upset when I uploaded photos of our ancestors onto a family history site. My mom thought some of the photos were unflattering. She also reminds me every week or so that I don't have to reveal the various diseases our ancestors suffered from.

I can see her point. In a sense, family history is simply highbrow Google-stalking of the dead. And while it can be fascinating, it can also make you feel queasy. Take the conversation I had with a genealogist who volunteered to work on the Global Family Reunion. He said, "I hope your great-grandparents had a good time on that cruise to Mexico for their honeymoon."

"What's that now?" I asked.

"I was researching your family, and I found a ship manifest with them that was dated a week after your great-grandparents' marriage. I figured it must have been their honeymoon cruise."

On some gut level, I felt invaded. Which I know is ridiculous, since I'd asked this nice man to look into my ancestors, and a tropical cruise is no crime. But still, it felt odd, like when the guy in the next airplane seat keeps glancing at your computer screen.

A honeymoon is one thing, but what if the personal details are damaging? This happened to one of my third cousins. She found out that some of her Jewish ancestors survived the Holocaust by cooperating with the Nazis. She emailed this information to a couple of relatives. A few weeks later, the info ended up on one of the semipublic genealogy sites. She was devastated.

You might recall that one of my favorite genealogy podcasts (yes, there are several) has the tagline "Your ancestors want their stories to be told." But do they really? I don't have a definitive answer. I try to imagine my third-great grandkids digging around in my records. Do I want them peeking at the list of every Google search I ever made in my life? (By the way, I can explain the search for "Most Phallic Termite Mound." It was for an essay. Really.)

Honestly, I don't think I'd care that much. I'll be dead, which is a great way to mitigate embarrassment. Plus, my job consists of writing books about my life, so already I'm a bit of an outlier in terms of exposure.

I guess this is where I come down: I'm for moderate invasion of dead people's privacy. Especially if the value of illuminating history outweighs the embarrassment it may bring to our family's reputation. To take an extreme example: I'm glad that we know about Sally Hemings, even if it means Thomas Jefferson's legacy has been harmed.

So that's my thinking on privacy for the dead. What about privacy for the living? This is also a huge controversy in family history. Mega-trees like Geni and WikiTree have been careful about privacy controls. They don't reveal the full names of living people. On Geni, for instance, my name shows up as "[Private] Jacobs," unless you have my permission to see my first name.

But there's still a ton of concern among users. I've emailed hundreds of potential cousins asking for their parents' and grandparents' names. Among the responses:

What are you doing with this information? Are you going to steal my identity?
Am I going to get a bill for $8,000 from a Hong Kong appliance store? WTF?

Partly it's generational. As a rule, older folks are more private. As the genealogist Adam Brown points out, Jews who survived World War II are understandably reluctant to give any information. No good came from divulging details in the past.

So far, I have yet to hear of an instance of anyone using family tree info to steal identity.

I can always count on Randy Schoenberg—the maverick genealogist and lawyer—to have a strong view. "I get in raging Facebook debates with people about privacy," he says. "I call them the paranoid narcissists. It's a form of narcissism: The world is out to get me! If I disclose who my mother is, they'll come after me. There are seven billion people in the world, but they're after *me*."

Here's one of Randy's Facebook posts:

My birth date? As far as I can recall everyone I grew up with knew what it was. So no, it's not private. Names of my wife and kids? Hardly private. There were something like 300 people at our wedding. We send out holiday cards to 300+ folks every year. Again, nothing private. Home address? It's in the phone book, on the Internet. Again, not private. Parents' names? Same as my name, nothing secret there. My social security number has been used countless times by countless companies and government entities. It's no secret either, I suppose.

I'm not nearly as certain as Randy. I've read enough articles about password breaches and Julian Assange's massive ego to be terrified of hackers. But I do think, with safeguards, the benefits of the World Family Tree will outweigh the privacy risks.

That brings us to one final privacy issue: DNA tests. The writer Maud Newton, who has agreed to speak at the Global Family Reunion, summed it up well: "I think it's crazy to take DNA tests. And I've done it three times."

That's my view as well. I've taken several DNA tests and even gone the full Monty and had my entire genome decoded by both NYU and Harvard professors. My data is encrypted, but for how long? As one MIT study showed, a smart and motivated hacker could unmask my full genome results without much trouble.

When I think about that, I conjure up frightening scenarios out of *Gattaca*. My health insurance premiums could triple. Potential employers could discover I have the gene for stealing office supplies. (I don't, and it doesn't exist, but maybe something like it does.) What if I'm subjected to the greatest scourge of all: more pop-up ads? Imagine if someone sells my DNA data to marketers and pharmaceutical firms. "Since you have the gene for sweaty feet, please check our fragrant insoles."

Or else think of my descendants. Imagine my grandson is at a bar in fifty years, and he's chatting with a cute woman. She googles his genome and sees he has genetically low oxytocin levels (the so-called monogamy hormone). She excuses herself to go to the bathroom and never returns.

I got a taste of this potential dystopia recently. A few years ago I interviewed the actress Mila Kunis for *Esquire* magazine, and it turns out she'd read and enjoyed my books. Learning this was the fifth-most-exciting moment of my life, after my wedding and the birth of my sons. Since then, I've exchanged a handful of emails with her.

Like me, Mila is an Ashkenazi Jew, and I figured we shared some genes. So for the reunion, I asked her if she'd want to compare our 23andMe results. She was happy to. And my guess was right: we are related. We both belong to haplogroup H7, which means we have a common female ancestor who lived several thousand years ago in West Asia.

But here's the thing: Mila shared too much. I was just asking her to use the "are we related" feature on 23andMe. Instead she sent me screen shots of all her DNA results. So I got to see, for instance, if Mila has the gene for dry or wet earwax. It is a secret I will take to the grave.

It made me feel like a Peeping Tom 2.0.

So privacywise, there are plenty of downsides to doing DNA testing. But, of course, DNA testing also has extraordinary potential benefits. I get these glimpses into the lives of my distant ancestors. I get peeks into my health risks, which someday may help me choose medications and diets. And since I'm part of the Harvard Personal Genome Project, my results could help lead to medical breakthroughs.

So that's why I spit into a tube. Maybe it's a mistake. Maybe my fourth-great grandkids will read my ancient emails and see not only how much time I spent watching videos of people on treadmills doing faceplants but also that my mom warned me about privacy. "Why didn't he listen to his mother?"

REUNION COUNTDOWN: 23 WEEKS

My son Lucas has told me that he wants to be in charge of security at the event. He's forty-six pounds, but on the upside, he does have a green belt in karate. So maybe.

Back when I came up with the idea for the reunion, my hope was that it'd be a family project, my version of building a kayak in the basement with my sons. A boat would have been easier. But the family—in some cases reluctantly—is rising to the occasion. Julie is organizing a scavenger hunt at the reunion. Jasper and Zane are working on games for our younger cousins. My dad is reading the vendor contracts to make sure I'm not inadvertently awarding the portable toilet company my birthright.

It doesn't make up for the amount of time the reunion has taken me away from my family, but it's something.

CHAPTER 27

The Genius of Isaac Newton

I want to interview Neil deGrasse Tyson, the renowned astrophysicist and host of *Cosmos* on the National Geographic Channel, who is, of course, my distant cousin.

I send an email to his website with my pitch. Tyson emails back: "I'm going to tell you the same thing that I told Henry Louis Gates" (Gates had asked Tyson to appear on his show *Finding Your Roots*):

My philosophy of root-finding may be unorthodox. I just don't care. And that's not a passive, but active absence of caring. In the tree of life, any two people in the world share a common ancestor— depending only on how far back you look. So the line we draw to establish family and heritage is entirely arbitrary. When I wonder what I am capable of achieving, I don't look to family lineage, I look to all human beings. That's the genetic relationship that matters to me. The genius of Isaac Newton, the courage of Gandhi and MLK, the bravery of Joan of Arc, the athletic feats of Michael Jordan, the oratorical skills of Sir Winston Churchill, the compassion of Mother Teresa. I look to the entire human race for inspiration for what I can be—because I am human. Couldn't care less if I were a descendant of kings or paupers, saints or sinners, the valorous or cowardly. My life is what I make of it.

It's a fascinating response, and I ask Tyson if I can talk to him about it further. He doesn't respond. I don't give up. I ask if I could at least print his email. He says yes and sends me a revised version. (For which he bills me $200, which I thought was a little odd, but I send off the check. I guess I'm not giving this book away for free, so I can't hold a grudge. And besides, he's family.)

I've heard versions of the Tyson Position before. My brother-in-law Eric says he finds it strange that people are obsessed with these ancestors who often share no more DNA with them than a stranger on the street. A friend's dad put it more succinctly: "I don't care about dead people."

I've wrestled with this myself. On the one hand, I agree. The Tyson Position is perfectly in tune with my project. We're all part of the human family, so I should focus on the most inspiring figures, even if they're not on my particular branch.

On the other hand, I'm drawn to my own specific line of ancestors. Maybe it's narcissism or lack of imagination, but I'm more interested in those who made me. I think it's a pretty common trait, perhaps even a deep-seated part of human nature. I don't think it's necessarily a bad thing. It's a crutch, but an effective crutch. It's motivated me to research history that I otherwise might have ignored. It's allowed me to feel more connected to the rest of the world.

Everywhere I look nowadays, my mind pings with connections to my family. This morning, visiting a friend's office, I spotted the bright yellow-and-red Exit sign by the stairs. I flashed to my grandfather, who once told me that reading about the Triangle Shirtwaist Factory fire and its locked exits inspired him to pursue labor law. Which then made me think of a cousin on the other side of my family who married a Korean-American architect who won a contest to design the memorial plaque for the Triangle Shirtwaist Factory fire. All is linked. No man, woman, or object is an island.

I even think of my family when I put on my underwear every morning, which isn't as creepy as it sounds. I recently discovered that my mom's mom's mom's dad owned a dry goods department store in St. Louis that sold, among other things, underwear. And not just any underwear. It was among the first underwear in history to use elastic seams for a snugger fit. My family's underwear featured pink stretchy bands on the sides and back—a great leap forward in the millennia-old battle against droopy drawers.

It was a controversial technology. Another company sued my ancestors, claiming they owned the rights to the phrase "elastic seam" underwear. The case went all the way to the Supreme Court of the United States in 1911. In a historic decision, my family won the case. I found a copy of the decision online, and it gives me great pleasure to think that my family is responsible for Oliver Wendell Holmes's having to learn about the design subtleties of underpants.

I love it when my kids get on the all-is-connected bandwagon. The other day we were at my mom's house, and Zane was trying to juggle. One of the balls got away from him and looked destined to smash into my mom's knickknacks. Instead, the ball thudded safely into a wastepaper basket.

"Thank you, wastepaper basket," Zane said. "And thank you, Grandma, for buying the wastepaper basket. And thank you, Grandma's parents, for having Grandma. And thank you, Grandma's parents' parents for having her. And their parents . . ."

I'm hoping that this idea isn't just a pseudo-deep notion that my kids will talk about in their dorm room someday while vaping. I'm hoping it reminds them—reminds me—that our actions affect others. That we should strive to be less self-involved.

Perhaps you've heard of the Native American idea of seven generations—that we should behave with an eye toward the seven generations to come. I'm embarrassed to say I first heard of this notion from an eco-friendly diaper brand. (Possible link to elastic bands in underwear? Or am I pushing it?) Regardless, I still love the notion.

As Oren Lyons, chief of the Onondaga Nation, writes, "We are looking ahead, as is one of the first mandates given us as chiefs, to make sure and to make every decision that we make relate to the welfare and well-being of the seventh generation to come. . . . What about the seventh generation? Where are you taking them? What will they have?"

The seventh generation will probably be affected most by big international actions like the Paris Agreement. But maybe little actions are worth something too. Maybe I should get off my ass and fill up a stainless-steel water bottle from the sink instead of buying a tiny Poland Spring bottle that will end up in the Great Pacific Garbage Patch. I want my seventh-great grandkids to have a good life, perhaps one with even more advanced underwear than we have now.

REUNION COUNTDOWN: 19 WEEKS

I'm in awe of the group of women leading the charge on the branch parties. "Branch party" is the appropriately tree-related phrase that Angel Hundley, a volunteer, came up with for the simultaneous family reunions around the world. The branch parties will livestream the talks and encourage attendees to sing along remotely with Sister Sledge.

I feel like I'm watching these women—Angel, Eowyn, and Cherie—play a masterful game of Risk, conquering territory after territory. So far twenty-one parties are scheduled, each paid for locally.

There will be branch parties in Texas and Detroit. There will be parties in Peru, the Netherlands, and New Zealand. There will be one at the Cherokee Heritage Center in Oklahoma.

In Buffalo, a branch party will be held at Forest Lawn Cemetery. Forest Lawn writes that it has "160,000 souls under our perpetual care, including President Millard Fillmore." Eowyn asks if we can count the 160,000 as cousins for the record. Something to consider.

CHAPTER 28

Fathers and Sons

I t's Sunday and I'm off to learn about my sixth-great grandfather, the Vilna Gaon.

I was invited by Barbara Sontz, the genealogist from the Genealogy Event, to a lecture at a Jewish cultural center about the famous rabbi. How could I say no? I'm curious to hear more about my brilliant Lithuanian ancestor; plus the Vilna Gaon has something like eighty thousand descendants. Imagine I get just 10 percent of them to come to the Global Family Reunion? I'd crush the record.

I tell Julie and the boys that I'll see them later—they're meeting friends at a street fair downtown—and set off for midtown Manhattan. I arrive late to the lecture, but Barbara has saved me a seat with her coat.

The speaker is a Yale professor of religion and history named Eliyahu Stern. He's written a book called *The Genius: Elijah of Vilna and the Making of Modern Judaism*. Stern is wearing a brown jacket and black glasses and is handsome enough that he could play the young professor in a Netflix dramedy about academia. He's also a great talker.

Stern explains that the Vilna Gaon, born in 1720, is sort of the Jewish version of Daniel Boone, but instead of wrestling alligators, he's famous for his mighty feats of brain power.

It's said he memorized the first five books of the Bible by age five. He could recite the entire Hebrew Scriptures by age nine. According to another source, he never slept more than two hours out of twenty-four, and never more than thirty minutes consecutively.

His very name is a tribute to his brilliance: *Gaon* in Hebrew means "wise man," a term that had been out of use for centuries before he started interpreting Torah. Plus, he has not one but two Facebook fan pages.

Onstage, Professor Stern is talking about the Gaon's legacy. The key, he says, is that the Vilna Gaon made learning cool. He elevated the act of studying to an end in itself, the highest aspiration. After the Gaon, millions of Jewish kids wanted to be scholars the same way my friends wanted to be arena rock superstars. Nerds everywhere owe him a debt of gratitude.

And just as important, the Gaon revolutionized Jewish study by expanding its boundaries. He argued that a complete understanding of Jewish law and literature required a broad education—the study of mathematics, astronomy, geography, botany, zoology, and philosophy. I love him for that. He was a Semitic version of a Renaissance Man.

So definitely a role model, right? Not so fast, says Stern. "He's a family man," Stern adds, noting that the Gaon had eight children. "But what kind of family man? I'll tell you a quick story."

One day the Vilna Gaon was getting ready to go off to the woods to study. Before he left, one of his younger sons fell deeply ill. Another of the Gaon's sons, Abraham, wrote about what happened next, and Stern gives the short version of what Abraham said.

"Father was going to go off into the woods to study. And well, his studies simply came first. So he packed up, went off into the woods, and spent a month there. And never once thought about us or anything to do with my brother. Then one day, he was on the toilet, and it's only in those moments that one can't think about the Torah. And he remembered my brother. And he said, 'Oh, I wonder how he's doing?' And picked himself up and went back home."

End of story. Stern shakes his head. "That's a father?" he nearly shouts. "That's a father?"

I agree. If this were a call-and-response sermon, I'd be yelling "Amen!" The Vilna Gaon may have had a superstar brain, but he could be a rotten dad.

Stern continues: "What you see there is that there are serious costs to his personality. You want to produce more texts? You want to write more texts than anyone in the annals of Jewish history? You want to be a Steve Jobs? You want to be an Albert Einstein? Don't ever confuse that with being a good family man, or a good human being. And I think unfortunately our society, we put such a premium, and I think Jews as a whole, we put such a premium on intellectual excellence that we sometimes don't realize that you don't always get your cake and eat it too. And we have to think: What do we really want to be teaching to our children?"

Oh man. This resonates. The work/life balance has clearly been a problem for centuries. Since long before my supersuccessful friend told me, "Family is an impediment to greatness." Since long before Harry Chapin wrote about cats and cradles and silver spoons. Since long before I chose to go to a lecture on a sunny Sunday instead of hanging out with my wife and kids.

Stern is right about Einstein. Here's an excerpt of a letter he wrote to his wife: "You will make sure that I get my three meals a day in my room. You are neither to expect intimacy nor to reproach me in any way." Despite this tender love poem, they got divorced soon after. Then again, in Einstein's case, maybe he had the right priorities. If he'd spent more time making pancake breakfasts for his kids and taking them to Swiss amusement parks, perhaps he'd have been too busy to come up with the theory of relativity.

My grandfather Theodore Kheel was better than Einstein as a family man. But he often put his work ahead of his wife and kids. I remember my mom telling me that she and her five siblings didn't eat dinner with their parents until they were thirteen. Instead, they would have "time" with their dad. That's what they called it, "time." It was five or ten minutes a night when the kids would come to the living room and have an audience with their dad. He was often traveling or working late, so time was precious.

It's a hard issue, and I don't have any answers. But I know that doing this Global Family Reunion project is making me a worse family man, at least to my immediate kin. Jules Feldman, the dairy farmer who sent me that initial email, warned me this might happen. "My wife says, 'You spend so much time on your tenth cousins, you forget about your wife and kids,'" he told me. So there's that guilt. Not to mention my twinge of guilt for criticizing the great Vilna Gaon's lifestyle choices.

A few weeks later, I was talking to my brother-in-law Willy about the Vilna Gaon, and he said, "Your grandmother never liked him."

This was surprising. My grandmother rarely said anything bad about the family.

"She didn't like the way he wrote about women," Willy said.

So there you go. That helps allay my guilt over the Vilna Gaon. By being critical of my sixth-great grandfather, I'm honoring my grandmother.

CHAPTER 29

Twins and Twins. Also More Twins

We're going on a road trip to attend another record-breaking family event. We're off to the annual Lollapalooza for multiple births: the Twins Days Festival.

I've wanted to go to Twins Days ever since I learned about it from a scientist a decade ago. This year I've got the perfect excuse. I'm hoping to get some inspiration, borrow some ideas.

The festival has been held every summer since 1976 in the appropriately named Twinsburg, Ohio. Twins from around the world—along with a smattering of triplets, quadruplets, and any other 'plets—descend on this farming village for three days of food, parades, contests, and requests from scientists to fill out questionnaires. It's got the Guinness Record for most twins in one place: 1,181 sets.

So, on a Saturday morning, Julie, the twins, and I (Jasper is off at sleepaway camp) board our flight to Ohio. We arrive at the Twinsburg High gymnasium, where we get our welcome packets and rubber Twins Days wristbands.

And then we gawk. It's hard not to. We are in the midst of hundreds of twins. The four of us gawk at old and young twins, big and small twins, blond and brunette twins, Asian and Latino twins. We gawk at twins taking selfies, twins hugging and laughing. We gawk at a quadrant of teenage twins engaging in some intertwin flirting.

We gawk at the excess of wacky T-shirt slogans. One pair of twins wears matching shirts that read "Save water, share a womb." Two teen-age girls bear identical slogans: "I'm my evil twin's evil twin." Even the nontwins get in on the T-shirt game. I spot a fortysomething dad. He's pushing a pair of baby girls in a stroller and wearing a shirt that says "Real Men Have Twins."

I won't be buying one of those, since my slogan would have to be "Real Men Have Twins, but Only Because They Had Trouble with Fertility and Had to Do IVF Which Resulted in Twins."

I make a note for the Global Family Reunion: T-shirts are key.

The next day we attend the Twins Double Take Parade, cheering on hundreds of twins as they belt out songs like "When the Twins Come Marching In." Just in case multiple births isn't enough of a theme, Twins Days has a secondary theme every year. This time it's the 1960s—Twinstock. Attendees are encouraged (aka required) to wear the same clothes as their twins, so the parade is a stream of double flower girls, double Barbies, and double Jimi Hendrices.

The parade ends, and we wander the fairgrounds eating Fritos tacos. We buy Lucas and Zane tie-dyed "Twins Days" T-shirts, which they put on right then and there.

"Peace, dude!" Zane says, and holds up his fingers in a peace sign.

"Peace back at you, dude!" Lucas says, and holds up his fingers in a peace sign.

Then they begin to poke each other in the face with their peace signs. Sort of Three Stooges meets Haight-Ashbury. I'm impressed that they can take an age-old symbol for peace and somehow turn it violent. Love and conflict—an excellent summary of family.

We check out the many contests: most different-looking twins, most similar twins, oldest twins, youngest twins (six *hours*, straight from the hospital). I make another note for the global reunion: More contests—people love their contests.

Lucas (left) and Zane (right) and their fellow hippie twins.

For our last stop, we arrive at a grassy field crawling with scientists. Scientists adore Twins Days. From their point of view, it's a convention of lab rats. With their identical DNA, twins can help scientists puzzle out which traits are due to nature and which to nurture. The field has booths where researchers are studying smell, hearing, and fingerprints.

A couple of years ago, one scientist was conducting a particularly unusual study. According to Katie and Kristy Barry—videojournalist friends of mine who have been attending the Twins Days for decades—this scientist was investigating the following topic: differential breast size among twins. Which sounds more fishy than an email from an eighth cousin. I'd like to see the diploma of this "scientist." Are we sure he wasn't a thirteen-year-old boy with a rented lab coat? Katie and Kristy swear he was legit, and they proudly participated in the study.

Despite this cautionary tale, I figure that maybe my twins could help further science. I approach a clean-shaven researcher at the vision booth.

"Fraternal?" he asks.

I nod.

"Sorry," he says.

That's the not-so-secret secret of Twins Days. There's a hierarchy of multiple births, and not just among scientists. At the bottom are the fraternal twins, who get the least amount of respect from the crowd. If this festival were a bird sanctuary, fraternals would be the sparrows and pigeons.

Above them are the identical twins, the equivalent of cardinals and blue jays. But above the identical twins are the identical triplets. And rarest of all, the albino horn-billed woodpeckers of the festival, are the quadruplets, who attract selfies and "oohhs" wherever they go.

Some of my friends back home think Twins Days is exploitative, a little too Coney Island Freak Show. But it doesn't bother me. The twins who are at Twins Days are a self-selecting group. They're happy to be twins. They revel in it. It's their tribe.

It's not for every twin. A few years ago, my friend Abigail Pogrebin wrote a great book called *One and the Same: My Life as an Identical Twin and What I've Learned About Everyone's Struggle to Be Singular.* For research, Abigail attended Twins Days, but she came alone. She couldn't convince her twin, Robin, to join her. Abby had to lie to the hotel clerk and say her twin was joining her later. Robin loves her sister, of course, but sometimes finds being a twin confining, an impediment to becoming her own individual.

I understand the tension. On the one hand, twins have a best friend for life—a little impenetrable club, total membership two, outsiders need not apply. On the other hand, twins are forever lumped together. Shared birthday parties, shared haircuts, and shared pronouns: "Are *they* happy at their school?" I can see how it'd get frustrating.

It occurs to me that the tension is actually a concentrated version of the push-and-pull in all of us. On the one hand, we want to be a unique individual. On the other, we want to be a member of a family/tribe/community. It's a modern paradox: we aspire to both stand out and fit in.

For most of my life, I tilted too much toward the individual side. My intense desire to be unique and apart from the crowd resulted in all types of negative consequences (e.g., selfish attention to my career, an ill-advised silver ear cuff in high school). I'm now forcing myself to think more about my place in the human tribe. The balance is still off, but I'm trying.

Before boarding our plane to leave Ohio, we stop at the airport gift store, and Zane and Lucas get souvenirs, but different ones. Zane gets a Cleveland Indians baseball hat and Lucas opts for a mug that says "Cleveland Rocks." My sons are, after all, different people—though united by their love of overpriced crap.

REUNION COUNTDOWN: 18 WEEKS

As Twins Days has reminded me, T-shirts are key to a mega-event.

I spend the day with Aaron, the event producer, brainstorming T-shirt slogans. At one point, I want to go with "Kiss me, I'm your cousin." Aaron wisely talks me out of it. He suggests I may have spent too much time talking to my friend K.C.

In the end we choose a couple of G-rated slogans, including "I'm your second cousin's wife's third-great aunt's husband's grandson. Practically siblings!"

It's probably too long, but we aren't being charged by the word.

CHAPTER 30

Five Mothers

Back in New York, I'm still in the twins frame of mind, so I pursue a twin-themed idea for the Global Family Reunion. At a party recently, I'd met the producer of a documentary about twins who suggested I screen her movie at the reunion. "It'd fit right in," she says.

The movie is called *Twinsters*. And as soon as I start watching it on my laptop, I see what she means. At the beginning of the movie, we meet a twenty-five-year-old actress named Samantha who was born in South Korea and adopted by a white family in New Jersey. She now lives in Los Angeles. One day in 2012 Samantha helped make a silly video about the pitfalls of dating; her scene features her kicking a suitor in the crotch.

Soon after uploading the video to YouTube, Samantha got a weird Facebook message from a French woman living in London. The woman was named Anaïs. She didn't know Samantha but had been forwarded the video and found it eerie that they looked so much alike: same nose, same cheeks, same freckles. Anaïs had also been adopted from South Korea and had been born on the same day as Samantha—November 19.

"I don't want to be too Lindsay Lohan," Anaïs wrote. "But . . . how to put it . . . I was wondering where you were born."

I later talk to Samantha about the moment she read Anaïs's message, and she tells me, "I was trying to be rational. I was saying, 'Calm down,

Samantha. The odds of me having a twin I've never met are too crazy.'
But another part of me was like, 'This has to be true.'"

Anaïs had grown up in Paris and was now studying design in London.
Samantha and Anaïs started videochatting and texting every day. They
compared tastes. They both have fingernails painted aquamarine. They
both love pickles. They clicked. They coined a nickname for each other,
"Fish," and developed a private greeting, "Pop!"

"You're already annoying," a friend said, lovingly, after watching them
make faces and weird sounds to each other on videochat.

They took the DNA test and yes, they are officially identical twins,
born of the same biological mother.

Neither Samantha nor Anaïs had ever been able to get in touch with
their biological mom. They didn't even know her name. But now, through
the adoption agency, they sent a note to Samantha and Anaïs's biological
mom. The woman denied she'd had twins. She said they had the wrong
person. When they heard the result, Samantha cried. "Maybe it's better,"
Samantha says now. "It leaves so much hope and possibility, like maybe
she's a superhero and that's why she can't tell us who she is."

A few months after Anaïs's initial message, Samantha flew to London
for their first in-person meeting.

The video of this meeting is both adorable and awkward. When
Anaïs arrives in the apartment, they can barely talk. They both giggle
for what seems like ten minutes straight. They don't hug or even touch
for a long time.

"My sister, Anaïs, has the best description of that meeting," says Samantha, when I interview her later. "We were like polar magnets. We'd
get close to each other, but then we'd rotate around, trying to see how we
could fit in the same space."

Finally their friends made them stand back-to-back to compare
heights, and they touched shoulders. "It was like a jolt of energy," Samantha says.

Long-lost twins Anaïs (left) and Samantha.

Turns out Anaïs is about half an inch taller than Samantha ("She never lets me forget that," Samantha says). They also have slightly different personalities. Befitting the stereotypes, Californian Samantha is a bit sunnier, and French Anaïs is a bit moodier.

I tell Samantha that I'd find it traumatic to find a carbon copy of me as an adult. What if the other A.J. is more successful, more generous, and shoots hoops with his pal Barack Obama? I don't need that stress.

Samantha laughs. "People ask if we're upset that we were separated at birth," Samantha says. "I'm just happy we found each other now. I try to focus on the good." And although they were separated, they had other families. "Family is what you make of it," Samantha says. "It doesn't have to be this physical lineage; it can be anyone you choose to accept."

Samantha recently cofounded a nonprofit with actress Jenna Ushkowitz to help foreign-born adoptees in the United States. It's called Kindred, and the motto is "Family has no boundary." "As an adoptee," Samantha says, "it would be so horrible if a mother said, 'Oh, my sons that are biological are my family and you're an extension of my family.'"

Toward the end of the movie, Samantha says that she may not be in touch with her biological mom, but she doesn't lack for moms. Not at all. She says she has at least "five other moms": her adoptive mom; Anaïs's adoptive mom; the foster mother who had her for a few months in Korea, and with whom she keeps in touch; her longtime manager, whom she calls a "momager." The list goes on.

I tell Samantha it reminds me of the scene in the movie *Her* in which the computer voiced by Scarlett Johansson says she loves Joaquin Phoenix's character, but also loves 641 other people.

I'm not evolved enough to be okay with Julie having 641 lovers, or even one other. But I do believe humans are more elastic with our love than we think. We can sometimes make room in our hearts to love others without diminishing what we feel for those already dearest to us. Love is not a zero-sum game.

REUNION COUNTDOWN: 17 WEEKS

Oh man, a tough few days. If I could cancel this whole event without suffering massive humiliation and weeks of angry calls, I'd do it in a second. I'm worried about money. I'm worried I'll embarrass my kids even more than I normally do. I'm worried there will be a riot. I'm worried there won't be enough people to sustain a riot. I'm worried that the festival of YouTube stars—on the same day, right near by—means no one will show up to mine.

I'm getting rejected multiple times a day by potential speakers and press outlets. I was booked to go on the talk show *The View*, which would have been huge. They canceled at the last minute because the hosts were worried I was poking into their private lives.

Worst of all, I have doubts about the thesis that we should treat our global family better. There was a guy on line at the drugstore who, with no provocation, pointed at my coat and said, "I was going to buy that same coat, but then I decided it was too ugly." Do I really want this bastard in my family? Maybe better to live in separate bubbles.

CHAPTER 31

Black Sheep

The World Family Tree has some bad apples. The worst apples, actually. Today I spend a disturbing forty-five minutes typing the most evil, cruel, and sadistic humans in history into the Geni search bar.

More often than not—*ding!*—out pops the chain connecting these spawns of Satan right to me.

Joseph Stalin, just fourteen steps away.

Serial killer/child party clown John Wayne Gacy, just fifteen away.

Murderous cult leader Reverend Jim Jones: he's twenty-one steps.

Every time the connection works, I let out a groan. I must have emitted twenty-five groans in under an hour. It makes me feel dirty, as if I've just inadvertently eaten a horseburger. Intellectually, I know that if I'm related to everyone, that includes the worst of humanity. But it's another thing to see the chain on my laptop screen so concretely, a series of arrows from Stalin right to me. I just hope the warm-and-fuzzy vibes from the World Family Tree outweigh this nausea.

After a while, I forced myself to stop connecting to the truly bad apples. On the other hand, the moderately bad apples? The gray sheep? Those are fun. I do want some of those on my tree. I want some gangsters and carneys and embezzlers.

I've thought about why. I feel that there's some genealogical street cred in having morally ambiguous ancestors. But I also think it's oddly

healthy. A sprinkling of criminals on your family tree can have a democ-
ratizing effect. It's proof that nobody's pedigree is pristine. Everyone has
unappealing people in their bloodline, and maybe we shouldn't be quick
to judge others. We aren't defined by our ancestors. In fact, good or bad,
they may inspire us to be better people.

This may be rationalization. Maybe I just want gangster relatives because I loved *Goodfellas*. Regardless, I want some bad guys on my tree,
and I want them close, not fourteenth cousins six times removed. I want
great-great-uncles and first cousins three times removed.

Julie's got the advantage here. Her great-uncle was rumored to have
been an accountant for the mob and was found murdered in his car.

So far, I've got barely anything. After scouring newspaper clips for
weeks, I've discovered that in 1924 my great-great-uncle Leon Sunstein
was arrested in Pittsburgh for stealing about five thousand dollars' worth
of microscopes. Microscope larceny. Well, at least it was a geeky crime,
which as a fan of science I have to respect. Later, in the 1940s, Leon became a bingo operator, which was apparently a shady profession, but it's
still not a story that's about to be optioned by Martin Scorsese.

If anyone can help, it's Ron Arons. He's the guy I spotted at the Genealogy Event wearing a black-and-white-striped prison suit. Born in
Manhattan, the tall, gray-haired sixty-one-year-old now lives in Oak-
land. Ron has written a couple of books on wayward ancestors and is the
founder of a company called Criminal Research, which will dig up your
family tree's rotten apples.

I call Ron to ask how he found this niche. He tells me the tale: His mother
never mentioned that her grandfather was a criminal. But Ron became interested in his family and tracked down his ancestors' census records at the
library. On an index card, he discovered that in 1900 his great-grandfather
had an unusual place of residence: Sing Sing prison. Ron was surprised but
still dubious. So he hopped a plane and went to the New York State Archives
in Albany. He started looking through the admissions records for the prison.

"Within an hour, I found it, and I just went nuts," Ron says.

Black sheep expert Ron Arons.

His great-grandfather was convicted, oddly enough, of bigamy: he had been secretly shuttling between two wives in New York. He spent three years in a seven-by-four-foot cell.

When Ron unearthed the record that day, he called up his brother from a pay phone and they both laughed for several minutes at the sheer oddness of it. But the news also had a profound effect on Ron.

"The notion that I've got criminal blood in me was life-altering," Ron says. "I never thought of myself as anything but a Goody Two-shoes. This was a very different view of my world."

"Did it change the way you acted?" I ask. "I mean, not that you'd knock over a liquor store, but maybe it made you more rebellious?"

"I think it definitely made me a bit more rebellious," Ron says. "I think writing this book was a little rebellious."

Ron was so inspired by his discovery, he dove full-time into black sheep research and wrote a book called *The Jews of Sing Sing*, in which he describes the most colorful Jewish inmates in the notorious prison.

He says not everyone loves the idea of highlighting bad Jews. "I gave a talk in Detroit and there was an elderly lady who said, 'You can't talk about this.' She said there were no such things as Jewish criminals. Luckily, everyone in the audience came to the rescue and said, 'Shut up, lady.'"

His business, Criminal Research, takes clients in search of the naughty side of their family. "This morning, this woman emailed me. Her father had told her, 'Definitely do not investigate Uncle Willy!' And she said, 'That's all the more reason why I have to.'"

"I do believe the truth will set you free," Ron says. For instance, his discovery about his great-grandfather gave him some insights about his childhood. Like the time Ron made a joke, asking his grandmother if she'd send him to Sing Sing if he was bad. "And my grandmother said, 'Don't you dare use those words in front of your grandfather. That will upset him greatly.'"

And Ron thinks he understands his grandfather—the son of the bigamist—better now. "He had a very sad, troubled childhood, and he dealt with it by being a clown for his grandchildren. He went into his closet and would put on different hats that my aunt had purchased from her travels across the globe. He would put on a show for us. That was his way of coping with it."

Ron also discovered details of the arrest in several newspaper articles. It's a wild yarn that takes place in 1897 Brooklyn, with Ron's bigamist forebear jumping from trolley cars to avoid the cops, before being dragged into the police station, where both his wives confront him, shouting at him to be ashamed, one of them holding up Ron's grandfather and saying, "Do you deny your own son?"

Ron asks me about my own family's black sheep.

"I did find out my grandfather was once arrested for selling pretzels without a license."

"Oh my God, that's terrible. How do you even go out in the morning!" Ron says. "Such a *shonda*."

PHARMACIST SLAIN; PARTNER IS HELD

Shot Dead in Rear of Store as Women and Children Sip Sodas at Counter.

BUSINESS ROW INVOLVED

Lost $85,000 in Lexington Av. Venture, Leonard Josephie, the Prisoner, Says.

While women and children sipped sodas at the counter, Leonard Josephie, head of the insurance brokerage concern of Josephie & Son, 116 John Street, shot and killed his partner, Abraham Ross, in the drug store they jointly operated in the George Washington Hotel, Lexington Avenue and Twenty-third Street, at 9:30 o'clock yesterday morning.

The police said Josephie had taken this means to end a long-standing quarrel over a venture that his attorney said had cost him close to $85,000. Ross, who was 42 years old and lived at 81 Irving Place, was the pharmacist of the partnership, while Josephie furnished most of the money, according to the police.

Mrs. S. Henry Preston Jr. of Tazewell, Va., who is stopping at 52 Gramercy Park, was at the counter with her two young daughters. Miss Mary Harmon Pritchard of Bluefield, W. Va., was also in the place. Ross was behind the prescription counter when Josephie walked in.

Heated Argument Starts.

Immediately a heated argument began, the sequel of an unsatisfactory conference with attorneys the night before. Apparently not wishing to disturb the customers, the police said, Ross suggested they go into the basement to talk things over. Josephie agreed and Ross went to the basement, but his partner did not follow.

Ross called up to Josephie, the police said, and when he got no response he began climbing the stairs at the rear of the store. Suddenly Josephie drew one of two revolvers, according to the police, and fired six shots. Then he pocketed the weapons and walked to the front of the store.

Josephie told Robert Pyle, the soda clerk, and Charlotte Watt, the cashier, to request the customers to leave. Then, the police said, he telephoned to the police and to his attorney, Sidney J. Loeb, 19 Cedar Street. Soon radio cars arrived and a large crowd collected. Josephie was taken to the East Twenty-second Street station.

He Charges Mismanagement.

Josephie told Deputy Inspector Michael J. McDermott that he and Ross had been partners in the drug store venture for five years and that he furnished most of the money. He charged that Ross was stubborn and was not cordial to customers and he said he had lost considerable money through mismanagement.

On Thursday night, according to Josephie, a conference was held in the office of Jack Goldberg, Ross's attorney, at 50 East Forty-second

---

Okay, okay. Good one. Ron is not much more impressed by the microscope thief. He says he'll help me find better black sheep after he's finished with another project. I ask him if he'd come speak at the Global Family Reunion, and he agrees.

A few days later, I'm talking genealogy on the phone with a cousin of Julie's, Joan Pollak, who is the family historian on my wife's side. I tell her about my lack of gangsters and bootleggers.

"Well, there's Leonard Josephie."

"Who?"

Leonard Josephie, she explains, is five steps away from Julie. Okay, a little farther than I wanted, and it's on Julie's side, not mine. But Leonard sounds intriguing.

Joan emails me some newspaper articles. In 1936 Leonard Josephie was the co-owner of a pharmacy in lower Manhattan. He was having a long-running dispute with his partner, who he believed was ripping him off for eighty-five thousand dollars.

On August 2, they began arguing at the pharmacy. The partner suggested going to the basement so as not to disturb the customers. The partner descended the stairs. Josephie did not follow. As the *New York Herald Tribune* wrote, "Suddenly, Josephie drew one of two revolvers . . . and fired six shots. Then he pocketed the weapons and walked to the front of the store. . . . Then he telephoned the police and his attorney."

I email Ron with the good news. He emails me back within a day. He congratulates me and has attached a copy of Leonard's admittance record to none other than Sing Sing prison. I click on it. It's a handwritten list with Leonard's information—forty-eight years old, Hebrew, attends services weekly, convicted of murder in the second degree. For now, Leonard, the calmest killer in the world, will have to do as my black sheep.

REUNION COUNTDOWN: 16 WEEKS

I spend much of my week responding to concerned emails from distant cousins, like this one.

> Dear A.J., I did consider joining your family tree project, but then I had second thoughts. Many years ago, my father discovered that we had distant relatives in Argentina. He went to Argentina with a photograph of my great-grandfather, and they exchanged many stories. It was very interesting, but there was one downside. Soon after contacting these people, we started receiving requests for money from them. My father, being the good guy that he was, actually sent some money to them. To make a long story short, my question is this. If I take part in your family tree project, is there any danger that I could receive hundreds, thousands, or even millions of requests for money from people that I don't even know claiming to be my relatives? Have you thought about this problem?

I have not. There are only so many worries I have time for in a day.

CHAPTER 32

My Presidential Cousin

I f I held the reunion today, I'd get maybe a thousand cousins—less than a quarter of my goal.

It's clear I need to get the word out. And for better or worse, the loudest megaphones in today's society are famous people. So I've decided to recruit some notable cousins to spread the one-world-family gospel.

I've already gotten a couple of celebrities. I took a photo of the comedian Mike Birbiglia, whom I've known for years. He gamely held up a piece of paper that said, in large handwriting, "I am a Cousin." I got similar photos with NPR host Ophira Eisenberg and actor Nick Offerman holding up "I am a Cousin" signs. I love those folks, but I've got my sights set on global figures—names my parents would recognize without having to ask Siri. My best shot? Former President George H. W. Bush.

I'm a Democrat, as is legally mandated for those who live on the Upper West Side of Manhattan, but I'm also a fan of the elder Bush (who, by the way, seems like a free-love Trotskyite compared with today's Republicans). I interviewed him a few years back for *Esquire* magazine and have been a speaker at a couple of fund-raisers for the Barbara Bush Foundation, which battles illiteracy.

So I put in a call to his chief of staff. I ask her if I could perhaps interview the former president again. I explain that I want to ask him about family for my book and reunion. She tells me the president rarely grants interviews anymore. At which point I play the cousin card.

"Just so you know, the president is my first cousin once removed's husband's third-great-grandfather's wife's third great nephew. So . . . maybe he'd do it as a favor for a relative?"

She chuckles and says she'll get back to me.

A week later, I'm on a plane to Houston. Bizarrely, my tactic actually worked. The World Family Tree is more powerful than LinkedIn. I'm missing a long-planned dinner date with my wife and her friends, but I promised Julie it'd be worth it. I spend the flight scanning the notes from the *Esquire* interview I did with the president years back. It was for a feature called "What I've Learned," and it reminds me why I liked him so much.

That previous interview took place at his home in Kennebunkport, Maine. The former president, his wife, Barbara, and I ate lunch on a patio overlooking the waves crashing onto a rocky beach. I asked him about his memories of the Berlin Wall coming down, and his World War II service: he was shot down over the Pacific and rescued by a nearby American submarine, narrowly escaping the fate of other airmen in his squadron who were captured by the Japanese. He told me his favorite phrase, "insurmountable opportunities." He told me the best advice his mom ever gave him. "She'd say, 'Give the other guy credit. Nobody likes braggadocio, George.'"

We also talked about more important matters. As a journalist, I felt it incumbent upon me to ask the president, "What was your favorite bathroom in the White House?"

He seemed surprisingly eager to discuss this. "It's in the Queens' Bedroom," he said. "We stayed there when George [his son] was president. There was kind of a wicker thing over the toilet. There I was, sitting where Barbra Streisand had sat. I couldn't believe it!"

Before I got to ask why, of all people, the star of *What's Up, Doc?* came to his mind, Mrs. Bush chimed in. "You can't say that! This is going in a magazine."

"Why not? What's wrong with it?" said the president.

Throughout the lunch, the president and his wife bantered like they were in an episode of a CBS sitcom. And as in sitcoms, it was clear they loved each other deeply.

WHEN THE PLANE lands, I take a cab to the former president's office, which is on the third floor of a nondescript office building. The president's assistant, a young former marine, escorts me past a George H. W. Bush bust in the lobby (it appears to be an homage to drip sand castles) and into an office with a large wooden desk and an American flag–themed chair. There's the president, sitting in a wheelchair, wearing a blazer, khakis, and pink-and-yellow argyle socks. Mrs. Bush and her Maltese dog are by his side.

I explain to them why I'm here. "I'm helping to put together a family tree of all seven billion humans. And you are on this tree. Because you are humans."

"Well, thank you," the former first lady says drily. "That's very flattering."

I tell them how we are related. "I thought we were more closely related than that," says the president. He actually sounds a bit disappointed. He then adds, "Family is everything. And I'm blessed to have a large one."

I tell them about some of their distant cousins, including Bill Clinton, who is President Bush's tenth cousin once removed.

"I always felt that Bill Clinton was my son from another mother, so I suppose it makes sense," says Mrs. Bush.

I tell them that Mrs. Bush, whose maiden name is Pierce, is a blood relative of the fourteenth president, Franklin Pierce.

"That I knew," she says. "I remember reading in high school or grammar school that he was one of the worst presidents ever. And it humiliated me. But I don't think it's true."

And then President and Mrs. Bush held up the "I am a Cousin" sign and smiled for the camera. The official Presidential Seal of Approval. Or at least the Seal of Not Disapproval.

To my surprise, the Bushes invite me to lunch at a steakhouse nearby. Over lunch, we talk about a grab bag of topics: twins, the president's favorite portrait painters, and LBJ (who once told Bush that the difference between the Senate and the House is like the difference between chicken salad and chicken shit). After a discussion of the wackiness of social media and wearable technology, Barbara Bush looks at her husband and says, "I'm glad we're eighty-nine and ninety. I'm going to slip off to heaven before it gets crazy."

I'm not sure how, or if, to respond. Instead, I change the subject. I want to know how they've stayed so seemingly happy in their marriage.

One of my favorite moments from my *Esquire* interview was when the former president talked about the first time he met the future first lady. It was at a Christmas dance in Greenwich, Connecticut, in 1941. I asked him what struck him about her.

"Her beauty. Her sheer beauty. And her dress! She had on a green-and-red dress. Spectacularly beautiful woman. And I asked somebody, 'Who is that beautiful girl?' 'That is Barbara Pierce. Why?' I said, 'Well,

I'd like to meet her.' And whoever it was brought her over. We said hi. Then they started playing a waltz. I said, 'Barbara, I don't know how to waltz.' And she said, 'Well, let's sit down.' So we sat down, and the rest is history. Been sitting down for sixty-five years."

That'd be about fifty years longer than Julie and I have been sitting. So I ask the Bushes, "What's the secret to a long-lasting marriage?"

Mrs. Bush answers: "I think you ought to treat your spouse like you treat your friends. You clean your house for your friends, you make sure they're taken care of. A spouse often comes second. So treat your spouse like the friends. Don't just go halfway. If each spouse goes seventy-five percent of the way, it's a perfect match."

Those are wise words. When I get home that night, I thank Julie for taking care of the boys. I unpack, which usually means leaving clothes in random piles. But this time, thanks to Barbara Bush's marital advice, I fold my sweaters and tuck my shoes away in my closet. I want to make it to at least my seventeenth anniversary.

REUNION COUNTDOWN: 15 WEEKS

I'm beyond frustrated. The Guinness World Records company seems to hold the world record for most attempted upsells.

I call the Guinness folks to see how I can get the reunion into their record book. The saleswoman suggests that I might want to get an "adjudicator" to come to the event, and guess what? The adjudicator isn't free. She sends me the list of packages, which include permission to use their logo and range from eight to twenty thousand dollars. I try to butter her up. I tell her it's a charity event to benefit Alzheimer's. I even find out how she's related to me. No luck.

If I want to get into the Guinness World Records without hiring the adjudicator, I have to submit—no exaggeration—seventeen separate pieces of evidence, including a statement from an auditing firm and a video of the entrance/exits. I'd heard from a friend that Guinness was "as flexible as a steel pole." I think he's right.

I do have another option that might be more flexible. A friend of mine started the scrappy competitor to Guinness called RecordSetter. It's more DIY, more like Wikipedia. You videotape your feat, email it in, they review it, and put it on their site.

My friend said, as a favor, he'd get someone to come to the reunion in one of RecordSetter's trademark retro yellow blazers. I love RecordSetter, but it's not ideal. The reunion's sponsors want the more famous Guinness. This will be tricky.

(Note: A few years ago, I actually invested some money in RecordSetter, so you could reasonably argue I'm motivated to be harsh on Guinness. But please, if you don't believe me, try dealing with Guinness yourself.)

CHAPTER 33

Tradition!

Today I'm taking Lucas to see *Fiddler on the Roof* on Broadway. It is, appropriately, a tradition.

When I was eight, my parents took me to see *Fiddler*, my first musical. I remember exactly one thing from that show: That the actor who played Tevye, the beleaguered Russian-Jewish dad of five girls, talked really loudly, weirdly, and wetly. That is to say, whenever he spoke, he'd spit. The stage lights would illuminate the arcs of saliva that departed from his mouth every time he said a word with the letters *T* or *K*.

Tevye, you might remember, is a milkman, and in one scene, he was schlepping around several buckets of milk. He's singing and spitting and the saliva is landing right in the buckets. I was horrified. As a young germophobe, I couldn't focus on anything else.

I asked my mom, "Do his customers know he's spitting in the milk?"

"I wouldn't worry about it," my mom said. "Just watch the play."

"But why doesn't he put tops on the buckets so the spit doesn't get in there?"

When I told Julie that was my only memory, she said, "Well, I'm glad you picked up the real purpose of the play: a public awareness campaign about the dangers of food contamination."

I'm hoping Lucas will get more out of *Fiddler* than I did. Specifically,

I'm hoping it'll give him a little understanding—even if a slightly cartoonish one—about the lives of our ancestors in Russia and Poland.

We get to the theater. The lights darken. The show begins. And unexpectedly, half an hour in, I'm a mess. I'm wiping my eyes with my sleeves, trying not to sob out loud or embarrass my son. This time, it's not the hygiene issues that I notice. It's the song "Sunrise, Sunset."

I mean, come on. It's so true. The days really are flowing far too swiftly. Stop flowing, days! I look at Lucas and think, Is this the little boy who sat on my lap while I read him *Pat the Bunny*, his eyes widening with amazement when we got to the furry page? Is this the little boy who pounded on his high chair for more syrupy peach slices, like a little King Henry VIII? That was yesterday. Now he's taking standardized tests and quoting the vulgar robot from *Futurama*. I really don't remember getting old. How did they?

The intensity of my reaction surprises me. Usually I'm only moderately sappy, not this blubbery. I blame it partly on just plain old exhaustion. I brought this on myself, so I'm not looking for pity, but planning this monster event is depriving me of huge amounts of sleep. I'm often frazzled and disoriented, like a hostile prisoner on *Homeland* after a month of interrogation.

A few minutes later at *Fiddler*, I find myself getting teary again, this time during the scene at a tavern. The Russian men and the Jewish men are both doing their respective folk dances in unison. See? Russians and Jews may be different, but they're both people, and they both enjoy stomping their boots heavily on the floor while wearing hats and clasping other men. We are all just loud, manic, and sometimes unsanitary people. It's the same message I'm trying to get across at the Global Family Reunion. Maybe we should do a *Fiddler* dance number as a warm-up to Sister Sledge?

After the show, I ask Lucas how he liked it. Overall, pretty good, he says, though he was bothered by the ending. In the end—spoiler alert—

the tsar's army kicks the Jewish people out of their little town, and the Jews all have to pack up their pushcarts with pots and pans and trudge off to a new land—in Tevye's case, America.

"Usually plays are sad in the middle, then happy at the end," Lucas says. "This was happy, then sad at the end."

He's got a good point. But I tell him it wasn't necessarily all that sad. Getting kicked off their land was a mixed blessing.

I believe this more and more. I've been reading about my ancestors' lives in nineteenth-century Eastern Europe. I've been studying the tiny towns in Poland, Ukraine, and Russia where they resided in simple wooden houses. About how they spent their days as storekeepers and farmers. The luckiest of my ancestors got a job selling peacocks to nobles, which was apparently a prime gig and allowed him to travel to other, slightly less-tiny towns.

Some parts of life were good. "Everybody knew everybody," says an oral history of Izbica, a Polish shtetl where my family lived. The villagers were close-knit. They looked after each other. No one starved.

But the flipside of this intimacy is that there was no relief, no privacy, no chance to escape the insularity. Everybody was up in your business. The narrator of the Izbica oral history recounts that "people were called mostly by nicknames. One or two words often described perfectly someone's beliefs, social standing and family lineage, or physical attributes. There was Lume (Lame) and Dziobaty (Chicken Pox). My father was called Leibele Goy, because he was a so-called freethinker who ate ham and associated closely with Christians."

When I read that passage on nicknames, it stayed with me. I know it was probably one of the lesser indignities of life back then, but still, it struck a chord. I tried to figure out what my Izbica nickname would be. My guess is Mole Man. For most of my life, I had a mole on my nose, until it threatened to become cancerous and I had to have it removed—an option my be-moled ancestors didn't have.

"Life was hard in those towns," I tell Lucas. "Think about it this way: if Tevye's family hadn't been kicked out, they wouldn't have moved to America."

And in America, I explained, Tevye probably lived on the Lower East Side and got a job as a peddler. Then maybe his son went to accounting school at night and opened a small practice, and that man's son went to Amherst and became an entertainment lawyer for Broadway actors, and he got house seats to *Fiddler on the Roof* for everyone in his daughter's class.

"See?" I say. "It was all for the best."

He nods, half-convinced.

I don't say it to Lucas, but I imagine that in a few years, the entertainment lawyer's daughter will go off to college, just like my sons will someday, and the dad will be lucky if she texts him once a week, and sunrise, sunset, how swiftly flow the days, and dammit, Lucas is right, the whole thing is sad.

REUNION COUNTDOWN: 13 WEEKS

Things are getting weird. I've decided that anyone who is willing to perform for free is invited to do so. We need to both boost attendance and bolster the entertainment. So we've got someone coming who is doing life-size origami dancing on the main field. I've seen her YouTube video and I still am not sure what this means. Also, we've got Gary Auerbach, the Freestyle Frisbee World Champion from 1995, who will be there teaching our cousins Frisbee tricks. We've got a freestyle rap artist specializing in evolutionary theory. I have no idea what this event will be like, and I'm supposed to be planning it.

CHAPTER 34

The Kevin Bacon Delusion

If we're going to throw a party for family, we should probably figure out how the attendees are, in fact, family.

Everyone is a cousin in the broad sense. But if we're going to break the record, we'll need proof. We need the paths. We need documentation. All of which is far more complicated than I anticipated. Hundreds of those who have said they're coming are still not connected. I've been freaking out.

Thankfully, this week, I get the news that two of the biggest mega-trees in the world are doing me a huge favor.

Both Geni and WikiTree have added notices on their websites about the Global Family Reunion; and more important, both have added a button that will allow users to figure out their path to me. A sort of Six Degrees of A.J. Jacobs. This is both highly flattering and deeply unsettling. As a friend of mine said, "Your project is all about uniting the world. But somehow you've made yourself the center of it all."

Dammit, he's right. And it underscores something I've noticed about family history from the start: it's a paradoxical pursuit that lends itself to both healthy and unhealthy perspectives. So far, I've identified three big tensions.

1. NARCISSISM VERSUS HUMILITY
On the one hand, genealogy is the most self-aggrandizing hobby ever.

Look at all these thousands of ancestors who all teamed up to create their ultimate masterpiece: Me!

On the other hand, once you get started, you see that the tree is enormous and you're just a tiny leaf. If you flip your perspective, you understand that each of your ancestors spawned thousands of descendants. You're not the center. You're nothing special. Suppose your seventh-great grandmother time-traveled to the twenty-first century. She'd barely have time to pinch your cheek before she'd be off to visit her other offspring.

Despite the fact that I'm the Kevin Bacon of my own reunion, the overall effect of studying the tree has been humbling. I know that someday I'll be just one of hundreds of ancestors on a chart, and that my birth date will probably be wrong and my middle name misspelled (it's Stephen with a *ph*, in case any descendants stumble across this manuscript).

2. EXCLUSIVITY VERSUS INCLUSIVITY

Genealogy has historically been a tool of the elite. The idea has been to prove your link to royalty, to show you deserve respect and/or an inheritance.

It was so associated with aristocracy that, back in Colonial times, some Americans found genealogy distasteful. It was seen as un-American, a holdover from the corrupt British caste system. The antigenealogy sentiment continued for a century. Ralph Waldo Emerson wrote that we should leave behind "the sepulchres of the fathers" and quit searching "among the dry bones of the past. . . . When I talk with a genealogist, I seem to sit up with a corpse."

But increasingly, genealogy is being used for the opposite purpose: to demonstrate how broad our connections are. If you go back far enough, almost all of us have some kingly or queenly blood in our veins: it's a simple numbers game. Take the *Mayflower* descendants: There are an estimated 25 million Americans who are direct descendants of *Mayflower* passengers, so we're not talking about a small, gated community. And if you count relations by marriage—as I like to do—everyone on earth is a *Mayflower* relative.

3. SCIENCE VERSUS EUGENICS

On the one hand, the field of family history holds great scientific promise. You may recall the Columbia professor named Yaniv Erlich who has been studying the big data of the Geni family tree. He's crunching the numbers on millions of relatives to discover patterns of longevity and learn how diseases are passed down. The World Family Tree is one of the richest data sets we have in human biology. It could help us cure ailments and improve how we live.

On the other hand, genealogy has a long and ugly history of being co-opted by racists and eugenicists. Christine Kenneally's book *The Invisible History of the Human Race* has a section about genealogy during the Third Reich. The Nazis hired genealogists—a profession previously considered unimportant—to search for those with impure blood. One genealogist at the time said, "People dismissed us with a pitying laugh. That has now changed thanks to the regime of Adolf Hitler. Today genealogy has tasks of state-level importance to fulfill."

Likewise, in Japan in the 1920s, there was an obsession with keeping blood unmixed. There were eugenics-minded matchmakers and genealogy detectives who would comb through prospective husbands' and wives' family trees in search of non-Japanese ancestors.

The problem persists. As you might remember, some white supremacists today are using DNA tests to figure out who among them has the "purest" pedigree.

This conundrum reminds me of the Internet as a whole. It's an open question whether, in the end, the connectedness offered by the Internet will be good or bad for society. The comedian Kumail Nanjiani is on the pessimistic side. He recently wrote this assessment of the Internet: "Hope: Internet will allow people from different backgrounds to communicate and understand one another. Reality: All the racists found each other!"

I'm more optimistic than Kumail. But it's going to be a battle.

REUNION COUNTDOWN: 11 WEEKS

We've got a crisis. A celebrity with 1.3 million Instagram followers wants to attend, but he's not allowed. Because he's a dog. Waggles, the Irish terrier. I tried to get permission from the New York Hall of Science to bend the no-pets policy, but sadly, no exceptions.

This is how I spend my days—drowning in minutiae. The magician David Blaine has agreed to come, which is great, but needs a place to keep his bike. We find a secure office that can store a bicycle. Then it turns out the "bike" is actually a motorcycle. So we have to grapple with motorcycle parking.

Having never planned a large event before, I was repeatedly told there were a lot of moving parts, but I didn't realize quite how many. My brain isn't equipped. Thank God for Eowyn and Aaron and the rest of the Global Family Reunion team. My respect for event planners knows no bounds.

CHAPTER 35

The Pilgrimage

A few weeks ago, I landed the biggest gig of my career: I'm scheduled to be the warm-up act for Donny Osmond.

This momentous occurrence will take place at a family history conference in Salt Lake City. I'll give a talk about my upcoming reunion, and then out will come the main event: the man with the flawless hair and the snow-white teeth and purple socks and a soul that's just a little bit rock 'n' roll.

The conference is called RootsTech and it's put on by FamilySearch, the genealogy company operated by The Church of the Latter-Day Saints. Osmond is, famously, a Mormon, so he's a perfect fit. The conference is huge: more than twenty-five thousand people attend, many but far from all affiliated with the Church of Jesus Christ of Latter-day Saints. The Mormons, as you may know, are genealogy superstars. They dominate the field. Think of how Brazilians dominate supermodeling. Or how the Austrians rule skiing. Or how Floridians excel at driving naked while high on bath salts.

So it would be enormously helpful to have the Mormons as allies on my quest. At first I wasn't sure this would be possible. I figured they'd be leery of a secular Jew who is on the record as being pro–gay marriage. And in turn, I find the Church's official views on same-sex marriage deeply troubling. But my project is all about finding common ground. So I'm giving it a shot, as long as no one asks me to self-censor.

The kids are on spring break, and Julie and I decide to take the family on a mini vacation to Utah. At the airport in Salt Lake City, we are met by Cherie Bush, one of the RootsTech staffers. Cherie is blond and smiley and brilliantly organized. She's also passionate about her job.

When I first contacted Cherie several weeks ago, she warned me some of her emails might contain multiple exclamation points. She lived up to her promise. And now, here she is, welcoming me with literal open arms.

"My cousin!" she says, giving me a hug.

Cherie is delightfully enthusiastic!!! And I'm not being sarcastic! I love it! I need it! Seriously! Over the past few weeks, whenever I'm feeling stressed about my potentially disastrous reunion—which is often—Cherie sends me emails like "I know it's going to be amazing!!" She's my Utah-based Paxil.

Cherie and her husband, Dennis, take us to dinner at Brigham Young's former house, which has been converted into a cafeteria-style restaurant. Over mashed potatoes and turkey potpie, we talk genealogy. It turns out Cherie's husband is a distant relative of the presidential Bushes, which makes him my relative, too. They've never met the presidential Bushes, but the name has come in handy. "We were once upgraded to the presidential suite at the Marriott." Cherie laughs. We spend the next hour talking family trees.

Why are Mormons drawn to family history? Partly it's for the reasons I've heard from every family historian: It makes them feel a sense of belonging. Family is everything. They owe it to their ancestors who sacrificed so much (and the Mormons were indeed persecuted). But for Mormons, it's more than that. It's also part of their religion. "It's crucial for us to turn our hearts to those who paved the way for the rest of us," says Eowyn, who is Mormon herself.

Here's a vastly oversimplified explanation: In Mormon belief, families can be joined together for eternity after this life. And you're not just joined to your parents and siblings, but also to all your ancestors.

To ensure your family relationships continue in the afterlife, you need to undergo a ritual at a Mormon temple—a ritual called "sealing." For instance, kids are sealed to their parents and grandparents.

But Mormons believe it's not just the living who can choose to join their family for eternity. The deceased can, too. Those who die without accepting the Gospel are given a choice in the afterlife. This is done by proxy. With the permission of the family (assuming the person died in the last 110 years), the Mormons perform the rituals of sealing and baptizing. If the deceased accepts the rituals—and the LDS Church does believe they make a choice—he or she will pass from "spirit prison to spirit paradise," in the words of one Mormon writer. So genealogy isn't just a hobby. You are researching which ancestor needs to be sealed with which family in paradise. You are saving souls. The stakes couldn't be higher.

Which means that for the past seventy years, The Church of Jesus Christ of Latter-day Saints has been on a quest to build a family tree of the entire world. They've been collecting data. Unimaginable amounts of data. The Church's informational Fort Knox is a huge vault drilled into the side of a quartz mountain in Utah. It contains 3.5 billion images on microfilm, microfiche, and digital media. Drawer after drawer and server after server preserve names and birth dates from all over the world.

Here's a statistic to give you a sense of scale: every year, more data is *added* to this vault than is contained in the entire Library of Congress.

And where do they get this information? Thousands of Mormon missionaries have been at it for decades. They fan out all over the world—from Thailand to Kenya to Bolivia—and scan millions of pages of public records. They interview designated family historians in rural Africa who have kept hundreds of years of ancestor names in their heads. The vault holds parish records from England in the 1500s and Chinese family trees that date back to before Christ.

Cherie told me I won't be visiting the vault. The public isn't allowed inside. But surprisingly, almost all the information is shared online at the website FamilySearch or at the Family History Library in the heart of Salt Lake City, a fact I find commendable, as do many in the genealogy world.

"They could have kept all the data for themselves," says Gilad Japhet, the founder and CEO of MyHeritage, one of the biggest family history sites. "But instead they give it away to all users for free, and share it with other organizations. In that sense, the Church is really remarkable."

At Cherie's suggestion, I visit the library the next day while Julie and the kids go off to check out the local trampoline scene. The library is an impressive place. It's a sleek five-story building of glass and white stone filled with more than a million books, hundreds of whirring microfilm machines, and dozens of well-groomed Mormon helpers. I know plenty of Kingsbacher and Sunstein records are tucked away in there, waiting to be discovered, unseen for decades.

During RootsTech, the Church sometimes keeps the library open late, past midnight. Even at that hour, it remains packed. It's like the world's quietest rave. But I go in the afternoon, accompanied by Eowyn.

Eowyn suggests I look for the records of some of my Polish ancestors; the library has an impressive Eastern European collection. Thus ensues three hours of threading microfilm—a skill I haven't employed since high school—and scrolling through page after page of old marriage and death records from the late 1800s.

I'm starting to fade when Eowyn says, "Wait! That looks like Flug."

She's right. This handwritten document from Zamosc, Poland, does look like it has my grandmother's maiden name. We zoom in. Yes, in handwritten script, I see a clear *F-L-U-G*. Our library helper, a woman with a Polish accent named Maria, translates the document for us. Yes, it's the marriage certificate of Moszek Kozes and Szandla Flug, who is a cousin of my great-grandmother.

"It's such a beautiful find! Such a beautiful document!" she says. "Some people come here and don't find anything for days!" Maria is choked up.

It's true. The calligraphy is gorgeous, more appropriate to a founding national document than a bureaucratic marriage form.

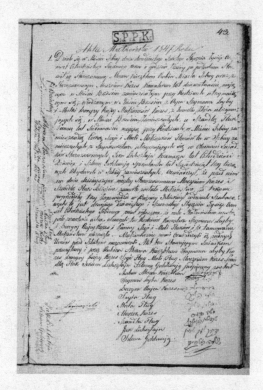

The couple is described as "Old Covenant," which is the nineteenth-century Polish way of saying "Jewish." The bride's parents are listed as tavern keepers. They posted a notice of the couple's engagement on the synagogue door for three weeks, as was the custom. This was their Face-book announcement. It had a serious purpose, though: to alert any other suitors who might have a claim to the engaged. This was the time for skeptics to speak up. Luckily, no one did.

I suppose I should be happy for Moszek and Szandla. They're getting hitched! But instead, I feel a mixture of sadness and worry. It says Moszek is nineteen and Szandla is seventeen. So young! When I was nineteen, I was barely able to commit to buying a blacklight poster.

Is it possible to have paternal feelings for relatives who have been dead a century? Because that's what I'm feeling. I want to hug them and tell them it'll be okay. Or maybe warn them that it won't be okay at all. Get out. Because the next century is not a good one for Jews in Zamosc. There will be pogroms. There will be the unspeakable horror of World War II, and Zamosc was not spared. The Nazis shot five hundred Jewish people in the Zamosc streets and dumped their bodies in a mass grave.

Oh man. All this from a wedding document.

The following day Cherie picks me up in her car for a prearranged tour of Mormon sites. She drives me to a factory with hairnet-wearing volunteers who are busily canning applesauce for the indigent. I see thousands of T-shirts and socks bound for the Third World. I meet a series of friendly Mormon men and women with rectangular black name badges pinned to their well-ironed shirts. "Our job is to feed the hungry and clothe the naked, whether or not they are members of our religion," one tells me.

Cherie is proud of her faith, and wants to show me her community in the best possible light.

Because Mormonism doesn't always get the best PR. Much of the criticism is focused on the Church's policy toward gay rights. Like most evangelical Christians and ultra-Orthodox Jews, the Latter-day Saints are opposed to gay marriage. The Mormon website says that "sexual relations are proper only between a man and a woman who are legally and lawfully wedded as husband and wife. Any other sexual relations, including those between persons of the same gender, are sinful and undermine the divinely created institution of family."

In some ways my project meshes perfectly with the Mormons' goals. They share the belief that humans are one big family. They have the quixotic notion that strangers should treat each other less awfully.

But in another way, my thesis is totally at odds with the Mormons. I embrace all sorts of family structures, including gay marriage and gay parenthood. In fact, by pointing out that everyone on earth is family, I'm hoping to de-emphasize the "traditional" family and embrace a thousand variations.

When I first talked to representatives of the Church about my reunion, I told them I'd be advocating for an expanded definition of family, including gay marriage, and to their credit, they didn't complain. Part of this may be because the Mormons aren't monolithic. As with every large group, you'll find Mormons with a wide variety of beliefs. At RootsTech, I met a woman named Erika Munson. A few years ago Erika cofounded a movement called Mormons Building Bridges, which urges a more accepting view of gay and transgender Mormons. She thinks it's not just morally right, but also crucial to keeping younger Mormons in the Church. One of her five kids, a thirty-two-year-old son, left the Church, and one of the reasons for his departure was the Mormon policy on gays and lesbians. Erika's group marches in the Utah Pride Parade and holds events introducing gay and straight Mormons where she serves what she calls "the casserole of reconciliation." Another group called Mormons for Equality are fighting for the legalization of gay marriage in the Church.

The gay-rights Mormons are a minority, for now. But if I had to place a bet (which, I suppose, is also not allowed in Mormonism), I predict an eventual acceptance of gay marriage by the Latter-day Saints. This could be delusional optimism on the part of a blinkered liberal, but that's my long-term guess. After all, Mormon doctrines do change. In 1890 the Mormons outlawed polygamous marriage. (Polygamy is still practiced by a handful of radical splinter groups, but not by those in the mainstream Church.) In 1978 the Mormons finally allowed African-Americans to receive the priesthood. Religions usually—not always—adapt to the mainstream.

CHAPTER 36

An Ocean of Cousins

I t's the day of my big RootsTech gig. I arrive early at the convention hall. It's an intimidatingly enormous room, like a half-dozen high school gyms put together.

"How many people are coming?" I ask Cherie, when I get to the green room.

"We expect about eight thousand," she says, smiling.

Eight thousand. Or about seventy-nine hundred more than my typical speaking gig.

I'm going to need help. It's only ten a.m., but it's time to start violating Mormon rules. I begin surreptitiously taking alternate swigs from two stainless-steel water bottles I filled up at the hotel—one with coffee and one with white wine. Yes, I know. Quite gangsta.

A few minutes later there's a flurry of murmuring among the staff, and in comes Donny Osmond. He's wearing a black leather jacket. He still looks boyishly handsome at fifty-seven, but also tired. He did a show in Vegas last night and took a private jet to Salt Lake City this morning.

I introduce myself and we pose for photos. I'm pretty sure Donny can tell I'm nervous to be his warm-up guy, because he goes out of his way to reassure me. He puts his arm around my shoulder. He tells me, "This is going to be great, A.J."

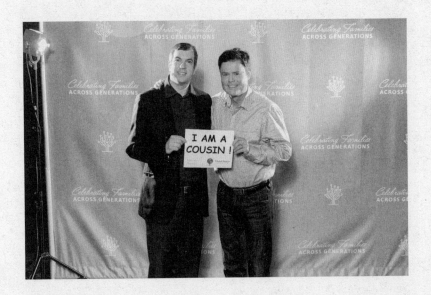

We start talking about families. His is famously big.

"When my parents started a family, the first two children were deaf," Donny tells me. "And my parents were told, 'Don't have any more children.' But they did. And I'm glad they didn't stop at six because I'm number seven."

Donny now has five kids of his own and a bunch of grandkids. I ask him the secret to a long marriage.

"I always tell people that if Debbie and I ever have an argument and I know that I'm wrong, I am man enough to know that I'm wrong . . . but if I know that I'm right, I am man enough to know that I'm wrong."

It's a classic Borscht Belt joke, one that would have fit right in to his seventies variety show. But I need all the levity I can get.

"How'd you meet your wife?"

Donny tells me, oddly, that he met her at this very convention center. He went to an Elton John concert here on a double date with his brother.

"My brother was dating this girl named Debbie. And when Elton sat down to sing 'Your Song,' I remember looking over and thinking, 'I'm going to marry my brother's date someday.' And now we're going on thirty-seven years."

Huh. I didn't expect such a scandalous pickup tale from Donny Osmond.

"And how did your brother feel about that?" I ask.

"We haven't spoken since." He pauses. "No, it was fine!"

I spend the next half hour on the green-room couch, bouncing my leg, muttering my speech to myself, and emptying my wine-filled water bottle. Finally, RootsTech organizer Shipley Munson calls me onstage.

"Okay, everybody, please hold up your signs!"

I look out into the vast sea of eight thousand Donny Osmond fans. In unison, they dutifully lift up eight thousand cardboard signs with the message "I am a Cousin." Yes, Cherie and the RootsTech folks have distributed a sign to everyone in the audience. It's a dazzling sight, these rows upon rows of signs. It's almost too much. I feel like a South American dictator.

I look over at Cherie. She's in the front row, beaming. If she had a thought bubble, it would contain several hundred exclamation points. Without her, this wouldn't have happened. Next to her are Julie and my kids. I'm not sure, but I think I spot something unusual on my kids' faces. Is that pride? Or embarrassment? Probably a combination.

My speech goes fine. I talk about how we're all family and invite them to the Global Family Reunion. I'm praying that at least some of them will show up in New York in the summer.

And then Donny comes out to near deafening whoops and hollers. I have to remind myself: There's no shame in being less popular than an Osmond in a predominantly Mormon crowd.

REUNION COUNTDOWN: 9 WEEKS

When my friend Andy finds out I'm holding this event, he calls me.

"Are you kidding me?" he says. "You're the worst person to throw a party for the world! You're an introvert and a misanthrope."

There's a bit of truth to that claim, which makes my project seem ironic—well, perhaps ridiculous—on the surface. But let me clarify. Yes, left to my own devices, I'd be tempted to spend months at home avoiding all human interaction with the exception of the occasional Indian restaurant delivery guy.

But I also know that this default state isn't good for my mental health. When I'm alone, my brain goes to dark corners. I worry, I stew, I construct elaborate revenge fantasies against people who made fun of my buck teeth in sixth grade. If I'm alone for too long, I can work up some impressive antipathy for the human species, myself included, what with our flawed brains and cruelty and tendency to loudly chew apples in elevators.

My job doesn't help. Being alone is an occupational hazard of writing, which—and I'm not being flip here—might explain why so many writers take their own lives.

Thank God for Julie. Julie is a natural extrovert. She forces me to go out and have dinner with her friends and colleagues. I grumble beforehand, but

I'm almost always pleasantly surprised. I'm reminded that most humans aren't so bad in reality. They have experiences and ideas and generally want to be good and probably don't know how much I hate apple chewing in elevators. I come home in a much better mood.

Being married to Julie has been like fifteen years of cognitive-behavioral therapy. She's coerced me to be social, and it's made me happier. During a wedding a few years ago, she even convinced me to join her in the Electric Slide, though that was a bridge too far.

Planning the reunion is stressful and horrible in many ways, like arranging a hundred bar mitzvahs at once. But it's also doing what Julie has always done: it's compelling me to interact with other human beings. I have no choice but extroversion, or I'll fail. And as much as I dread the meetings when I wake up, I'm usually energized afterward. Maybe *usually* is too strong. Often. Sometimes.

CHAPTER 37

Cheers to the Dead

I've got a decision to make: booze or no booze? Should the Global Family Reunion serve beer, wine, and hard liquor? Or should we keep it to juice and lemonade only?

I can see it both ways. On the one hand, there shouldn't be alcohol: It's a family event with a lot of boisterous kids running around. On the other hand, there should be alcohol: It's a family event with a lot of boisterous kids running around. And those kids have parents. And those parents will need a drink.

There's also the Mormon wrinkle. Alcohol is forbidden in the Mormon religion, and if all goes well, hundreds of Mormons will be coming to the reunion. Hopefully some non-Mormons too, but I expect the Mormons will be there in clean-cut force.

I call Cherie, my main LDS contact: Would the Mormon folks be okay if alcohol is served? She says yes. I talk it over with the event producer, Aaron. We decide we will have beer and wine.

On reflection, it seems only appropriate. My family's history is drenched with booze. For starters, in my family's archives, I found a poem written for my great-great-grandmother's eightieth birthday party in 1922. One stanza reads:

At blue laws we wink
We'll walk a mile for a drink!

And then there's my great-great-uncle, my coincidental namesake: A. J. Sunstein. A. J. was a liquor dealer in Pittsburgh before Prohibition. I have a photo of his store in which you can see the employees—men with mustaches and bowler hats and scowls—standing among whisky barrels. (The store was located in a section of Pittsburgh called Temperanceville at the time. So A. J. was already thumbing his nose at the dry crowd.)

A. J. shows up in dozens of newspaper clips in the years approaching Prohibition. He wrote impassioned editorials arguing against banning alcohol. He said that the saloons would be able to regulate themselves. Saloon owners were responsible folks and wouldn't sell whisky to anyone who posed a danger.

The Anti-Saloon crowd wasn't buying A. J.'s argument. One wrote a newspaper rebuttal entitled "The Naïveté of Sancho Sunstein." The rebuttal asserted that saloons will self-regulate when humans have figured out how to "extract sunshine from cucumbers. When the fashion in pigs runs to side pockets, when figs are gathered from thistles and money from trees, and the secret of perpetual motion is discovered, we may expect the saloon trade to cure itself."

Which is my all-time favorite bit of snark directed at a relative.

A. J. had his good side. According to the papers, he contributed to a lot of charities, including ones helping Russian Jews fleeing persecution. But he may not have been completely on the up and up, to put it mildly. In July of 1919 A. J. was arrested by federal agents. He was selling beer that was 2.5 percent alcohol, and the limit at the time was 2 percent.

And then there's this 1924 *Pittsburgh Post-Gazette* headline about Sunstein being called before a Senate hearing about price-fixing in the liquor industry: "Sunstein Tells Committee He Burned the Papers Because They Were 'in the Way.'" The senators didn't seem happy with A. J. But who doesn't like to keep their office tidy by constantly burning suspicious documents?

The liquor store of A. J. Sunstein and his father, circa 1905.

A. J.'s store went out of business when Prohibition passed. But don't worry. Other relatives of mine kept up their part in the vice trade. My great-great-grandfather on another branch, Morris Kingsbacher, started a cigar-making business called Kingsbacher and Sons cigars.

So my tree can boast tobacco and booze—two-thirds of the way to the ATF jackpot! No firearms dealers I know of, but I'm still looking.

According to a letter in the family archive, Kingsbacher's factory, at one point, employed a cigar roller named Samuel Gompers. If that name sounds familiar, it's because he later went on to be the founding father of the American labor movement, which railed against the corrupt and harsh practices of factory owners.

So that's a nice contribution to history, helping to inspire the labor movement!

And don't forget my great-grandfather Sam Kheel, who was in the fur trade. There's an article about his hauling forty thousand rabbit pelts back from Europe (and witnessing the murder of another fur trader who was accused of being a spy). Every time I read about Sam, I wonder how much my aunt Marti, an animal rights activist who died of leukemia a couple of years ago, knew about her grandfather.

My immediate family tree doesn't seem filled with truly evil types like hit men and loan sharks and TMZ editors. But at the same time, not all of them were working on the polio vaccine or spending their free time digging wells in El Salvador. I wouldn't call the money that my ancestors made dirty. But it's certainly got a few stains. And without that money, my forebears wouldn't have been able to afford to send their kids to college, an advantage that cascaded down to my trip to college, which led to my current job.

So what's the appropriate feeling? How much guilt should I inherit, if any, for the sins of my ancestors? I know I can't control the actions of my vice-pushing great-great-grandfather. Yet I can't deny that I've reaped at least some advantages from his behavior. Should I be giving more money to animal rights charities and the American Cancer Society? Yes, probably.

But there's also another way to look at the situation, one that might be more empowering. I recently read a *New York Times* article that gave me some perspective. It said one advantage to family history is that it can inspire your kids to be more compassionate and charitable. Tell your kids about a charity or good Samaritan that helped one of their ancestors. That way they'll see how crucial helping others is: we wouldn't be here without it.

In short, maybe focus on gratitude, not guilt. Instead of wallowing in the shortcomings of your ancestors, be moved by those who aided them and follow their example.

REUNION COUNTDOWN: 7 WEEKS

I screwed up. Here's what happened: I have about fifty super-close relatives coming—aunts, uncles, first cousins, and so on—and I got worried they wouldn't be able to find each other. The grounds are sprawling. Plus, some of them are elderly and I wanted to make sure they had a place to gather and sit. So I've arranged for the fifty superclose relatives to meet at a tent. The Jacobs family tent. So a reunion inside a reunion. Then I got this note from one of my more left-leaning cousins:

> Though I am immensely grateful to have been born into our family, it would be uncomfortable for me to be at a table and tent especially for us amongst a throng of others who do not each have a table and tent especially set up for their more immediate families or group they more closely belong to.

Dammit. He's right. An exclusive tent for my immediate family goes entirely against the whole point of the Global Family Reunion. What the hell was I thinking? I remind myself not to put the name Jacobs anywhere near the tent. No need to rub it in the face of my fourth and seventh cousins.

CHAPTER 38

My Celebrity Cousins

I've noticed another paradox about my project. My big thesis is that we're all equal. We're all cousins. Genealogy should be inclusive, not exclusive. Doesn't matter if you're famous or unknown, a *Mayflower* descendant or the offspring of a Latvian barmaid. We're all linked. So don't be intimidated by someone's supposed connection to a notable ancestor.

And yet, to spread this idea that we're all equal, I've been doing just the opposite: I've been feeding our infatuation with celebrity. When I invite people to the Global Family Reunion, I play up the celebrity angle in my emails: You too can figure out how you're related to Beyoncé and Albert Einstein! To paraphrase Alanis Morissette (sixteen steps from me), it's a tad ironic.

I've been aware of this tension for a while. But my friend, a genealogist named Pamela Weisberger, put it to me bluntly over coffee the other day. "In ten years, there'll be a psychiatric disorder where people are obsessed with how they're related to celebrities, and they're going to name it after you. The Jacobs Syndrome. You're the ultimate enabler." (Pamela, by the way, is a close blood relative of Shemp from the Three Stooges.)

This aspect of the project is, alas, a bit of a throwback to the early days of genealogy. In eighteenth-century Europe, aristocrats traced their lineage to see how they connected to the king. And European kings and

queens manufactured family trees that linked them straight back to biblical times, directly to King David of Israel, and then to Adam himself.
"See?" they could say. "I'm descended from biblical kings! It's God's plan
that I have unlimited power and you clean outhouses."

I'm not alone, of course. Celebrity genealogy is huge right now. I've
spent many hours watching PBS's *Finding Your Roots* and TLC's *Who Do
You Think You Are?*—in which an actor or singer gets a guided tour of his
or her ancestors.

Professional genealogists occasionally grumble about the shows' flaws.
One complained that Lisa Kudrow didn't need to go to Poland to find her
cousin Yuri's phone number. It's on the Internet! (Apparently, footage
of actors typing names into search bars for half an hour just didn't test
as well.) They also take issue with the shows' climactic scenes, where
the celebrities reverentially page through yellowing documents while
wearing white gloves. The white gloves are like the hazmat suits in a
medical show: they break them out for maximum drama. But according to
archivist Tom Perry, gloves are a bad idea when handling old documents.
You can't be as nimble. You're more likely to tear the ancient paper.

And yet, despite the nitpicks, most genealogists appreciate the shows.
They spark interest in our geeky pastime. They inspire people to trace
their own pasts. That's my hope for my paradoxical quest as well: That
the ends will justify the means. That the celebrity angle will hook my
distant cousins on family history, but that they'll soon realize their non-
famous ancestors are just as fascinating.

So, with that hope in mind, to spread the word about the Global Family Reunion, I pitched a monthly column called "Chat with My Famous
Cousin" to *People* magazine in which I'd figure out my link to a celebrity
and then interview him or her about family.

I got the green light. The interviews have been surprisingly delightful, perhaps because everyone—no matter how big or small their Twitter
following—has interesting ancestors. Here are three notable moments so far:

1. MOST ENLIGHTENING INTERVIEW

I already admired Daniel Radcliffe, the star of the Harry Potter film series and many other good nonwizard movies. He's the rare former child star who turned out thoughtful and well read and has never been arrested for head-butting a maître d' or whatever.

I admire him more when he asks me this question: "I know this is a bit creepy, but if you find out how I'm related to my girlfriend, would you email me?"

We meet at a New York restaurant, and Daniel tells me the tale of his grandmother, who seems worthy of a biopic herself.

In 1938 Daniel's grandmother met a South African miner named Wilfred when he visited England. She fell in love, got married, and moved with him back to South Africa. According to Daniel:

> She said that as soon as the plane touched down, she felt him change as a person. He had gone along with English society. But now that he was back in South Africa, he was back to being a racist, vile man who did not treat people well. And then, during my grandmother's pregnancy, he tried to have her put into an asylum.
>
> My grandmother says she was sitting in her living room one day and there was a knock at the door and it was the police. They said they had a warrant to take her away. And she said, "Who signed it?" and they said, "Wilfred, your husband." Then he emerged from behind her, saying, "Oh yeah, I did sign that."
>
> My great-grandmother had to fly to South Africa to rescue her daughter and my mum. My mum was two weeks old and became the youngest child to ever fly out of South Africa.

At the end of the interview, Daniel is so polite, he says he hopes to come to the Global Family Reunion. But in case he can't make it, he records a welcome message I can play for attendees.

Cousin Daniel Radcliffe.

2. MOST AWKWARD CELEBRITY INTERACTION

The actor and hip-hop artist Ludacris also has an amazing family history. But in this case, Ludacris doesn't know about it until I tell him.

While preparing for the interview, I asked genealogist Abby Glann to help with research. She turned up an astounding document—a 115-page transcript of an interview that Ludacris's great-grandmother gave thirty years ago for a university oral history project.

It is vivid stuff. Ludacris's great-grandmother told tales of life as an African-American growing up in Illinois and Kansas in the 1910s. She spoke of her one-room schoolhouse. She talked of a cousin who fled the KKK by swimming across a lake at night.

I knew he'd be interested. The problem is, my conversation with Ludacris isn't face-to-face. We talk over the phone while he is riding in a car, distracted by a babbling chorus of voices in the background. I'm not sure he even knew beforehand that the interview was about his family and not a normal Q&A to promote his new movie. In short, not ideal conditions for an intimate discussion about his family.

I start out with smaller revelations—for instance, that a distant relative of his was a Harlem Globetrotter.

He seems moderately interested at best. Then he puts me on hold for a couple of minutes to deal with some problem.

When he comes back on the line, I start to tell him about his great-grandmother Bertha Craig, who was born in Kansas, had five kids, and worked as a maid most of her life. I tell him Bertha's mother was African-American. Her father, she believed, was Jewish.

There is a pause.

"Are you trying to tell me my great-great-grandfather was a Jew?"

"That's true. That's according to this interview with your great-grandmother. She said she thinks he was Jewish. I'm Jewish too, so you and I are probably *mishpokhe*."

Another pause.

"Are you sending me all this shit in an email?"

"Yeah, I'm happy to send you all this."

"I'm going to have to do some homework on it."

"I didn't mean to freak you out."

"No, it's all good. I'm just trying to figure all this out."

"It's an amazing document by your great-grandmother."

"I'm going to give you my email. Are you getting reactions for the interview or, what the hell is going on right now?"

By the end of the interview, Ludacris seems to have warmed to his newly discovered heritage. I ask him if I could email him any additional questions.

"Yeah. Hey man, we're family!"

I email him later to ask how (or if) all this knowledge had changed his view of his identity, but got no response. The lesson: When you reveal someone's heritage to them, it should be done with care, face-to-face, perhaps over some tea and soothing acoustic guitar, not on a cell phone or email.

*Cousins Ricky Gervais, Olivia Munn, Nick Offerman, John Legend,
Dr. Oz, Olivia Wilde, Jason Sudeikis, Penn Jillette, and Christina Hendricks.*

3. SECOND-MOST-AWKWARD CELEBRITY INTERACTION

Another odd brush with famous cousins wasn't for *People* magazine, but it fits the theme, so I'm including it here. It happened during an appearance on *Good Morning America* to publicize the Global Family Reunion.

GMA wants me to explain to their celebrity guests how they're related to each other. Originally, the plan is for me to sit on the couch with the stars and chat. But later the producers say this plan isn't working out. Logistics. Timing. Celebrities. And so on.

So here's the backup idea: Maybe, as the celebrities enter the studio on Forty-Fourth Street, I can stand outside and reveal that we're cousins. And by "reveal," I mean shout at them as they walk by. A few days later, I find myself next to a police barricade at seven a.m. Behind me are dozens of fans holding signs and autograph pens, waiting for this morning's crop of A-list talent.

An hour later, a black SUV pulls up. Out steps Mark Wahlberg.

Cameras click. Fans shriek.

I try to make myself heard. "Hey, Mark! I'm your cousin!" I holler. "It's your cousin A.J."

Mark Wahlberg looks at me. His face is a mixture of puzzlement and alarm, much like the face I made when I first saw SantaCon.

"We're cousins through the Donnellys!" I say, waving a printout of the tree connecting us.

"Oh?"

He edges away from me to sign some autographs, occasionally glancing my way nervously.

"Hey, Mark, remember to come to the big family reunion next summer."

He looks at me a little longer than felt comfortable. "Okay," he says. "Thanks."

A little while later, along comes Melissa McCarthy, the actress and comedian.

"Hi, Melissa! I'm your cousin," I say, when she steps out of her chauffeured SUV.

Melissa smiles, sort of. Her publicist—a bulldog of a woman—comes marching up to me. "What are you doing?" she demands.

I explain the idea: we're all related, Melissa is my distant cousin, and I'm holding a reunion. "So if Melissa wants to come," I say, "and maybe bring a dish, like couscous, she should give me a call."

"Couscous?" says the publicist. "That's very specific."

I can't argue with that. I'm not sure why couscous popped into my mind. I guess when I'm nervous, couscous is my go-to grain.

It wasn't what the publicist wanted to hear. The publicist finds my *GMA* producer and complains about the couscous guy crowding into Melissa's space.

In terms of humiliation, this is about equal to the time in sixth grade when I drooled on the piano in music class and the popular girl noticed and announced it to the other students. I tell my kids that sometimes it's okay to look ridiculous for a greater cause. Still, I never show them the *GMA* segment.

CHAPTER 39

51 Percent of the Family Tree

I'm at the living room table, scouring old newspaper articles of my maternal great-grandfather Elias Sunstein (I was pleased to see he won his 1907 local tennis tournament in Pittsburgh) when Julie comes into the room.

"I have a bone to pick with you," she says. A bone to pick. It's a metaphor my vegan aunt Marti once scolded me for using, but I decide now might not be the time for me to bring this up.

"What's the matter?"

"Go to the Global Family Reunion site," Julie says.

"Okay."

I click on the event's home page, which I set up a few weeks ago. It consists of photos of notable people, such as John Legend, George H. W. Bush, comedian Nick Kroll, all holding up "I am a Cousin" signs.

"I'm noticing there's something missing," she says.

I study the site again, then look at her quizzically.

"Estrogen. There's no estrogen."

She's right. The photos are all of men—not a female in sight.

That's not good. An affront to 50 percent of my cousins. I promise her I'll add photos of female cousins to the home page.

But it's not just a problem with my website. It's one of the biggest issues in the field of ancestry, at least among the more progressive genealogists. Female ancestors get much less face time.

Even if we find the names of women from our past on various government documents, we often know little beyond that. Women are frequently ciphers, lacking stories, feelings, opinions. As one blunt-speaking researcher told me, "It's a historical sausage party." Which is cruelly ironic, because genealogy attracts more women than men.

The difficulty stems largely from the paper trail. "For the most part, it's very much a man's world, records-wise," says genealogist Jane Wilcox, host of *The Forget-Me-Not Hour* podcast. War records, land deeds, business filings—all traditionally male-dominated.

Sometimes I like to blame the British.

"If the Dutch had won North America instead of the British, women would be a lot better off," says Judy Russell, a family historian with a law degree who goes by the moniker "The Legal Genealogist." "The seventeenth-century Dutch were far more liberal than the English. The Dutch allowed women to own land, open businesses—everything except vote. There were actually two kinds of marriage, one where they retained their rights and one where they forfeited them." (By the way, the phrase "going Dutch" is not related to Dutch marital feminism, though it should be.)

To research women, Russell and Wilcox suggest trying unorthodox methods. Perhaps scour the records of shopkeepers in the area, which often listed clients' names, addresses, and purchases.

Personally, I lucked out. My grandmother's insanely detailed archive has yielded amazing facts about my female ancestors. And I have some great, strong ones in there. Perhaps my most feminist relative was just one generation back: my beloved aunt Marti, the one who died recently. She lived in Berkeley and taught feminist philosophy. (Actually, Berkeley wasn't liberal enough for her, so she lived outside Berkeley.) She was pushing for gender-neutral language from the time I was able to form words. If my grandfather said *mankind*, she'd remind him it's *humankind*.

My cousin David, of the leprechaun-at-the-wedding fame, found this an endless source of amusement.

"Manhole cover," he'd say.

"Personhole cover," she'd correct him.

"Chairman of the board."

"Chairperson of the board."

"Manicotti."

"I'm not going to say it, David."

I've taken Marti's message to heart, at least partly: I try to use the word "humankind." She'd still be appalled by my indiscriminate use of "you guys." Point is, if Marti's soul is with a gender-neutral deity looking down from a nonphallocentric heaven, I'm sure she's nodding her head with approval at Julie's activism. I adored Marti, so she's yet another reason I have to make the Global Family Reunion less male-heavy.

I knew about Marti's feminism, of course, but the family archives introduced me to another activist in the bloodline—Gertrude Kingsbacher Sunstein, my mom's mom's mom. And I've grown to love my feisty great-grandmother as well.

Her kids called her "the iron woman," which is probably vaguely sexist, but was meant as a compliment. According to an oral history of the family, she carved the turkey at Thanksgiving and drove the car instead of her husband. I show that passage to Julie.

"Look! You carve the turkey and drive the car too! It's a family tradition."

(I've been mostly banned from driving since I got too entranced by an audiobook biography of Albert Einstein and lost control of our rental car on the highway, jumped the median *Dukes of Hazzard* style, and spun into the oncoming traffic. No one was hurt. The author rejected my offer to blurb his book as "dangerously good.")

Gertrude was also a suffragette. Actually, let me rephrase: she was a suffra*gist*. Marti always told me the word "suffragette" was terrible because -*ette* is a diminutive suffix. She believed "suffragette" was the equivalent of saying, "Aw, look at those cute little women asking for their right to a participatory democracy. Isn't that adorable!" So Gertrude was a suffragist. She marched. She wore a sash. She held fund-raisers. She handed out pamphlets.

We still have one of the pamphlets Gertrude handed out in the 1910s. It's a fascinating twenty-page peek into the concerns of the day. The writer tries to dispel the myth that women are too emotional to vote. And also not smart enough. It argues that, despite having a body part pointed inward instead of outward, women can still grasp the basics of economic theory.

The pamphlet's oddest section addresses the apparently widespread concern that too many disreputable women would vote. The dreaded harlot-and-strumpet coalition. Don't worry, the pamphlet said: "Women of the half-world are not willing to vote. They are constantly changing their residences and their names. They do not wish to give any data concerning themselves, their age, name or number and street."

In 1920 the Nineteenth Amendment was ratified and women gained the right to cast ballots. Soon after, my great-grandmother wrote her husband perhaps my favorite family letter of all time. She was with their three kids on the Jersey Shore, and he was working in Pittsburgh. Her writing is historic, inspiring, and delightfully cranky.

She starts by saying sorry-not-sorry for taking so long to reply to his last note: "Now you have had a chance to see how pleasant it is to wait all week for a letter from one's spouse."

In your face, Great-grandpa Sunstein.

She then informs him that "vacation" with the kids isn't exactly paradise. "The weather here is cold and rainy—too disagreeable for bathing. Dickie has been quite miserable, and doing his best to make life miserable for me."

So don't think that women have it easy.

And then she gets to the big news:

Great-grandpa Lazarus "Elias" Sunstein and great-grandma
Gertrude Kingsbacher Sunstein.

"Congratulations on the suffrage victory! Now we can go to the polls together and I won't have to wait outside—as I have done so frequently before."

An epistolary mike drop.

I love that she congratulates her husband; universal suffrage is good for everyone, not just women.

I'm proud of Great-grandma, and proud of my great-grandfather for supporting her, if not helping out on the vacation. He probably got some ribbing from his friends, because male supporters of universal suffrage were often mocked. I found one 1909 postcard online that featured an illustration of a sad, apron-wearing man washing clothes in a wooden tub. The tagline: "I want to vote but my wife won't let me."

There was one other Gertrude Sunstein nugget in the archives that struck me. It was her obituary in the *Pittsburgh Post-Gazette*. It included mention of her suffrage work. What it did not include was her first name. She was referred to throughout as "Mrs. Elias Sunstein."

Yes, Mrs. Elias Sunstein.

My aunt Marti would have gone berserk over that one. Here Gertrude is, trying to get equal rights for women, and her entire identity is subsumed by her husband.

Marti always disliked the patrilineal naming system, where kids are named for their dads. She'd argue—correctly, I think—that it gives undue weight to the male. It creates a lopsided view of the family, where the dad of the dad of the dad of the dad gets all the glory. Think of it this way: you have sixteen great-great-grandparents but you probably share your last name with only one of them.

What would a totally fair and truly gender-unbiased naming system look like? Maybe if I gave equal weight to all my great-great-grandparents? "I'd like to make reservations. Okay. My name is A.J. Jacobs-Weinstein-Kaufman-Fliegelman-Flug-Weissman-Szuch-Tomashoff-Kheel-Schecter-Herzenstein-Saphier-Sunstein-Fink-Konigsbacher-Friedenheit. Right. That's J-A-..." Perhaps a tad unwieldy.

Maybe the secret instead is the portmanteau approach. My friends Gary and Jodi combined their last names, Ruderman and Wilgoren, and ended up with Rudoren. I just spent two productive minutes mixing up my great-great-grandparents' names. The result: Jaweikkaffsutshisskoff. So maybe not the perfect solution.

REUNION COUNTDOWN: 6 WEEKS

I'm going to be repaying favors to friends and acquaintances for the next several decades.

Jeopardy! champion Ken Jennings has written a trivia quiz about family for the event. (Sample question: What San Francisco 49ers quarterback attended a university named for his own great-great-great-grandfather? Answer: Steve Young.)

A wonderful songwriter I know named Jill Sobule has composed a theme song for the event. Sample lyric:

There's Janis and Tupac and Kurt Cobain
We're all going home on the very same train
You're my cousin, you're my kin
Let the party now begin.

And it's not just people I know. A man from Denmark named Niels Bjerre Hansen volunteered to create a chart linking one hundred historical figures, from Gandhi to Kanye West.

I've never been in charge of a cause that people actually believe in. It's terrifying. About half the time I feel like a fraud. But it's also exhilarating and inspiring—a good way to chip away at my misanthropy.

CHAPTER 40

The Melting Pot

I'm trying to figure out whether to fully embrace the Epcot vibe of the Global Family Reunion. I've already had Scottish-American cousins tell me they're coming in kilts and Peruvian-American cousins tell me they're wearing ponchos. Maybe I should go full Small World and set up pavilions for each of the global family's different cultures. I could have two hundred simultaneous mini-reunions.

On the other hand, as Julie points out, wouldn't this Balkanization be contrary to the idea that we're all one big family? She might have a point. (Sidenote: Aunt Marti once told me the word *Balkanization* is Balkanizing, because it unfairly singled out Balkan culture as being divisive. So apologies to the Balkans.)

While organizing this reunion, I've been thinking a lot about the pros and cons of assimilation and identity. My own family's history has provided a lens. As in most Jewish families, my relatives run the gamut. Some of my family remained black-hat Orthodox, and others assimilated with force.

My grandfather Theodore Kheel was one of the latter. He was passionate about civil rights and equality, but Judaism held no interest for him. He never went to synagogue as an adult, never had a seder. Many of his friends and coworkers had no idea my grandfather was Jewish.

I found a speech by President Lyndon Johnson in which Johnson praises my grandfather for fighting for civil rights by saying, "On the weekends, Ted was working tirelessly on Civil Rights, when he could have been at church with his family." The sentiment is nice. But it's a little odd to have the leader of the free world refer to my Jewish grandpa as a Protestant churchgoer.

My grandfather was so non-Semitic, he was one of the first Jewish people to join a super-WASPy country club near his home. When I was a kid, I always fantasized about showing up to the club's tennis courts wearing a pink-and-green madras yarmulke and a tallit with little whales on it.

I'm not completely sure why Judaism held so little allure for him. He once told me he saw the history of the world as moving away from religion and embracing science. As a labor mediator devoted to resolving conflicts, perhaps he saw clinging to culture as polarizing.

But my grandfather wasn't even the most hard-core assimilator in the family. My third cousin Lisa Grayson told me a story about her dad. In 1968, when Lisa was eleven and living with her family outside Milwaukee, her dad went on *Jeopardy!* and won enough money to take her mom to Europe. He needed a passport, so he gathered a bunch of government documents for proof of ID. While he was out one night, Lisa peeked at the papers on his dresser. One of them was a government document that said, in effect: "Herbert Goldberg" will henceforth be known as Herbert Grayson.

Until then, she thought she didn't know any Jewish people all. Now she was a Jewish person herself. Or at least half. She became fascinated. She wrote about her experience in an article in *Avotaynu*, a Jewish genealogy journal:

> By the time I was a teenager, I was obsessed with all things Jewish; this manifested itself in secret excursions to Milwaukee's old delis and synagogues and a passion for Chaim Potok novels. . . . At 16, I finally gathered the courage to talk to my father, and he scheduled a restaurant dinner alone with me to discuss what he called "the subject."

My third cousin Lisa and her dad.

How strange it was to watch my gregarious, unflappable dad squirm—and, I am ashamed to admit, I was not above baiting him to see what elaborate sentences he could devise to avoid using the dreaded words "Jew," "Jewish," or even "Judaism."

So focused was I on getting a reaction from him that I never asked the questions I really wanted to: Had something awful happened? Why was he so afraid of being found out? Even if he didn't want to be Jewish, why couldn't we know his family? All my (usually articulate) dad told me was that, yes, his family members were "those people," but life was easier for "people who weren't of that religion." . . . He wished I had never found the paper on his dresser.

Lisa's father never told her his reason for secrecy. She figures a lot of it had to do with his fear that being Jewish would hurt him at the ad agency where he worked. And as a boy, he may have been embarrassed by his own father's immigrant parents, with their heavy Yiddish accents and Orthodox ways.

Of course, Lisa's dad was right that "people of that religion" did have a harder time. Anti-Semitism was and remains an ugly force. Reading through my family's archive, I got glimpses of what they faced. One particular reference to anti-Semitism sticks out in my mind. It's from the sixtieth wedding anniversary of Fannie and Gerson Friedenheit. (You may recall, Gerson was my third-great grandfather who was in the Civil War for about three minutes.)

To give you the context: This was 1919, and America was in the midst of a eugenics obsession. A few years earlier, Teddy Roosevelt had popularized the notion of "race suicide." He feared the superior white race would be overwhelmed by all these inferior child-spawning immigrants. He gave speeches and wrote articles on the need for white people to have more kids, lest they be swamped by the lesser races, which included African-Americans, Latinos, Catholics, and Jews.

So at the wedding anniversary, my ancestors gave a toast to Gerson and Fannie's stunning fertility, poking fun at them for having fourteen kids. My grandmother, God bless her, kept the program with the words to that toast. And in the speech, Gerson's grandkids made a startling joke: they said Gerson and Fannie had single-handedly scared Teddy Roosevelt into starting his campaign to encourage WASPs to procreate.

This seems a very Jewish thing to do: cope with the hatred by making it into a gag.

I realize my own views on assimilation are filtered through my mostly pro-assimilation family. I'm not a super-assimilator like my grandfather, but I also don't find *assimilation* to be a dirty word. I think partial assimilation is a good thing. My project is all about the follies of tribalism and how we shouldn't build unscalable walls between different cultures. I do cherish some cultural identity, but I'd prefer that the partitions between cultures be low, maybe ankle-height, and somewhat porous, like cheesecloth.

To use another, more delicious metaphor, the melting pot doesn't have to turn us into an undifferentiated puree. It's okay to have some identifiable ingredients. But they shouldn't be so chunky that they can't mix with the others. There needs to be some unifying values, like freedom of thought and speech. I'd love for all of us to identify as humans first and members of our ancestors' culture second.

My kids are getting a taste of their heritage. We light candles on Shabbat. We hold a seder every year. They will have bar mitzvahs complete with the requisite Talmudic themes, such as Coney Island carnival games. But the most important Jewish lesson I want to pass on to my kids comes from my grandfather. Not my maternal grandfather who played tennis at the WASPy country club. The other grandfather—my dad's dad, Charles Jacobs—who sold pretzels on the street during the Great Depression.

My aunt Carol told me a story about how my grandfather was at home on Yom Kippur. He told Carol, "You may wonder why I'm at home on Yom Kippur instead of at the temple. The reason is, I believe that you can pray to God anywhere you are, not just in temple." And he said,

There are only three things I want you to take away from your Judaism:

1. Love of family.
2. Love of learning.
3. Love of responsibility toward others.

"It was one of the most profound things he ever said," Carol says now. "He was a beautiful, gentle, wise man."

Amen.

REUNION COUNTDOWN: 4 WEEKS

I've nixed the Epcot idea. I'm certainly happy to have kilt and poncho wearers aplenty, but I don't want to set up separate stations for each culture. Julie's right: that'd be more like a Global Family Disunion.

CHAPTER 41

The FBI and My Grandpa

As I mentioned, my pro-union grandfather Theodore Kheel probably possesses the most impressive FBI file in the immediate family. I've wanted to read it for years.

A few months ago I filed a Freedom of Information request with the FBI, as did my aunt Jane. We each got sent packets, though, oddly, the contents were slightly different. Together, these files totaled an impressive 349 pages.

I spend a weekend reading every word that wasn't blacked out. Here's what I learn:

1. The FBI grilled my grandfather as a suspected communist at their Washington, D.C., offices. He said he was not.
2. In 1962 my grandfather helped organize the forty-fifth birthday party for John F. Kennedy where Marilyn Monroe wore a tight dress and sang the most suggestive rendition of "Happy Birthday" in history. I'm not sure why this is in his file, but it was news to me.
3. My ultraliberal aunt Marti was under serious surveillance for years. One of her close friends in the Students for a Democratic Society was an informant and reported on Marti's trip to a lefty conference in 1967.
4. The FBI was highly suspicious of my grandfather's ties with Martin Luther King Jr. Page after page on seemingly every meeting they ever had.

Reading the file makes me alarmed and proud. Alarmed at the depth of knowledge the FBI had about the minutiae of my grandfather's life—his vacation spots, his daughter's dorm at college, etc. But I also feel proud of my grandfather, especially because of what I learn about his relationship with King. I knew he'd had some dealings with him, but I didn't know the extent of them.

They worked on several projects together. My grandfather assembled a group of lawyers who defended Dr. King pro bono in his Supreme Court lawsuit brought against him by an Alabama police department. Dr. King and the *New York Times* were being sued for libel by an Alabama officer of public safety for an advertisement they ran alleging racism. The Supreme Court found 9–0 in favor of King.

My grandfather was president of a lobbying group called the Gandhi Society for Human Rights, of which Reverend King was honorary president. And he also threw a 1964 fund-raiser at his home in Riverdale to help defray King's legal costs.

After reading the file, I call my aunt Kate and ask what she remembers of that party.

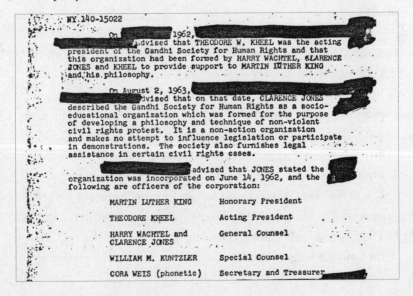

```
NY 140-15022

         On _____ 1962, _____
         ____ advised that THEODORE W. KHEEL was the acting
    president of the Gandhi Society for Human Rights and that
    this organization had been formed by HARRY WACHTEL, CLARENCE
    JONES and KHEEL to provide support to MARTIN LUTHER KING
    and his philosophy.

         On August 2, 1963, _____
         ____ advised that on that date, CLARENCE JONES
    described the Gandhi Society for Human Rights as a socio-
    educational organization which was formed for the purpose
    of developing a philosophy and technique of non-violent
    civil rights protest.  It is a non-action organization
    and makes no attempt to influence legislation or participate
    in demonstrations.  The society also furnishes legal
    assistance in certain civil rights cases.

         _____ advised that JONES stated the
    organization was incorporated on June 14, 1962, and the
    following are officers of the corporation:

         MARTIN LUTHER KING         Honorary President

         THEODORE KHEEL             Acting President

         HARRY WACHTEL and          General Counsel
         CLARENCE JONES

         WILLIAM M. KUNTZLER        Special Counsel

         CORA WEIS (phonetic)       Secretary and Treasurer
```

Martin Luther King Jr. and my grandmother Ann Kheel
at my grandparents' house in New York.

"You had to pay twenty-five dollars to attend," Kate tells me. "Your aunts Jane and Connie and I gave our allowance to Dr. King. It was about three dollars. I remember him being visibly touched. He said, 'That's so sweet of you.'"

Kate then asked Dr. King to sign her stuffed penguin. He agreed and signed it on the belly.

A stuffed penguin? The symbolism seems almost too tidy: black and white coexisting together.

"Actually," Kate says, "the penguin was aquamarine."

Oh well. Still, pretty amazing.

I made one more surprise discovery about my grandfather's civil rights activism: in 1971 he organized a conference on the social conflicts of the day. Here's how a *New York Daily News* columnist described it: Kheel has made a "daring new, and almost ecclesiastical, effort to put out almost all the nation's social fires with one unusual conference. Single-handed, he has convinced men of industry, of black communities, of the highest government echelon, to fly to New York for a national summit conference."

My grandfather wanted to use his conflict resolution skills to try to find solutions at the conference. "It's Ted Kheel's theory that the angry racial and religious conflicts searing our nation can be eased by the techniques of collective bargaining. . . . With his passionate quest for mediation and his fervent appeals to reason, he may have started this nation on the road to full fraternity."

When I read this, I practically do a cartoon spit take. What's this now? My grandfather held a quixotic conference that he delusionally believed would lead to world peace? I'm holding one of those too!

Of course, my grandfather's was a much more substantial effort, with historic figures like Bayard Rustin in attendance. And it's unclear if the conference had any impact. We are certainly a long way from full fraternity. But I love that he tried.

CHAPTER 42

The Great Surname Challenge

We're launching a contest: the Great Surname Challenge. The winners will be announced at the reunion. The idea is to see which last name can raise the most money to help battle Alzheimer's. (As I mentioned, Alzheimer's is the cause we are supporting at the event. All profits from sales and sponsors go directly to two Alzheimer's charities.)

This is how the Great Surname Challenge will work: You join the team with your last name and donate five or ten dollars or more. The team with the highest tally wins. We're going to see which last name can bring in the most bucks. The Jacobses or the Schoenbergs? The Kennedys or the Bushes? The Hatfields or the McCoys? (And don't worry, there's a prize for money raised per capita, so the Smiths and Joneses won't automatically crush the Spitzers and the Jeurgenses.)

"I like the idea," Julie says, "but it's kind of weird."

"Why?"

"Doesn't it kind of go against the whole point of the reunion? That we're all one big family? It's like when you were going to have separate reunions for separate ethnicities."

Damn. She's got a point. Names are tricky. On the positive side, your last name is a touching tribute to your ancestors (or one specific male ancestor, in most cases). In another sense, it's tribal. I'm a Montague and you're a Capulet, so we must kill each other.

Genealogists deal a lot with surnames, so I've actually learned a bit about the topic. The use of surnames has varied wildly from culture to culture and era to era. Some cultures had none. Others put the "last name" first and the "first name" last, as in Japan or Korea, where the surname is the one that goes first.

Jewish surnames arrived relatively recently. For most of Jewish history, my ancestors had no last names. Then, in the early 1800s, the Prussian government enacted laws to force Jewish people to take surnames to help officials keep track of them.

Some Jewish families chose last names inspired by the Bible, such as my own last name, Jacobs. Others chose last names based on towns or landmarks, such as my wife's ancestors, who went with Schoenberg, or "beautiful mountain" in German.

Still others chose job-related last names. Julie's mom's maiden name is Zuckerman, which means "sugarman" in German, presumably because one of Julie's fifth or sixth great-grandparents was a sugar salesman. According to Zuckerman family lore, one of the Zuckermans lost all his money and became bitter, so he changed his name to Salzman, which means saltman. The story sounds suspiciously neat, but maybe that's just my cynical inner Salzman talking.

Oddly, I've been fascinated with job-related last names for years. While working at *Esquire*, I once pitched the editor in chief an article in which we'd ask famous people to act out their last names: What if Anderson Cooper spent a day trying to make a barrel (that's what a cooper does)? Or what if Will Smith spent an afternoon hammering glowing iron into a horseshoe (as a smith does)?

My boss at the time never responded to my email. I'm guessing it's because he was so inspired by my brilliant concept, he immediately left the office to go harvest some wheat (his name is Granger, which means "farmer").

Or else he thought it was a terrible idea. Hard to know.

I'm sad we no longer create career-related surnames. As Christine Kenneally writes in *The Invisible History of the Human Race*, we should be seeing more people with last names like "Analyst," or, God forbid, "Podcaster" and "Lifecoach."

Overall, I like my family's surname of Jacobs. But other Jewish families weren't so lucky. According to the excellent book *The Language of Names*, by Justin Kaplan and Anne Bernays, "Some local authorities [in Eastern Europe] recognized that the name decrees offered them an opportunity for extortion and bribery. They gave attractive names to those who paid for them . . . and gave comic and derisory names to others." In the latter category:

Eselkopf, which means "ass's head"
Fischbaum: "fish tree"
Kusemich: "kiss me"
Gimpel: "dunce"
Karfunkel: "carbuncle" or "boil"

Many names changed, of course, when immigrants came to American shores. My mom tells the story of how the Friedenheits (my mom's great-grandparents) got their name. Apparently, the official at Ellis Island asked Gerson "What's your name?" And Gerson said, in German, "Anything is satisfactory." Which in English sounded sort of like "Friedenheit." That's what the Ellis Island official wrote down, and thus was born the Friedenheit family.

Nice story but almost surely not true. It's a long-standing myth, this idea that Ellis Island officials saddled immigrants with bungled names. "If you want to get a professional genealogist really angry, tell them that your family's name was changed at Ellis Island," one genealogist told me.

The most famous tale of an Ellis Island snafu is about a Jewish man who ended up with the Irish-sounding name "Sean Ferguson." How'd that happen? According to the tale, when this Jewish fellow arrived at Ellis Island, the immigration officer asked him his name. The man nervously replied, "*Ich habe schon vergessen!*" Which is German for "I've already forgotten." The officer waved him through: "Sean Ferguson, welcome to the United States."

Again, almost certainly apocryphal. Truth is, the Ellis Island officers simply checked off the names on the ship's manifest. They didn't transcribe them. If anyone is to blame for a wacky transliteration, it's the ship company's workers back in Europe. But most immigrants who changed their names did so after arriving in the States, as my paternal grandfather did. My grandfather went from Jacobowitz to Jacobs. The motivation was usually the urge to blend in and avoid discrimination.

So what to think of Americanized names? Were the immigrants abandoning their ancestors? Selling out their heritage? Even back in Ellis Island's heyday, this was the subject of debate. *The Language of Names* authors dug up several old newspaper articles about the controversies.

For instance, in 1923 a weekly Jewish magazine called *The American Hebrew* wrote about a man named Harry Kabotchnik who wanted to change his surname to Cabot. The magazine deplored the loss of the name Kabotchnik, "with its rich, sneezing tonal effects."

In 1898 an immigrant told the *New York Tribune*, "We honor our fathers just as much, even if we drop their names. Nothing good ever came to us while we bore them; possibly we'll have more luck with new names."

The immigrants' requests weren't always granted. The *New York Times* reported that "a Civil Court judge in Brooklyn [in 1967] refused to change Samuel Weinberg's family name to Lansing 'for future business reasons, such that my sons shall not bear any possible stigma.' The judge's name was Jacob Weinberg."

Unlike Judge Weinberg, I reserve judgment on the ethics of name changing. I don't resent my ancestors. And I'm not going to change my name back to Jacobowitz as a political statement. In one sense, yes, name changes could be seen as a betrayal of our forefathers, a surrendering to the dominant culture. But in another sense, can I blame my ancestors for trying to make their difficult lives just a little less difficult?

The truth is, names do have real-life effects. There are studies that show that employers hire certain types of last names more than others. Even your last name's placement in the alphabet might have an effect. Julie claims she has been the victim of alphabetic discrimination. She says she was glad to shed her maiden name's *S*, the nineteenth letter, for *J*, the tenth. She still holds a grudge about how her college housing was assigned *A* to *Z*, and she got stuck with a lame dorm room.

I support my wife, of course, but I never saw this as a pressing social justice cause—until I recently discovered there is actual research on "the tyranny of the alphabet," as *Slate* phrased the phenomenon. A 2006 study by professors at Stanford and CalTech found that faculty members "with earlier surname initials are significantly more likely to receive tenure at top ten economics departments. . . . A likely reason is that academic papers by economists typically list the authors' names alphabetically."

Perhaps the most generous view of name altering is to consider it my ancestors' act of self-invention, even rebellion. Name changes for Jews were forbidden by the Third Reich. According to *The Language of Names*, in Hitler's Germany, it was illegal to change a Jewish-sounding name. "Those who weren't readily identifiable had to take 'Israel' or 'Sarah' as a middle name."

You could also argue that surname switching was a foreshadowing of things to come. More and more, according to the Pew Research Center, America is a nation of self-namers. The practice is everywhere, among all sorts of people—hip-hop stars, Twitter users, transgender people.

The oddest name-changing story in my immediate family concerns my great-grandfather, who was born in 1883. His granddaughter once told me that he "was not given a name at birth. Family legend has it that he was known as Baby Sunstein until age three or four, when he

picked his own name: Laz. His parents then named him Elias, which I
guess was long for Laz. His formal name was Elias, but he was known
as Laz till the day he died."

It's unclear why his parents never got around to choosing a name for
him. Perhaps they liked the generic simplicity of "Baby."

But it occurs to me, maybe Baby's parents inadvertently stumbled
on the secret to overcoming the clannishness and tribalism of names.
Maybe we should all adopt the same last name, something like "Human"
or "Person." In the meantime, though, the Jacobses are crushing the
Schoenbergs in the Great Surname Battle. And both are being crushed
by those bastards the Brauns.

REUNION COUNTDOWN: 3 WEEKS

The team is stretched too thin. Take Eowyn, who is connecting cousins while
wrangling vounteers while writing a blog while editing a reunion cookbook
with recipes from far-flung cousins. I'm so frazzled that today, when trying
to get my family to make a decision about what to eat, I actually heard this
phrase come out of my mouth: "Every second counts." No excusing that.

CHAPTER 43

Awkward Family Photos

Here's what I know about how my ancestors looked, based purely on textual descriptions:

My great-grandfather Sam Kheel was missing three toes on his left foot (as reported without explanation on a draft card).

His father, Aaron Kheel, had a "proportionate mouth," according to the US Passport office. It's a lovely phrase, by the way, and one I plan to use when I next sweet-talk Julie. "Come kiss me with that proportionate mouth."

A great-uncle had a "Roman nose," according to a visa application, a euphemism for Semitic features (this was the era of phrenology, so such facial shape mattered).

What I'm trying to get across is this: it's hard to conjure up the faces of my ancestors from descriptions alone, which is why I'm thankful my ancestors were early and enthusiastic shutterbugs. My grandmother's archive has more than a thousand photos. There's image after black-and-white image of unsmiling patriarchs with elaborate facial hair, unsmiling daughters in wide skirts, and unsmiling young boys in sailor suits. There are baby photos of my grandparents which give me emotional whiplash. I get a jolt of oxytocin—look at that cutie with the chubby cheeks!—followed by a wave of melancholy. Oh right. They grew up, got old, and died. I understand why my grandmother covered up clocks with masking tape. We get it, Time. You're a relentless bastard.

In the genealogy world, photos are king. Ancestry sites are basically Facebook for dead people. Users respond to photos more than text. Randy Schoenberg told me early on: If I want my distant cousins to look at my family tree and add to it, I need to upload images. They are, he said, "cousin bait."

So on a Tuesday night, I put dozens of my family photos on Geni and Ancestry and go to bed with a sense of accomplishment.

On Wednesday morning, my mom calls. She's upset. She doesn't like the indiscriminate photo sharing and wants them taken down. The shot of her grandmother in the black bathing suit? Highly unflattering. And do I really need to share the infamous Missing Cat Photos with my aunt Marti?

The Missing Cat Photos are my all-time favorite family images. They're of my mom and her siblings as kids. The family is in front of a fireplace, all dressed up, all smiling. Except for Marti, who is assuredly not smiling. In one photo, she's sticking out her tongue. In another she has her back turned. In a third, she has her arms out, as if she's cuddling an invisible object.

The problem? My grandmother—Marti's mother—wouldn't allow Marti's pet cat Bootytat to be included in the family photo.

"I don't think she'd want to be remembered like that," my mom says of Marti.

"I disagree! That's exactly how she'd want to be remembered. She always said it was her first protest."

As I've noted, Marti would grow up to become a passionate animal rights activist. She was not a moderate. She was vegan, of course. She avoided leather belts, shoes, and car seats (she owned a Toyota Corolla because it's an animal-free car). And she was vigilant about speciesist language. I once made the mistake of uttering the phrase "kill two birds with one stone" in her presence. She corrected me. The proper phrase is "liberate two birds with one gesture."

Marti, who loved photography, carried a long-lens Nikon camera at all gatherings. She'd snap photos but would never instruct us to "Say cheese!" because of the treatment of dairy cows. Instead she'd tell us, "Say soy cheese!"—until she decided the soy industry was corrupt.

So I'm confident Marti would be happy the Bootytat photos were on display. But I don't blame my mom. She's getting increasingly nervous about my project and its potential privacy invasions. She is, perhaps rightly, concerned about family legacy.

After a few minutes of discussion, my mom relents on the Marti cat protest photos. They can stay. But I do have to remove the bathing suit shots. I'm too nervous to tell her that I haven't just uploaded photos, I've also sent them to be analyzed. I've emailed them to Maureen Taylor, aka "The Photo Detective," whom I met at the Genealogy Event.

Maureen, a genealogical consultant who lives in Massachusetts, has an intriguing specialty: she'll inspect your old family photos and find clues about identity or date or behind-the-scenes stories. A few days later, I do a videochat with Maureen to go over her discoveries. But before I get to my family, I have questions about photos in general.

"How do you figure out the date of a photo?" I ask.

"There are a ton of clues," Maureen says. Cars, facial hair, even the shape of the photo. "Rounded corners were big in the 1870s." And most of all, clothes. Maureen wrote a book called *Fashionable Folks: Bonnets and Hats, 1840–1900.* It's more interesting than it sounds, because historical headwear got nuts. Hats got so unwieldy in New York that legislators introduced a bill requiring female theatergoers to remove their massive headgear so the poor saps behind them could see the stage.

Or consider the trend of stuffed birds atop hats. "People would raise birds in their homes and then sell them to hatmakers, who would kill them and put them on hats," Maureen says. The Audubon societies were formed, in part, to battle these disturbing bird hats. My aunt Marti would have been marching with them.

Speaking of the macabre, I ask Maureen, "Is it true that, in Victorian times, they used to prop up fully dressed corpses and take family photos with a dead relative?"

"It is true," she says. "And there were photographers who actually specialized in it."

"What's with the long faces? Why are so few of my ancestors smiling?"

"Taking a photograph was an important occasion, almost a solemn one," she says. Plus, our forebears had to pose in the same position for as much as thirty minutes, so it was easier on the mouth muscles.

After a week with my photos, Maureen has solved some puzzles. For instance, that shot of my great-grandma near a hotel? Based on the ruffles on her dress, it's from the 1930s. And it might have been taken by a street photographer—last century's versions of those folks at Disneyland who take your photo and then sell it to you later for a mere three hundred dollars. This information was good, though a little underwhelming. I'm not sure what I wanted: Look! My great-grandfather's got a bloody knife hidden in the couch.

Still, as a history nerd, I love talking about black-and-white photos. So much so, I am inspired to ask her a question. Would Maureen give a talk about family photos at the reunion? I figure it'll be a good warm-up to one of the main events: the Biggest Family Photo in History.

That is, if we can pull it off. The logistics will rival D-Day. Where will five thousand cousins stand? Where will the photographer stand? Is the photographer tall enough? Do I need to rent a crane? What about a drone? (Turns out we're too close to LaGuardia and a drone might be illegal.)

And of course, what should we all say when the shutter clicks? All

I know is that in honor of my vegan aunt Marti, it won't be a dairy product.

My great-great-grandmother Sophie Friedenheit, wearing a hat and not smiling.

CHAPTER 44

Brother Versus Brother

A troubling clip showed up on my Facebook feed. It was a video of Kathy Sledge—of Sister Sledge fame—singing "We Are Family" on BET's *Black Girls Rock!*

It was a rousing rendition. But where were the other Sisters? It was just Kathy.

Thirty seconds of googling reveals that Kathy, one of the original Sisters Sledge, is now solo. She no longer appears onstage with her other sisters—Joni, Kim, and Debbie, the ones signed up to sing at the Global Family Reunion. And the breakup doesn't look like it was pleasant. A little more googling turns up a lawsuit in which the three sisters forbid the one sister from using the name Sister Sledge to promote her gigs.

Oh no. This can't be good. I probably don't need to spell this out to anyone, but let me do it anyway: Sister Sledge—who sing the ultimate song about family harmony, the song played at weddings and bar mitzvahs for decades—apparently don't get along. Or at least had serious issues with one of the siblings.

I think back to how excited I was when they first agreed to sing at the Global Family Reunion. What a perfect musical encapsulation of my thesis! What symbolism. We are indeed family! Well, it turns out Sister Sledge are family, but apparently a somewhat dysfunctional one. Which isn't unusual. But still a bit of a bummer.

Shortly after I make this discovery, Julie and the kids and I join her brother Eric for an afternoon in downtown New York. Julie works for Watson Adventures Scavenger Hunts, and we are testing one out.

"How's the reunion going?" Eric asks. I tell him the Sister Sledge news.

"See?" he says, snickering. (He actually snickered.) "That's what I've said from the start."

I tell him that I know not all families get along. I'm well aware of family squabbles. I've watched *Downton Abbey*. I'm only saying that if we see someone as a family member, even a distant one, we may treat that person better than we'd treat a total stranger. Perhaps there's a way to increase the world's total quotient of kindness by hijacking the evolutionary bias that makes us favor those with our DNA.

Okay, I don't use those words exactly. But I try to make my case.

Eric disagrees. We are at a candy store that sells retro candies, like Bit-O-Honey and Necco Wafers. And we start to argue. Heatedly. Our voices get shrill. I start sweating. This is no longer funny. He is using phrases such as "Here's your problem." I'm using phrases like "Can I finish?" We are both as worked up as the most reprehensible of cable TV pundits.

Zane comes over to ask if he should get grape or strawberry Pop Rocks. I briskly tell him, "Strawberry," then go right back to arguing.

I can't even count the levels of irony here. I am fighting with my relative (Eric) in a dispute inspired by fighting relatives (Sister Sledge) about whether relatives fight too much. Okay, maybe that's three levels.

Eric isn't the only one in my family who's a skeptic. My cousin David— of leprechaun-wedding fame—posted the following on Facebook when I first announced my project.

I take issue with your dream scenario that if we find out we are all related, we will all act with more civility to each other. I am a jerk to everyone, related or not. You had to mute me during our project, due to your (admittedly true) belief that I am a "cocky bastard"; I would have acted this way if you were my brother, my cousin, or entirely unrelated. So unless you can find out that we are related to Andy Kaufman, Howard Stern, Richard Sherman, or Muhammad Ali, your newest project won't matter to me, which is frankly the only thing that matters.

I see David and Eric's point. It's not a panacea. A few weeks ago, I was at Chipotle with Lucas and his friend. The friend tossed a napkin on the floor. I said, "Would you pick that up? Because if you don't, one of the people who work here will have to."

The friend said, "Well, they're my cousins, right? So they won't mind."

That's not the message I'm hoping to impart.

On the other hand, I have plenty of anecdotal evidence that reframing strangers as distant relatives softens the heart. It certainly works for me, at least most of the time. The guy who took up three subway seats with his legs spread at a 170-degree angle was a challenge.

But I've often experienced what I referred to earlier as the Judge Judy Effect. When someone cuts in front of me at the bookstore line, I try to remind myself, Okay, that's not cool. But he's my cousin. He and I share a grandfather way back. And we'll have descendants in common. So maybe I should give him the benefit of the doubt. Maybe he has a sick kid who needs those Berenstain Bears books immediately.

Others who work on the mega-trees have told me they've had the same experience. Anecdotes, however, are not science. So I was kind of down.

And then a few weeks after my fight with Eric, an email dings in my inbox. It's from Eric. I open it warily. It says, "Well, I still don't believe it, but here's an article from Harvard that supports your thesis."

It was a recent study in which some Palestinians and some Israelis were randomly told that either they shared significant DNA or didn't. The ones who believed they were related treated each other more kindly in a memory game that followed. The players could either blast their opponents with loud noise, softer nose, or no noise. Those who believed they were closer cousins went easier on the eardrums of their opponents. Another part of the study showed the "cousins" were more open to hearing peaceful solutions to the Arab-Israeli conflict.

I could hug Eric! He's the bigger man after all. I love my relatives.

And thankfully, that was just one of the studies I've since found. A social scientist in Australia emailed me a link to his blog:

> Research has shown that kinship doesn't need to be real or even consciously understood to make us behave better towards others. A 2002 study found that participants were more likely to entrust money to people whose pictures had been slightly altered to resemble their own faces. Another study in the same year found people were more willing to help strangers who had the same surname as themselves, and a 2008 study showed that the greater number of perceived relatives in a group, the more cooperative people became.

A few weeks later, my cousin Cass Sunstein sends me a link to an article he'd just written. Cass is an actual close relative—first cousin, once removed. He's also a brilliant Harvard law professor and behavioral economist. He's agreed to speak at the Global Family Reunion, and his article in *Businessweek* is about what he calls the "Family Heuristic." It's the idea that evolution has trained humans to treat family members preferentially for the sake of preserving our DNA. The notion of a Global Family can hijack this bias. It nudges us to treat strangers with more kindness.

It's still not hard science. It's not quite Newton's $F = ma$, and most of the research concerns perceived DNA connections, not perceived in-laws. But it's a start. With luck, some postdoc psych student will do a more rigorous study.

And maybe, with some more luck, Sister Sledge will reunite.

REUNION COUNTDOWN: 1 WEEK

I am freaking out.

The Global Family Reunion

I t happened. Or something happened. I'm still processing. Let me get back to you after a six-day nap.

We Are, Without a Doubt, Irrefutably, Family

I'm back. And yes, the Global Family Reunion did occur a few days ago. And . . . it was horrible. And great. It was the best worst day of my life.

Also the oddest.

How can I sum it up? I started this adventure with a pro/con list, so maybe it's appropriate to end with one. I'll first give you the lowlights, because there are plenty to choose from:

THE FIVE WORST THINGS ABOUT THE GLOBAL FAMILY REUNION

1. THE WEATHER

I wake up at five thirty that morning to the sound of cars splashing through puddles on the street outside. Rain. Dammit.

The overnight storm has now tapered off to a light drizzle, but the damage is done. When I arrive at the field behind the Hall of Science where my cousins will soon be standing, I'm greeted by soaked grass and miniature ponds. Marshland. I half expect to spot some herons and muskrats.

The prospect of hundreds of soggy relatives is bad enough, but the rain has also short-circuited the electronic system, so we can't scan tickets. The event is supposed to start at eleven a.m. Doors don't open till half an hour later.

I brought a bottle of white wine for a postreunion celebration. At eleven a.m. I start guzzling. It isn't just my reputation I'm worried about. I'm concerned about disappointing my huge family. All these amazing volunteers have put in ridiculous amounts of time. All these distant cousins have shlepped to Queens from around the state, the country, the world.

2. MY SO-CALLED SPEECH

At eleven thirty, I walk onto the stage to welcome the several hundred people gathered in the field. By now, the rain has stopped.

But my speech—well, it isn't Churchillian. The anxiety is making me sweat, so I've already soaked through my shirt and look like I've just finished playing an overtime NBA final. The sweat must have used up all my body's water, because my mouth is parched, which makes it hard to pronounce basic consonants. I sound like I'm having a stroke.

"I'd like to welcome all my cuddins. The big cuddins, little cuddins, the old cuddins, the young cuddins . . ."

3. THE NEVER-ENDING PARADE OF SNAFUS

My grandfather once told me a fun little prank. The day after an event—a play, a party, a fund-raiser—simply go up to the person in charge and say, with a look of concern, "I was there last night. *What happened?*"

You'll almost always be treated to an anguished monologue—part apology, part finger-pointing—about all the blunders that ruined the event. The human mind works that way.

At least my mind does. All day long, things go haywire. There's the Marilu Henner incident. The actress has come to give a talk about how to form family memories. (In case you don't know, she has a famously amazing memory and can recall where she was on, say, March 15, 1982, as well as every other day.) Marilu pauses midtalk because the stagehands are chatting so loudly they're creating a racket. She walks to the side of the stage and says to one of them, "You know, I can hear you. You're very loud." She returns and says to the crowd, "Now he won't forget that and neither will I."

Writer Maud Newton's speech is interrupted by repeated announcements that Sister Sledge will be playing soon. The livestream flits in and out. The emcee forgets to introduce Eowyn, who has written a lovely speech about being adopted.

Julie keeps telling me, "You can't control everything. Just try to enjoy yourself as best you can."

"Uh-huh," I say, as I eye a drone with a camera hovering alarmingly close to the heads of the people in the crowd.

I turn around and ask Aaron, "We have insurance for that, right?"

I'm stressing about everything that's happening and everything that's not happening—the missed opportunities. I couldn't convince the Lillys from West Virginia to come so that we could have a combined record-breaking event. A friend was working on an app that would allow two random reuniongoers to bump smartphones and reveal how they're related, but it wasn't ready in time. Mila Kunis couldn't attend.

4. THE ATTENDANCE QUESTION

For most of the day, I have little clue how many people showed up. Could be a thousand. Could be ten thousand. It's hard to tell: the event is spread among the museum's buildings and fields.

Some moments I think it's a huge hit, and we'll definitely break the record. I mean, look at the speech by Henry Louis Gates that packed an auditorium of several hundred seats and an overflow room as well!

But then I go outside to the field to see the sponsors and tents and music, and it looks like forlorn, vast swaths of empty damp grass. The damn field is way too big. You could stage a Napoleonic battle on this field. I should have held it in a cozy restaurant backroom.

Plus, how many of these attendees are connected to the World Family Tree? Hundreds of them are, I know. But many aren't yet. A core group of volunteers is taking down people's grandparents' names, trying to connect them to the tree before they leave. But it looks like we'll have to connect some after the reunion.

I should have brought another bottle of wine.

5. THE FAILURE TO END ALL WARS AND RACISM
At least as of press time.

Okay, now the bright spots.

THE SIX BEST PARTS OF THE DAY
1. THE GLORIOUS RANDOMNESS OF IT ALL.
I can't say it was the biggest event in history, but this I can say: it was one of the weirdest.

This became clear to me at four p.m. I'm backstage with Julie. A huge crowd is assembled on the field watching Sister Sledge (or at least 75 percent of them) sing two songs that are not "We Are Family."

Finally, and fortunately for my stomachache, the sisters start to sing their big hit. Joni, who is wearing a bright-yellow cape, is banging a tambourine. A keyboard player is jamming. The crowd is waving their "I am a Cousin" signs in unison.

After the first round of "We Are Family"s, Joni motions for people to join the sisters onstage. So Julie and I step out and start dancing (awkwardly in my case, not in hers, as one tweeter helpfully pointed out later).

And it's then that I scan the crowd and notice what an exceedingly random collection of humans it is: There's a rabbi and a minister and Marilu Henner. A Harvard professor trying to clone wooly mammoths alongside a Daughter of the American Revolution. A stand-up comedian who just gave a speech about his coming-out alongside dozens of Mormon missionaries in their white shirts and black ties who have volunteered to help. *Love Boat* theme-song lyricist Paul Williams and UN ambassador Samantha Power. *Super Size Me* filmmaker Morgan Spurlock and a genealogist from Denmark.

Also, Frederick Douglass. I'd invited a bunch of historical reenactors—Abraham Lincoln and Ben Franklin and such—but Frederick Douglass is the only one who showed up. So there he is in his Victorian frock coat alongside a freestyle Frisbee champ and a street chalk artist. Not to mention a huge spectrum of different types of families: heteros, adoptees, sperm donors, diblings.

It's a Cobb salad of humanity.

"This is bizarre," Julie shouts to me, as we dance next to the saxophone player.

I nod. At that moment, I couldn't be happier.

2. ALL THE COUSINS WHO MADE IT HAPPEN.

I didn't get to hear all the speeches, but the ones I did hear were stellar. Henry Louis Gates summed up my project better than I ever could have: "Every schoolboy and schoolgirl now knows that we descended from a small group of people in Africa. From Mitochondrial Eve and Y-Chromosomal Adam. But it's one thing to know it. It's another to see it demonstrated fifty thousand years later. Despite all our differences—differences in geographical origin, skin color, hair texture, nose structure—despite all these differences, we are all related. We are all cousins, whether we like it or not." Damn, that guy is good.

My brother-in-law Eric gave a talk. He's a behavioral economist and, in between mocking me, talked about the pros and cons of family business.

DNA expert CeCe Moore spoke. She spends her days connecting relatives, and told the story of Jordanna, a woman who discovered at age twenty-one that her father wasn't her biological dad. Her biological dad was a sperm donor. It was upsetting, confusing, and exhilarating. Her parents had lied to her. But she'd also suddenly gained twenty-three half-siblings (he was a major donor). CeCe figured out who Jordanna's dad was and even tracked down his Facebook page. No one knew whether to reach out, but one half-sibling did. "I'm so happy you found me," the sperm donor said. "That's why I left my social media so open." All of them are now planning a family reunion.

The children's folk singer Tom Chapin showed up with sunglasses and a banjo, and sang the only song that could be more on-the-nose than "Kumbaya" or "We Are Family." It's called "Family Tree," and has been sung at thousands of kindergarten recitals over the last thirty years.

> The folks in Madagascar
> Aren't the same as in Alaskar
> They got different foods, different moods
> And different colored skin
> You may have a different name
> But underneath we're much the same
> You're probably my cousin and the whole world is our kin.

I wanted to tell Tom that, from an evolutionary biology standpoint, he can drop the "probably," though I guess it'd throw off the rhythm.

3. BONA FIDE HUMAN INTERACTION OCCURRED.

I have mixed feelings about hugging. For one of my books, I went to a convention of the high-IQ society Mensa. The Mensans all had colored stickers on their lapels. A green sticker meant "Yes, I like hugs." A yellow sticker meant "Ask before hugging." And a red sticker meant "No hugs at all."

Sure, a little odd. But as a longtime repressed person, I can see the logic.

Julie didn't think no-hugging stickers would go over well at the reunion. Which meant there was a lot of spontaneous hugging going on. Old friends hugging. Strangers hugging. Former sitcom stars hugging.

One of the most enthusiastic huggers I meet is named Melissa Uto. She's wearing a purple shirt and purple sunglasses and is part of a group of thirty people, all clad in purple.

A couple of years ago, Melissa took a DNA test and found out she's half Puerto Rican. "I got my results back and I open them and said, 'Holy shit, I'm Latina.'" She reached out to her new cousins, formed a Facebook community, and decided to have their first meeting at the Global Family Reunion. "A lot of us have a history of not-so-great family life. We wanted a break. A new start."

"So how's it going?" I ask.

"Great," says Melissa. "It's amazing not to be the loudest person in the room."

Melissa's cousin Victor gives me a handmade guitar with DNA double helices painted on it. I can't play a lick, but maybe someday I'll learn to mangle "Stairway to Heaven." I'm touched. I submit to a hug.

4. IT WAS, IN FACT, GLOBAL.

The volunteers had managed to set up forty-four simultaneous reunions around the world—New Zealand, Texas, Mexico, Canada, Mauritius, among them. The parties were connected by two-way live feeds. My brother-in-law Willy's family gathered about seventy relatives in Peru. They held up "Yo Soy Primo" signs.

The Salt Lake City Global Family Reunion had thousands of attendees—as well as Japanese drummers and bagpipers—because Mormons are better at organizing events than any group of humans on Earth.

Despite my invitation, the space station astronauts didn't call in. But a handful of cousins did organize a reunion in Second Life for our virtual relatives.

5. A FOREST OF THREADS.

On the second floor of its main building, the Hall of Science has a permanent plaque with a quote from a nineteenth-century Anglican priest named Henry Melvill: "We cannot live for ourselves alone. Our lives are connected by a thousand invisible threads, and along these sympathetic fibers, our actions run as causes and return to us as results."

I love that quote. It's my second-favorite passage about the metaphorical importance of threads. My favorite is from a book called *Invisible*

Cities by Italo Calvino. I read the book long ago and have always remembered it. Calvino wrote a fable of a city where people's apartments are connected by threads. The threads are strung from one apartment and across the street or down the block to another apartment. Each thread represents a different kind of relationship. If the people in the two apartments are blood relatives, the threads are black. If they are in business together, the threads are white. If one is the boss of the other, the threads are gray. Eventually, the threads grow so numerous and thick and multi-shaded, you can't walk through the city.

That passage popped into my brain several times during the reunion. At one point, while watching Paul Williams sing "Rainbow Connection," my mind started creating the threads. I could almost see them. Threads for blood cousins, threads for in-laws. Threads for friends, threads for colleagues. Threads for people from the same state. An infinite number of multicolored threads. Threads connecting coffee drinkers and Bananagrams players and people who love Norse mythology. You could do it a million ways.

I know this everything-is-connected idea is easy to mock. Recently, while watching reruns of the cult sitcom *Community*, I saw a scene where an obviously stoned dude says, "Everyone is my bro. Because everything in the whole, entire universe is connected. Rocks. Eagles. Hats." To which the main character replies, "Yeah, but some things are more connected than others. Like tarantulas and me peeing my pants."

So granted, the trope that we're linked to rocks and hats is kind of hokey. But like many hokey topics, it's also profound, important, and scientifically fascinating. This past year I've become obsessed with it. I've started keeping a file in my computer.

The file has an article about the history of the phrase "six degrees of separation." Turns out the psychologist Stanley Milgram did an experiment in 1978 to see how closely connected any two random people were. Milgram asked Random Person X to get a letter to Random Person Y using the US Postal Service and potential mutual friends. On average, it took about six people for the letter to reach its intended target.

There's a *New York Times* article about a reboot of Milgram's experiment: in 2016 Facebook studied its 1.59 billion users and found an average of 3.5 degrees of separation. There's a list I've compiled of unexpected historical connections, like Abraham Lincoln's friendship with Giuseppe Garibaldi, the uniter of Italy, whom Lincoln unsuccessfully asked to be a major general in the Civil War. There's a magazine article about how electrons can affect each other from light-years away. And a passage from Bill Bryson's book *A Short History of Nearly Everything* about how each of us likely contains at least one atom that was also in the body of Beethoven.

A single thread may not mean much. It may seem random and inconsequential. But millions of threads? When I see the world as a dense thicket of multicolored threads, it makes it harder for me to be a self-involved island, which is my natural tendency. It makes me feel less angry and alone. Even if I had the wherewithal or athletic ability to punch someone in the jaw, I imagine my arm would get all tangled up in multicolored threads.

6. THE END.

The day flies by. Before I can process it, the sponsors are folding their tents and the Sister Sledge roadies are packing up the drum sets.

Aaron and I debrief in a trailer. We've raised several thousand dollars for Alzheimer's research. However, despite the generous sponsors who funded most of the event, I still have to put up some of my book advance to cover the duct tape.

Luckily, there are no fatalities or looming lawsuits.

Julie and my sons return from a lesson with the freestyle Frisbee champ. We head to the Mister Softee truck nearby.

"Did you break the record?" Jasper asks me as we walk. "Did you get to five thousand people?"

"Aaron says we had thirty-eight hundred people in New York," I say.

"So . . . no, you didn't break the record?" Jasper asks.

"Well, it depends. We broke other records. We had the most simultaneous reunions around the world—over forty of them. And we had the most people around the world celebrating family at the same time," I say. "The total is close to ten thousand."

"But you didn't break the main record?" Jasper asks.

"Well, um. No."

"So was it a failure?"

A good question. I'm not sure what to say.

"It was a successful failure," Julie says.

I love that. *A successful failure.* That's the way I see most of my life. There's room for both. Our narrative oscillates all the time.

I grab Julie's hand and squeeze. She squeezes back, despite my absurdly sweaty postevent palms.

I adore my seventh cousins, of course, but these folks, the ones who are a mere single branch away on my family tree—they are my favorite human beings on planet Earth.

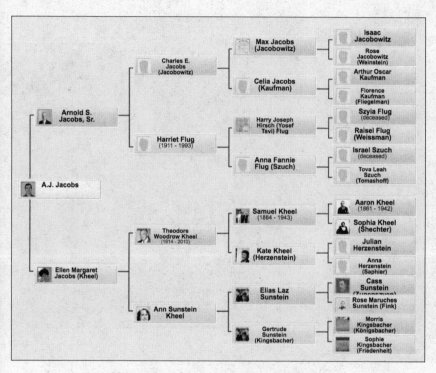

My immediate family tree, as seen on Geni.com.

Henry Louis Gates Jr. and Lucas, volunteers, a bunch of cousins, my sons Zane and Jasper and wife, Julie, with David Blaine, the Ramos Family Reunion in Peru, Tom Chapin, The Three Wise Guys (a minister, a rabbi, and an imam), and Sister Sledge.

Credits: Sharon Schuur, Ryan Brown, and Elana Goodridge

A Note from the Author

All the events in this book are true. Some of the sequences have been rearranged, and, in certain cases, the names and identifying details have been changed. The relationship links (for example, fourth cousin three times removed's wife's uncle) were recorded at the time of research. The World Family Tree is ever growing and changing, so the chains may show up differently today.

Acknowledgments

I just checked, and *The Guinness Book of World Records* does not have an entry for "Longest Acknowledgments in a Nonfiction Book." Which is a shame, because if it did, I'd be about to crush it.

What I'm trying to say is: I've got a couple of people to thank. At one point, I considered thanking all seven billion members of my family in microfiche-size print, on the theory that if even 10 percent of that list ended up buying the book, I'd rack up some sweet sales numbers. I decided against that.

Yet even without listing every human being on earth, I do have an unusual number of people to acknowledge. This is because I want to thank not only those who helped make this book a reality, but those who volunteered to help put on the Global Family Reunion. And that latter group is an astounding number of human beings.

Let me start with the folks at Simon & Schuster: My visionary and patient editor Ben Loehnen, the patriarch Jon Karp, the matriarch Carolyn Reidy, Julia Prosser, Richard Rhorer, Amar Deol, Sybil Pincus, Sherry Wasserman, and Lisa Healy.

Also many thanks to the people at ICM: Heather Karpas, Josie Freedman, Heather Bushong, and my Southern kinsman Sloan Harris.

I'm a big fan of the people who happen to share a large percentage of my DNA: Lucas, Zane and Jasper, and my parents, Ellen and Arnie Jacobs.

My wife, Julie Jacobs, gets her own paragraph, because she deserves it. Thank you for everything, Julie.

The following (moderately close) family members provided me with wonderful memories and insights about my ancestors: Carol Jacobs, Jane Kheel, Bobsey Colin, Lisa Grayson, Lauren Walter, Joan Pollak, Tom Kheel, Margie and Kevin Akin, Judith Stix, and Jenny Schwartzberg.

Here are a handful of crucial team members without whom the reunion would have been a dozen people playing hacky sack in Central Park: Eowyn Langholf of Turning Hearts Genealogy, Aaron Fisher of Revolution Marketing, Gilad Japhet, Cherie Bush, Shipley Munson, Barbara Sontz of Family Matters, Wesley Eames of Trace.com, Andrea Simmons, Lisa Cohen, and Henry Louis Gates Jr.

I'm grateful to the genealogy and science community, who taught me the meaning of phrases like *brick walls* and *pedigree collapse*: David Allen Lambert, McKelden Smith, J. Mark Lowe, Tim Urban, Judy G. Russell, Scott Fisher, Jane E. Wilcox, Dick Eastman, Edith Wagner, Jules Feldman, Jen Baldwin, Thomas MacEntee, Cyndi Howells, Megan Smolenyak, Tyler Moss, Diane Haddad, The Genealogy Guys, Yaniv Erlich, the New York Genealogical and Biographical Society, the New England Historic Genealogical Society, the Clayton Library, the Midwest Genealogy Center, Allen County Public Library, Family History Library, Federation of Genealogical Societies, Association of Professional Genealogists, Randy Seaver, Christine Kenneally, Eric Topol, David Ewing Duncan, Kevin Kelly, Spencer Wells, and Eviatar Zerubavel.

The following is a list of the official Very Important Cousins who were exceedingly generous in support of the Global Family Reunion and the fight against Alzheimer's:

Cheryl Berkof, David Berkof, Judy Louise Kennedy, Harris Scyster, Sherry McCutcheon, Gary Rudoren, Nathan Bowen, Fatima Costalaurent, Jade Walker, Tara Behrend, Hilary Steinman, Leila Tite, Kay Rose,

Kate Harvie, Wendy Kheel, James Cropcho, Adina Daar, Emily Greene, Chris Campbell, Mary Louis Trask, Amy Reiss, Maud Newton, Catherine Briner, Roland Arsenault, David Linn, Michael and Andrea Weitzner, Kathleen Tesluk, Ash Gupte, Lorie Wigle, Thomas Shaw, Becky Falto, Valerie Park, The Wymans, Dr. Steven G. Eisenberg, Dan Bodenheimer, Jennifer Jones Babuca, Leo Mader, Penelope Mader, Andy Goodwin, Samuel Hinckley, Dale Silverstein, Bettie and Bennie King, Edith Wagner, Frances Owens Haywood, Marsha Kamish, Donna Gail Stobaugh, Kharyn Sommer, Ryan Franklin, Todd Leavitt, Winnie Fraser, Jennifer East, Justin Stoney, Shannon Adkins, Anthony Lopez, Andrea Stancin, Jane Rosch, Chris and Megan Whitten, Heidi Prochnau, Ross Goodman, Jeff Boyer, Claudia Azula, Christina Fisher, Katie Gale, Amanda Jacob, Penny Van Vlerah, John Rockwell, Kimberly Schoen, Heidi Hanna, David Kuker, Marissa Kalman, Sue Silberstein, Kate Dickman, Athena Dalrymple, Dave Keeney, Cindy Mora, Irene Cruz, Stephen Reed, David Carter, Ron Brigmond, Gayle Carin, Deborah Waas, Michael Allen, Austin Dekle, Trina Selby, Steven Brown, Valerie Anderson, and Francine Silver.

Remember when I said I had a lot of people to thank? Was I making a joke? I was not. We got more.

Here are friends who helped spread the word about the reunion through radio shows, sermons, or by mentioning it to all the other patients at the ophthalmologist's office:

Peter Shapiro, Ethan Goldman, Matthew Galkin, Nancy Sheed, Vincent Rubino, Rabbi Angela Buchdahl, Jon Levy, Roger Bennett, Jayson and Kandis Gaignard, Alex Blumberg, Eric Mennell, Clay Hebert, Sara Simkin, Chris Guillebeau, Gail Sheehy, Eric Messinger, Peter Breslow, Scott Simon, Gabriel Sanders, David Patrick Columbia, Eric Jacks, Ben Sherwood, Rebecca Wallace-Segall, Mark Frauenfelder, Jean Becker, Hilary Neve, Jeff Tarr, Amanda Hesser, David Granger, Chris Anderson, Emily McManus, Rives, John Durant, Claire Odell, Doro Koch, Paul Mandell, Lisa Mandell, Eliza Chung, and Ross Benes.

I'm grateful to those who read the manuscript and gave wise advice, whether it was about the narrative arc or about the difference between polyamory and swinging: Rob Weisbach, Peter Griffin, Shannon Barr, Kristen Lasky, Jesse Rifkin, Andrew Lund, Kevin Roose, Jamie Bufalino, Michelle Caplan, Stephen Friedman, Lynette Vanderwarker, Victor Ozols, Riki Markowitz, and Emily Callahan.

Thanks to the folks at these excellent Alzheimer's organizations: Tim Armour, Sally Rosenfield, and David Shenk of the Cure Alzheimer's Fund, and Lou-Ellen Barkan and Danielle Robitaille at CaringKind.

I'm indebted to the amazing collection of speakers and entertainers who volunteered their time and talents, a list that includes two magicians, a *Daily Show* correspondent, a pair of long-lost twins, and the descendant of an illegal margarine kingpin. Namely: David Blaine, Jenna Ushkowitz, Sasha Martin, Adam Grant, Andy Borowitz, Bill Weir, Brady Rymer and the Little Band That Could, Bruce Feiler, CeCe Moore, David Ippolito, David Rencher, Dr. Oz, Eric Schoenberg, George Church, Gilad Japhet, Hasan Minhaj, Helen Fisher, James Altucher, Jonatha Brooke, Jordan Auslander, Josh Taylor, Kasia Bryc, Lama Surya Das, Lisa Loeb, Marilu Henner, Maud Newton, Nando Pelusi, Ophira Eisenberg, Pamela Weisberger (RIP), Paul Williams, Randy Whited, Ron Arons, Rudy Tanzi, Tammy Hepps (who uncovered the margarine scammers in her past), Ted Allen, the Three Wise Guys, Tracey Jackson, Tuelo and her Cousins, Tom Chapin, Baba Brinkman, Wesley Eames, Cate Smit, Karen Bergreen, Seth Herzog, Jared Freid, Abbi Crutchfield, Luke Thayer, Scott Rogowsky, Scott Fisher, Tom Shillue, Josh Beckerman, Lizzie Valverde, and Katy Olson. And, of course Sister Sledge (RIP Joni).

Thanks as well to these folks, who are on very close branches of my tree: My sister, Beryl, and her husband, Willy, Eric Schoenberg (who is smarter than I am), David and Allison (who I'm glad got married, the leprechaun incident notwithstanding), Barbara Brizdle, David Zuckerman, and Adam, Allison, Lisa, Doug, Natalia, Andrea, Alex and Barbara Schoenberg.

The following are just some of the people who volunteered their expertise for the reunion, everything from photography to trademark advice: Bret Watson and his team at Watson Adventures scavenger hunts,

Elana Goodridge, Ryan Brown, Cynthia Kaplan, Kate Harvie, Ryan Koch, Sharon Schuur, Rick Smolan, Steven Shewach, Pat Nixon, Andrea O'Dell, Candice Braun, Jack Braun, Annie Braun, Nina Hoffer, Matt Kuhn, Linda Grantham, Michael Carragher, Shantel Bancroft Gardner, Amanda Zitzelman, Ruby McCormick, Carol Rice, Frank Billingsley (Swabbed & Found), Sarah Klock, Todd Lowenstein, Andy Blazzard, Iris Mansour, Niels Hansen, S. James Boumil III, Dan Rollman of Record-Setter, Jill Sobule, Dan Bern, Ken Jennings, Weird Al Yankovic, Michael Ian Black, Nick Kroll, Ellie LeBlond, Zack Bornstein, Tom Schachtman, Stu Kotler, Jenifer de Wolf, Amanda Nussbaum, Kristen Mathews, Robin Spolanksy, Helene Fraymann, Ellen Seidensticker, and Michael Fire.

Here are the great men and women who held branch parties in Peru, New Zealand, and other places I'd like to visit someday: The Ramos family of Peru, John and Candace Ulmer, Cheryl Lang, Michaelle Cotton, Curt Witcher, Cynthia Theusch, Tamara Stansfield, Debbie Gutler, Susan Kaufman, Cari Lynn Postnikoff, Lisa Clark, Jeremiah and Nicole Arsenault, Valerie Walters, Roy Hamilton, Paula Hinkel, Laura Hedgecock, Jen Alford, Ann Sindelar, Ari Wilkins, Wacinque AK BeMende, Rod Tucker, Julie Hammons, Gabby Salazar, Benicio Samuel Sanchez Garcia, Douglas Harding, Roger Moffat, Jerry Oman, Marjorie Rhodes-Ousley, Sharon Rowe, Peggy Mouser, Lee Beingham Redgrave, and Donna Hartwig.

Thanks to the brilliant tree-builders at Geni who helped figure out connections of those attending the reunion, including Ashley Odell, Pam Karp, Hatte Blejer, Adam Brown, Kevin Hanit, Peter Rohel, Erica Howton, Malka Mysels, Jeff Gentes, Ann Fuller, and Dan Bodenheimer. As well as the Geni staff: Mike Stangel, Noah Tutak, and Amanda Tantisalidchai.

Equal thanks to the resourceful tree-builders at WikiTree who connected hundreds of other attendees: Chris Whitten, Abby Glann, Ron Norman, Lucy Lavelle, Karen Tobo, Erin Breen, Lucy Selvaggio-Diaz, Kim Armstrong, Elizabeth O'Neal, Lianne Lavoie, Roland Arsenault, Tami Mize, and Scott Fulkerson.

I'm grateful to the folks at FamilySearch and RootsTech, including Thom Reed and Jen Allen. Thank you to the team at MyHeritage, including Aaron Godfrey, Lawrence Harris, Daniel Horowitz, Yinon Glasner, and Mike Mallin. Also to the crew at 23andMe: Anne Wojcicki, Joanna Mountain, Catherine Afarian, and Andy Kill. And those at FindMyPast, including Ben Bennett and Annelies van den Belt.

There's also Bennett Greenspan at Family Tree DNA. Not to mention those at Ancestry who helped, including Tim Sullivan and John Dilworth. And the tireless warriors at the New York Hall of Science, Dan Wempa, Jennifer Brunjes, and Margaret Honey.

Okay, I know I missed a whole bunch of distant cousins, so if you want even more, go to my website and I'll have an updated list and apologies to those I forgot. But for now, that's it. Thanks!

A Brief and Subjective Guide to Getting Started on Your Family Tree

Plus: What The Hell Is a Second Cousin Versus a Twice-Removed Cousin?

By Eowyn Langholf and A.J. Jacobs

I've asked Eowyn Langholf—a professional genealogist and the Chief Cousin Connector of the Global Family Reunion—to help me draw up some tips for those interested in giving genealogy a shot. Here are our suggestions.

Gather What You Have Already

It's probably more than you think: letters, heirlooms, journals, address books, family Bibles, photos, and the backs of photos, where valuable, if barely legible scribbles lurk.

Get Out the Tape Recorder

Note from A.J.: My mother-in-law recently pointed out that if we wanted to ask her anything, she's "not going to live forever." An excellent point. So my wife and sons sat down and videotaped her for three hours telling stories, some fascinating, some baffling (when asked her favorite childhood hobby, she said "throwing potatoes into the fire"). But it was three of the most valuable hours we've spent recently. We do urge you to get out your pen and paper, tape recorder, or webcam and interview your parents, grandparents, great-uncles—anyone willing to remember and reflect.

We find it best to avoid yes-no questions and focus on open-ended queries. You can start with this list of fifty suggested prompts: (http://www.wikitree. com/blog/50-questions-for-interviewing-living-family-members/).

Also, this question is often an anecdotal gold mine: "What kind of trouble did you get into as a kid?"

Build Your Tree

Genealogists talk about the Big Four sites—Ancestry, FamilySearch, MyHeritage, and FindMyPast.

These four offer similar services—you can map your tree, link to relatives, control your privacy, find birth certificates and other documents—and they're all good. You can't really go wrong. But each one has its own strengths and weaknesses. Which is the best for you? To make an educated decision, watch this video: https://www.rootstech.org/videos/sunny-morton.

Or if you're in a hurry, here's a superquick rundown.

FamilySearch (familysearch.org, free)
This site, owned by The Church of Jesus Christ of Latter-Day Saints, is free and huge—it's got 4 billion profiles (by far the most) and a massive database of documents.

Ancestry (ancestry.com, paid)
This is the Coca-Cola of the paying family history sites—the most recognized brand name. It's got 2.5 million subscribed users, and it scours databases to provide you hints of possible documents related to your ancestors. It's also the most expensive of the four. (Note: Aside from saying whether a service is free or paid, we're not going to list prices, because prices change often and there are frequent deals).

MyHeritage (myheritage.com, paid)
Based out of Israel, this site also offers powerful databases as well as DNA features incorporated into its 35 million family trees. With 8 billion records, it's particularly strong internationally, such as Europe and the Middle East. Plus, it's affiliated with Geni.com (see below).

FindMyPast (findmypast.com, paid)
With more than 2 billion searchable records, FindMyPast is especially robust in British and Irish databases, though it's also building up a sizeable collection of records for the United States and Canada.

Connect to the World

If you want to help build a World Family Tree—and connect yourself to everyone from Jane Austen to Aziz Ansari—we recommend one of these sites. Both of them use the Wiki model: thousands of users from all over the world collaborating and sharing information. Both of them also combine DNA results with traditional genealogical research.

Geni (geni.com)
Note from A.J.: This is the site I use the most. It's got more than 100 million profiles and is an easy way to connect to cousins all over the world. I find the interface to be intuitive, and the how-are-we-connected

function far too much fun. It's got a free version, but the extra good stuff requires a subscription.

WikiTree (wikitree.com)
Note from Eowyn: First of all, it's free, which is nice. Its strength lies with its community—it's a collaborative, friendly, generous, and hard-working group. WikiTree has nearly 15 million profiles. I'm on staff at WikiTree, where my title is, no joke, Forest Elf and I help oversee day-to-day operations.

FamilySearch (familysearch.org)
FamilySearch also has a worldwide tree, though it can be more challenging to connect to others on this service because of the strict privacy controls.

Or Keep to Yourself

If you want to keep a tree off the Internet, safe and secure on your computer's hard drive, you can try one of several software programs. RootsMagic and Legacyfamilytree.com are among the best.

Dive into DNA

There are now more than 50 firms offering DNA testing, from the mainstream 23andMe to the lesser-known service "Who'z the Daddy" (check out the cartoon sperm in the logo on its website whozthedaddy.com).

DNA testing has its drawbacks: You may discover unpleasant family secrets, and in this post-WikiLeaks world, you might not be able to keep the results private forever. But overall, we're still pro testing. The benefits are too enticing for us.

DNA testing can give you an estimate of your ethnic breakdown and a list of people with whom you share DNA. Sometimes the revelations can be life changing. Eowyn is adopted and didn't know anything about her biological father except his name and two of his brothers. A couple months ago she was contacted by a match through AncestryDNA that showed as a close family member. The woman turned out to be Eowyn's father's sister—her aunt! Eowyn's aunt knew just enough information about their family that Eowyn was able to start piecing together their genealogy.

Most of these services are in the $100 to $200 range, but the prices fluctuate and there are often special deals (pro tip: especially around Christmas and National DNA Day, April 25).

Here are the major services we recommend:

23andMe (23andme.com)

More than 2 million have spit their way into 23andMe's database, which is well designed and easy to navigate. Also, 23andMe recently resumed providing health-related genetic info, such as whether you have a gene that makes you more likely to get Alzheimer's disease (please go over health results with a genetic counselor before freaking out).

AncestryDNA (ancestry.com/dna) and MyHeritage (myheritage.com/dna)

These sites are both appealing since they can easily sync up the results with your online family tree.

FamilyTree DNA (familytreedna.com)

Some hard-core genealogists think FTDNA gives the most detailed scientific data. For one thing, unlike most, you can test your mtDNA (which traces your mom's mom's mom's mom's-and-so-on line) and yDNA (which for men traces your dad's dad's dad's-and-so-on line). They also have surname projects, so you can get connected with other potential cousins.

Personal Genome Project (personalgenomes.org)

This project was started by Harvard professor George Church. Church and his team of scientists will decode your entire genome for free. In exchange, scientists around the world will have access to all the (anonymized) data to help crack medical mysteries.

One thing to remember is that when you take a DNA test you are only matched against other test takers on that particular site. So if you test on 23andMe, you are only matched against other people who have tested on 23andMe. It's a bit like the Tower of Babel out there.

But don't worry, there are universal translators—websites that allow you to connect with users from any other site. You can upload your info to GEDmatch (gedmatch.com) and DNAland (dna.land) and find loads of new matches.

Search Old Newspapers

One of the biggest advances in family history (or regular history, for that matter) has been the recent digitization of newspapers. We love them, and not just for the numerous sock-garter ads. Here are three of our favorite sites:

Chronicling America (http://chroniclingamerica.loc.gov, free)
The Library of Congress maintains this amazing database of historic newspapers. The oldest article we found is from the May 13, 1789, *Gazette of the United-States*—a scathing editorial against dueling. Very convincing.

Newspapers (newspapers.com, paid)
Another vast repository, currently at 282,000,000 newspaper pages dating back to the 1700s. Note from A.J.: This is where I found out my ancestor suffered from hemorrhoids. A turning point in my research.

Fulton History (fultonhistory.com, free)
This website has more than 39 million newspaper pages—all of them scanned by one obsessive and dedicated man. His papers are from the United States and Canada, many of them based in New York. The search function isn't so sleek, but we still highly recommend the site.

Other Online-Research Tools

One-stop surfing: Cyndi's List (cyndislist.com, free)
If there's one website you should know about, it's Cyndi's List. This is the mother lode, the index of all indexes. It's got thousands of links in every imaginable topic of genealogy, and these links are organized into categories ranging from Adoption to New Zealand, from Anabaptists to Lumber Industry records.

RESEARCH BY PLACE

One helpful research method involves digging into your family's geographical roots. Practically every city, state, and region has its own genealogy society. There are at least 187 in Texas alone. You can search their sites or ask questions on their message boards.

A comprehensive list of local societies can be found at fgs.org (Federation of Genealogical Societies).

The granddaddy of them all is the New England Historical Genealogical Society, which has plenty on the *Mayflower* set, of course, but covers non-*Mayflower* families too (americanancestors.org).

A.J.'s local group—the New York Genealogical and Biographical Society (newyorkfamilyhistory.org)—is also strong and surprisingly diverse.

RESEARCH BY ETHNICITY

Practically every ethnic population has its own genealogy society. There is JewishGen (jewishgen.org), as well as the magazine and website *Avotaynu* (avotaynu.com). African-American cousins can check out the Afro-American Historical and Genealogical Society (aahgs.org) and *The Root*, an African-American news site cofounded by Henry Louis Gates Jr. (theroot.com).

But that's just the start. Cyndi's List and FGS both have comprehensive lists of cultural groups.

RESEARCH VITAL RECORDS

Any of the Big Four will automatically link you to birth certificates and marriage records as soon as you start inputting your tree. But you can do more poking around on your own. Among the many useful sites are:

Fold3 (fold3.com, paid), which offers vast U.S. military records

Find A Grave (findagrave.com, free), which lets you see millions of tombstones and death records.

The Ellis Island database (libertyellisfoundation.org/passenger), which is great for immigration research.

Offline Research

Sadly for the sedentary among us, not everything is available online. There are still billions of records yet to be digitized, and they lurk in local courthouses, libraries, and municipal archives. (Check out Cyndi's List for the ones near you.)

The LDS also provide some astounding brick-and-mortar research centers called Family History Centers—there are 4,725 worldwide, and they have friendly staffers who will help you research.

The most impressive of them all is in Salt Lake City, simply called the Family History Library. It's the largest genealogical library in the world, has experienced guides to help you, and it's free. Their collection includes 1.4 million rolls of microfilm, along with more than 600,000 books, journals, and maps.

Other big-time non-Mormon libraries include the Clayton Library Center for Genealogical Research in Texas (http://houstonlibrary.org/location/clayton-library-center-genealogical-research), the Midwest Gene-alogy Center in Missouri (https://www.mymcpl.org/genealogy), and the Allen County Public Library in Indiana (http://www.genealogycenter.org/).

Podcasts

Extreme Genes
Scott Fisher has the best and deepest voice in genealogy. He and cohost David Allen Lambert chat about the news and conduct lively interviews. Note from A.J.: This is where I first heard the story of the family with one mother and eight dads.

The Forget-Me-Not Hour
Hosted by Jane Wilcox, this interview show has in-depth *Fresh Air*–type interviews with great historians and researchers.

The Genealogy Guys
It's like *Car Talk*, but without the accents or crankshaft references.

Twice Removed
Hosted by noted author A.J. Jacobs, this five-part miniseries from Gimlet Media introduces guests in the studio to a mystery cousin. You'll learn about Food Network host Ted Allen's culinary roots and writer Dan Savage's gangster ancestors.

Books

Ancestors and Relatives: Genealogy, Identity, and Community by Eviatar Zerubavel (Oxford University Press, 2012)
An anthropologist looks at the meaning behind our obsession with ancestry. He opens with the provocative question: "Why do we consider Barack Obama a black man with a white mother rather than a white man with a black father?"

Family Trees: A History of Genealogy in America by Francois Weil (Harvard University Press, 2013)

We love the section on the scam artists of the late nineteenth and early twentieth centuries. Among the most notorious was American con man Oscar Hartzell, who convinced thousands of people to join him in a fraudulent lawsuit against the British government. Hartzell claimed to represent the only living heir to English sea captain and politician Sir Francis Drake, whose princely estate he planned to recover.

Evidence Explained by Elizabeth Shown Mills (Genealogical Publishing Co., 2015)
If you happen to crave approval from genealogy geeks, this is good to have on your shelf. It's a guide to how to cite your research for virtually any type of source you can imagine.

Genetic Genealogy in Practice by Blaine Bettinger and Debbie Parker Wayne (National Genealogical Society, 2016)
If you're ready to dive into the genetic genealogy pool, this workbook is a solid one to help you interpret your DNA test results. Its practical and easy-to-understand approach will help you with your research with hands-on exercises.

How to Archive Family Keepsakes: Learn How to Preserve Family Photos, Memorabilia and Genealogy Records by Denise May Levenick (Family Tree Books, 2012)
Maybe you're the person in your family who collects all the family stuff— the memorabilia, photos, letters, etc. How to manage the clutter? Denise's book is an excellent reference on how to get started and be organized.

Hey, America, Your Roots Are Showing by Meg Smolenyak (Citadel Press, 2012)
Smolenyak is a genealogist for several TV shows—the flap copy calls her "the Indiana Jones of genealogy." She tells us highlights from her career as an ancestor sleuth. There are sections on Barack Obama's Irish roots and Alex Haley's Scottish roots, to name but a couple.

The Ancestor's Tale by Richard Dawkins (Houghton Mifflin Harcourt, 2004)
A backwards-in-time pilgrimage to our ultimate ancestor, Luca. It's 683 pages because we've got a lot of grandparents.

Websites and Magazines

Family Tree magazine (familytreemagazine.com)
The most established publication on the topic, sort of the *Sports Illustrated* for family history geeks. It also has a strong website.

Eastman's Online Genealogy Newsletter (eogn.com)
This is written by expert Dick Eastman, who has been at it so long he used to store his family data on punch cards.

The Legal Genealogist (legalgenealogist.com)
Judy Russell writes about genealogy, often with an emphasis on its intersection with laws. She's one of the most evidence-based, clear-eyed, and delightfully skeptical writers out there. See her post "Facts Matter!"

Genea-Musings (geneamusings.com)
Written by Randy Seaver, this blog is a mix of genealogy news, research tips, personal experiences, debates, and puzzles.

GeneaBloggers TRIBE (geneabloggerstribe.com)
This site is run by a team of genealogy bloggers who share news, tips, resources, stories, and the occasional great-grandmother's cookie recipe.

Genealogy Gems (lisalouisecooke.com)
Lisa Louise Cooke's blog often has surprising angles, such as how to use Google Earth for genealogy.

The Genetic Genealogist (thegeneticgenealogist.com)
Blaine Bettinger's DNA blog is entertaining and relatively jargon-free.
Blaine reports on breakthroughs, which seem to happen every minute
these days. He also offers a multitude of resources and tips.

The DNA Detectives (thednadetectives.com)
Founded by CeCe Moore, this site provides information to help people
discover more about their family heritage through DNA testing. CeCe's
work has connected thousands of adoptees with their biological parents.
She also runs a "DNA Detectives" Facebook group where members learn
to use DNA to find relatives, both recent and distant.

Wait But Why? (waitbutwhy.com)
Writer Tim Urban's brilliant nonfiction site has two great pieces on ge-
nealogy: "Meet Your Ancestors (All of Them)" and "Your Family: Past,
Present and Future."

Conferences

RootsTech (rootstech.org)
This is the Comic Con of genealogy but with less cosplay (not to say
there is no cosplay; we've seen everything from pirates to pioneers to a
walking, talking tree). It's held every February in Salt Lake City, and the
organizers expect more than 30,000 attendees next year.

   We also recommend the National Genealogical Society conference
(ngsgenealogy.org) and the Jamboree put on by the Southern California
Genealogical Society (genealogyjamboree.com).

   Many conferences live stream or post video of the sessions, in case you
can't make the trip. Schedules can be found at http://conferencekeeper.org.

Hire a Professional

If you don't have the time to research, if you want a more in-depth
exploration, or if you get stuck behind a brick wall, you can hire a pro.

Note from A.J.: I am now going to plug Eowyn's business, Turning Hearts Genealogy (turningheartsgenealogy.com), because she's too shy to do it herself.

But there are many other professional genealogists as well.

To choose one, you can go to the Association of Professional Genealogists website (apgen.org). It allows you to find a pro who specializes in your family's ethnicity or place of origin. Eowyn recommends interviewing a few before hiring one.

When you hire a pro, it's best to give a specific assignment. "I want to know more about my family" is vague and might leave you less than satisfied. Instead, ask about a specific branch or a brick wall you've encountered.

Prices vary from about $20 per hour to more than $100 an hour.

Research Tips

GO NARROW AT FIRST

Pick one ancestor or surname and focus your search there. Later you can come back to other parts of your tree. If you try to do every ancestor at once, you'll get lost in the tangle of branches.

USE PHOTOS AS COUSIN BAIT

If you are sharing your family tree online, add images. It'll get other family members more interested. It's the same principle as Facebook, but with dead people. (No dead-people selfies, please.)

SOURCE, SOURCE, SOURCE

Almost all new genealogists make the same mistake and regret it later: They don't record their sources. Make a note where information comes from.

If your aunt tells you your grandfather's birth date, don't just record the date. Record that your aunt told you the date. Even better, ask your aunt how she knows his birth date. It might sound overly fastidious, but it can make a difference. You'll sometimes find the day that's celebrated as a birthday isn't what's recorded on official documents.

And Finally, What the Hell Is the Difference Between a Second Cousin and a First Cousin Twice Removed?

The concept of "second cousin" is actually an easy one to grasp.

If you are first cousins with someone, you share a set of grandparents. If you're second cousins, you share a set of great-grandparents. Third cousins, you share great-great grandparents. And so on. Easy.

The "removed" notion is a little more complicated. It has to do with generations.

"Once removed" means that the person is one generation away from you—meaning this relative is in your parent's generation or your child's generation. "Twice removed" is two generations away—your grandparents or grandkids generation.

Note from A.J.: Here's an example from my own family: My mom's first cousin Cass (her uncle's son) is my first cousin once removed, because Cass is from my mom's generation. My mom's first cousin once removed (her great-uncle's kid) is my first cousin twice removed, because he's from my grandparents' generation.

Clear? Maybe not. All this is easier if you see it in a chart. So thanks to Alice J. Ramsay for the chart opposite this page.

Or you could adopt the Hawaiian kinship terminology, where every person of the same generation and gender gets the same term. Brothers and male cousins are referred to by the same word, while sisters and female cousins get another word. Uncles and fathers are grouped together, as are aunts and mothers.

This is definitely in the Global Family Reunion spirit.

The relationship in each box is what that person's relationship would be to you, where you are "Self." As you can see, you, your siblings, your 1st cousins, 2nd cousins, etc., are all in the same generation. Thus, "once removed" means "one generation removed."

Copyright Alice J. Ramsay
Designed January, 1987

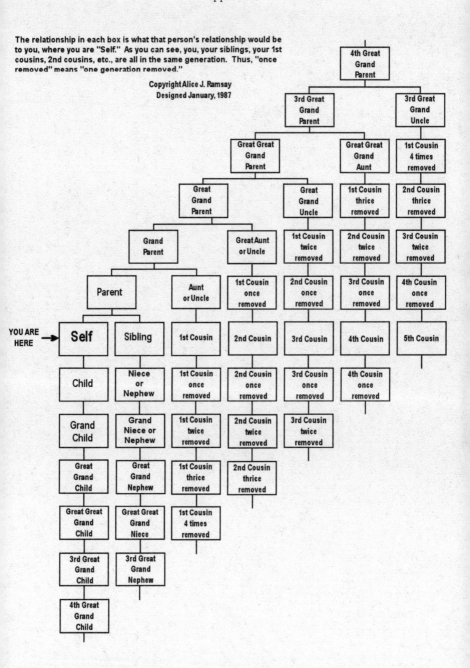

Notes

1   *I'd be happy to* trim *a few branches*: I'm actually very fond of both David and Eric. On the other hand, my second cousin who thinks global warming is a hoax . . . ? Not so much.

7   *"Okay, here it is . . . 70,420,308"*: This was a while ago. At press time, the World Family Tree on Geni has grown to 114,000,000 relatives.

9   *"Through the Zuckermans. Just twenty-one steps away"*: The World Family Tree is ever growing and changing. So the relationship links often shift. These were the links when I was conducting research.

13   *By some estimates we all share 99.9 percent of our DNA with one another*: There's a debate over exactly how much DNA humans share with each other. Until 2016, the accepted statistic was that humans share 99.9 percent of our DNA. A 2016 paper in the journal *Nature* challenged that, and some scientists now believe that the number could be anywhere from 99.0 to 99.9 percent.

I've spent way too much time wondering if the actual percentage matters from a philosophical and ethical point of view. On the one hand, 99.9 percent sounds good.

But two things could share 99.9 percent of ingredients and still be vastly different. Two apple pies could be 99.9 percent the same, but one could have 0.1 percent cyanide. You wouldn't want to mix them up.

So in my opinion, it's not the exact percentage. Instead, it's the idea that humans are all very much the same in that we share the desire for happiness, love, and a good night's sleep.

39   *I spoke with CeCe Moore*: The DNA companies are very good at predicting ancestral origins at the continental level, such as European, African, and Asian/Native American. The predictions are still reasonably accurate at the regional level—for example, Northern versus Southern Europe. But

the companies still have a long way to go with perfecting the accuracy of predictions at the subregional levels, such as German versus Scandinavian.

40   *But as intermarriage increases, I'm hopeful*: Intermarriage between ethnicities and races has increased over the last decades according to the Pew Research Center. However, some social scientists fear that DNA testing may reverse that trend in the future. Princeton sociologist Dalton Conley told me he worries that, as more people get tested, they will look for those with similar genes to marry. I hope his fear is unfounded and we continue our voluntary procreative ethnic deconstruction.

56   *Here's how philosopher Stephen Asma describes this dilemma*: Asma's book is titled *Against Fairness*, and it's an argument against utilitarian ethics that say we should treat everybody—family and nonfamily—equally.

59   *According to the book* The Intellectual History of Asia: Actually, the quote is from a book called *Ethics for Dummies*, but I like to pretend it's this other one.

115   *One of the sisters, Joni Sledge, called me to tell me that she likes the idea of a global family*: Joni died last year. It was a joy being part of her extended family. RIP.

118   *"That's what we're supposed to be! Fifty percent. If it were one hundred percent, we'd be identical twins"*: To clarify: Humans share somewhere around 99.0 percent to 99.9 percent of our DNA with everyone else on earth. But within that tiny 0.5-or-so percent, we also share DNA with those with whom we're closely related. So my sister and I share 99.5 percent of DNA, but also half of that 0.5 percent.

122   *"Well, it's the weirdest story I've ever heard"*: Michael has written a manuscript of his weird story. If any publishers are interested, please contact me. Also, Michael double-checked his dad's DNA using skin shavings from his dad's electric razor. It still didn't match.

133   *One Geni user, a New Jersey–based lawyer named Adam Brown*: Adam Brown spends several months a year in Antarctica as a radio operator. He is the founder of the Antarctica Jewish Genealogical Society, which is dedicated to studying the genealogy of scientists and workers in Antarctica.

142   *"We were born of risen apes, not fallen angels, and the apes were armed killers besides"*: This quote also appeared in my book *The Know-It-All*. In fact, full confession: There are a handful of short passages in *It's All Relative* that are eerily similar to my previous books, including the description of my uncle Gil and the *Family News* and the Italo Calvino story at the end of the book. I hope you agree with me that this is an example of efficiency and not laziness.

147   *I'm working with an event producer named Aaron*: That's Aaron Fisher of Rev-

olution Marketing. If you're throwing a massive event, he is your man. (I'm too lazy to set up a Yelp account, so consider this my Yelp entry on him.)

209 *A few minutes later there's a flurry of murmuring among the staff, and in comes Donny Osmond*: While in Salt Lake City, I was invited to sing with the Mormon Tabernacle Choir at their rehearsal. I thought it'd be rude to turn them down. We sang a song about birds and bees and blossoms. I figured I was singing quietly enough not to cause a disturbance—it was barely above a mumble—but the director stopped the rehearsal to announce that someone was off-key in the tenor section. He didn't name names, but I don't think it was a huge mystery.

262 *"You had to mute me during our project, due to your (admittedly true) belief that I am a 'cocky bastard'"*: This refers to an article I wrote for *Esquire* in which David, who is a professional poker player in Vegas, advised me how to play poker with my friends and son.

263 *a recent study in which some Palestinians and some Israelis were randomly told that either they shared significant DNA or didn't*: This study appeared in the *Personality and Social Psychology Bulletin*. Eric actually sent me the article after the Global Family Reunion. But it was too brotherly a gesture not to include.

264 *my cousin Cass Sunstein sends me a link to an article he'd just written*: Cass's article on the "Family Heuristic" appeared in *Bloomberg View*. It says, in part:

Here's how it works: Most of us feel a commonality with members of our family. At least in general, we treat them with familiarity and kindness. We sacrifice for them. We welcome them. We laugh with them. We are gentle with them; we give them the benefit of the doubt.

To qualify as a member of your "family," of course, a person must usually be part of a relatively small group—your parents, siblings, children, aunts and uncles, in-laws, first cousins, and those with a close relationship to any of the above. But modern genealogical tools make it easy to show that the universe of familial connections is extraordinarily large. Jacobs is exploiting the family heuristic by triggering the positive emotions and the strong feelings of commonality associated with small kinship units and applying them to the big world of distant strangers.

275 *each of us likely contains at least one atom that was also in the body of Beethoven*: This is actually a matter of some debate. You most likely have atoms from some historical figures, but perhaps not all historical figures. It depends on several factors, including when they died and whether they were cremated or buried.

Index

About the Author

A.J. JACOBS is the author of four *New York Times* bestsellers, including *The Year of Living Biblically*, *The Know-It-All*, and *Drop Dead Healthy*. He is a contributing editor at *Esquire* magazine, for which he wrote the article "My Outsourced Life." Jacobs is also a contributor to NPR, hosted the podcast "Twice Removed," and has given several TED talks. He lives in New York City with his wife and three sons (and several million cousins). You can visit his website at ajjacobs.com and follow him on Twitter at @ajjacobs.